GIBBO-IN MY LIFE

GIBBO-IN MY LIFE

Journey of an English — American Soccer Teacher

PAUL ANDRÉ GIBBONS

iUniverse, Inc.
Bloomington

GIBBO-In My Life
Journey of an English—American Soccer Teacher

Copyright © 2012 by Paul André Gibbons.

All rights reserved. No part of this book may be used or reproduced by any means, graphic, electronic, or mechanical, including photocopying, recording, taping or by any information storage retrieval system without the written permission of the publisher except in the case of brief quotations embodied in critical articles and reviews.

iUniverse books may be ordered through booksellers or by contacting:

iUniverse
1663 Liberty Drive
Bloomington, IN 47403
www.iuniverse.com
1-800-Authors (1-800-288-4677)

Because of the dynamic nature of the Internet, any web addresses or links contained in this book may have changed since publication and may no longer be valid. The views expressed in this work are solely those of the author and do not necessarily reflect the views of the publisher, and the publisher hereby disclaims any responsibility for them.

Any people depicted in stock imagery provided by Thinkstock are models, and such images are being used for illustrative purposes only.
Certain stock imagery © Thinkstock.

ISBN: 978-1-4759-0273-0 (sc)
ISBN: 978-1-4759-0274-7 (hc)
ISBN: 978-1-4759-0275-4 (ebk)

Printed in the United States of America

iUniverse rev. date: 05/02/2012

In loving memory of my mother
—Dorothy Rita Gibbons—
whose spirit lives on and whose frail and
loving heart beats inside of me.
And to the memory of my dad
—John Samuel Woodall Gibbons—
who taught me to live the common life
with a servant's heart.

I heap an abundance of love upon my children
—Nathalie, Daniel, and Sean André—
with hopes that they will learn from my mistakes.

To my grandchildren
—Maddison Poppy, Coco, Lottie, and Daisy Boo—
The thought of them gives me endless pleasure.

To Unk and Aunt Rene,
who have always been an inspiration to me.

And to my childhood hero, Rob Marsh.

*For what shall it profit a man
if he shall gain the whole world
and lose his own soul?*

Mark 8:36

*And did those feet in ancient time
Walk upon England's mountains green?
And was the Holy Lamb of God
On England's pleasant pastures seen?*

From Sir William Blake's *Jerusalem* before Milton's *The Poem*

CONTENTS

Prologue In a Place Called Trinity xi

Chapter 1.   Higher Ground 1
Chapter 2.   My England 7
Chapter 3.   Black Country 10
Chapter 4.   The Watering Trough 15
Chapter 5.   A Bucket of French Frogs 17
Chapter 6.   Just Two Blokes 26
Chapter 7.   One Sad Day 32
Chapter 8.   On Hadrian's Wall 37
Chapter 9.   Blue Coat C of E and Art College 45
Chapter 10. Chelly Baby 50
Chapter 11. Outside Influences 53
Chapter 12. Nathalie and Daniel 59
Chapter 13. Bustleholme Boys 64
Chapter 14. To Lose a Love 70
Chapter 15. Original Mocumentary 78
Chapter 16. Coaching at The Albion 81
Chapter 17. Sean André 84
Chapter 18. Iberian Moment 92
Chapter 19. Coming to America 94
Chapter 20. Backstage Passes 102
Chapter 21. Tobacco Town 106
Chapter 22. Mistranslations 114
Chapter 23. The Wren's Nest 117
Chapter 24. Picture on the Wall 123
Chapter 25. Best Moves—A "Footy" Bit 127
Chapter 26. Full Circle 134
Chapter 27. Princess of Grass 137
Chapter 28. A Better Club. A Better Life 145
Chapter 29. The Great Escape 150

Chapter 30. Heman, Horrors, and Hilarity 154
Chapter 31. Namaste 161
Chapter 32. Bonanza 166
Chapter 33. Beautiful People 169
Chapter 34. If You Gain the Whole World... 172
Chapter 35. Heart Strings 177
Chapter 36. Miguel Liam Lemming... 183
Chapter 37. Sliding Down the Globe... 186
Chapter 38. Botswana... 193
Chapter 39. This Time for Africa 199
Chapter 40. Youth Sports.. 202
Chapter 41. Fish 'n Chips 204
Chapter 42. World Class Partners 206
Chapter 43. One Spectacular Day.. 209
Chapter 44. To See Her Face Again.. 212
Chapter 45. The Village of Bloc... 215
Chapter 46. Proper Mountaineers 220
Chapter 47. For Old Times' Sake 224

Epilogue Cherish the Moments... 233

Acknowledgements

to those who have contributed to my life story and added
to the memories in ways past understanding.

Thomas Rongen
John Fleming
Al Soricelli
Lesley Boggs
Lloyd "the Virginian" Bayliss
Mark Stokes
Rick Batchelor
Dr. Timothy Snare
Allen Scott
Ed Hollowell

To all my soccer players and coaches.

And to Jon Anderson and *Yes*.
You have always inspired me with your songs and words,
especially *Close to the Edge, And You and I, and Awaken*.

To Jane.
You got my heartbeat and my voice,
and you properly told my story.

Prologue
IN A PLACE CALLED TRINITY

She wrote the book in my voice, not the easiest thing she's ever done, she confessed. When we met that day, it seemed all too strange, but the more I thought about it, the more it aligned with other things that were going on in my life at the time. People were crossing my path right and left. People interested in me for all the right reasons. Interested in the direction I was taking. I had to know it was for a purpose. I'm still not sure where it will all lead, but I do know this, I have ignored road signs before. I dare not allow history to repeat itself.

Time has passed quickly since the day I met Jane—personally, that is. That day was not the first time I had seen her. And she was always doing the same thing. I frequented that coffee shop, such is the type of gathering place that attracts readers and writers and users of all manner of electronic devices. Then one day there she was again. I sat at the round table in the window on a high bar stool. Sipping coffee. Staring. Wondering what on earth she was doing. This is the message I sent my children in England that first day I spoke to Jane.

> Kids, I met this lady today in Panera Bread (a Wi-Fi coffee shop); I saw her the other day and was a little intrigued by her as she was flipping through reams of typed and written notes. I wondered why I was so drawn. Today there was a seat available next to her, so I slid into it, sat down and drank coffee. It took me about five seconds to start talking to her, such was the magnetism and me being just plain nosey—"Can I ask what you are doing?" I said boldly. She smiled and said, "Just finishing off writing a book . . ."

Paul André Gibbons

>And that was it. An hour and a half later we exchanged emails . . . and the rest will be history . . . one day. Things are just meant to be sometimes. Right?
>
>The story continues . . . about *a dead pig full of air*.
>
>Love, love and God bless! Dad February 2010.

I met her in one moment and opened the beginning of a lifetime of friendship with the writer of my story. A lot of words have been spoken, a lot of the story told since that day. These are Jane's words as she reflects on how she connected with me and, in an hour and a half, agreed to *consider* helping me tell my story.

Paul André Gibbons

The thought of it was overwhelming. I left Panera Bread that day and chastised myself for even thinking of taking on another life story. I didn't have time, but far beyond that, I couldn't understand a word this man said. His accent was so thick—like nothing I had ever heard. I said, "Huh?" so many times that I quickly used up my allotment before we ever started exploring the possibility of a story. There I was a southern writer, a woman, attempting to get the voice of a man born and raised in a place unfamiliar to me—The Black Country of England. I doubted my ability to capture the accent on paper, and more than that, the wherewithal to understand the nuances of a game about which I knew nothing.

In just a few days, I got a crash course in the life and times of a kid born a continent away. And as I've written the story, I've visualized the "Little Viking" growing up, maturing, facing life's trials and hurts quite like no other, to become a seasoned and great soccer coach. I call him a world class soccer coach, for which he rebukes me. Mind you, I had never seen a soccer game in my life, and I had no idea that soccer in England is football, that the players are not soccer players but footballers with passion reaching biblical proportions when their heroes rise up out of the earth and appear on the pitch. The pitch? What the heck's a pitch?

In a few short weeks, I had filled my mind with stories of football heroes, both players and coaches, and Gibbo introduced me to the great soccer coach, Thomas Rongen. I've read portions of life stories of some of the greats, including Bryan Robson, Gibbo's all-time favorite footballer. He handed me Robbo's book published in 2006, entitled *ROBBO, My Autobiography*, and I got on football overload just trying to keep up. What a guy, or as Gibbo would say, "A proper bloke!" He won my heart. He has an amazing vitae and nostalgic ties to West Bromwich Albion, a story all its own.

I didn't know what to expect the evening I went to see the U14 girls practice in Tarpon Springs, the first time I'd ever watched a practice. U14, huh? I thought it was a submarine of sorts until I asked only to find out the girls were all "under" fourteen years of age.

My daughter, Andrea, and I arrived and sat on the bleachers. The girls were already heavy into their evening session, and I was energized, sitting on the edge of my bench just watching their attentiveness. It was easy to see love and devotion to their Coach Gibbo. After a few plays, they huddled and the next thing we knew, they were all running toward us. They stopped directly in front of where we were sitting and sang, "We're Climbing up the Sunshine Mountain." Andrea and I both choked up. The evening was special as the girls sat on the bleachers with me, one by one, telling me all about their coach, their Gibbo. It was as if I had known them always. I soon learned the reason for the joy on their faces and the song in their hearts. And to top off the evening, on the piece of grass adjoining Gibbo's, the boys were practicing and Peter Ward was on the field—their coach. What a surprise, for Gibbo had just loaned me Peter's biography, fresh from the publisher, and I had already begun to read it. I think everybody who knows English football knows *He Shot, He Scored, It Must Be Peter Ward*. And that's the title of his new book, *He Shot, He Scored*. What a pleasure to meet one of England's great footballers.

Gibbo has dictated his entire life story while sitting across from me at the Panera Bread where we first met in Trinity, Florida—every word written over loud voices, crying babies, clattering dishes, spilt coffee. Somehow we were able to block it all out. I watched Gibb's face as he talked about his family, his children and grandchildren, his country, tears rolling down his cheeks at the poignant lines, and hearty laughter at himself as he recalled life in The Black Country of England.

I like to believe it did not happen by accident, but that it was God-appointed. I was just finishing the manuscript of my third book, and I was deeply involved in writing a life story for someone else when I met Gibbo that day. There was no way I could fit this into my schedule.

There is a poignant line spoken by the Psalmist that says, *O spare me, that I may recover strength, before I go hence, and be no more* (Psalm 39:13). I needed that kind of strength to follow through with a commitment of this magnitude.

All of us who are worth our salt desire to leave a legacy of good *before we go hence*. In the beginning as Gibbo talked, I began to pull things out of him that had never been spoken, not that it was hard to do. At first he thought he was in therapy. He needed to be freed from the chains that had held him captive since the day his mother died, to say nothing of the grief and guilt over leaving his children behind in England when he came to America.

I heard this many times in the weeks that followed: "That's the first time I've been able to talk about it . . ."

Entwined in his personal story I have found another theme. Paul Gibbons lives to touch the lives of the young people for whom he is responsible. Does he have enemies? Of course. There is an abundance of jealousy in all professions, especially where competition is involved. How he deals with it is incredible. I have learned much from Gibbo's life and times, but mostly of his selfless desire to make life better for the young people who need him. Of his willingness to take *a dead pig full of air*—a round of leather—and in an unforgettable journey, touch the hearts and lives of young people the world over. And if he can answer *yes* when as his friend, Mark Stokes, always encouraged him to say, "Lord—lead me. I'll do it," then who would I have been to say *no* to the writing of his amazing story.

Jane Bennett Gaddy, Ph.D.

Chapter 1
HIGHER GROUND

*. . . there's a poignant storyline that clashes
with this charismatic spirit of mine,
taking me to the depths at the most inopportune times.*

The highest "ground" in England is the Hawthorns in West Bromwich, the Black Country in the West Midlands. Its name derives from the beautiful hawthorn bushes that grow thick and full, their blossoms as white as the Cliffs of Dover. Appropriately, the hawthorn bush was considered the emblem of hope, but in 1900 those that grew on the site of the stadium had to be uprooted to make room for the new home of West Bromwich Albion. I lived beneath its shadow as a boy, served in its School of Excellence as a man; and it has been a part of my life since I was big enough to walk the Old Roman Road from Tantany and climb the altitude of a mere five hundred and fifty-one feet to reach the gates of its hallowed ground. I know its history, its players, its wins and losses, its legends, its supporters. When Albion fans roar and swear allegiance, I feel the earth move beneath me. I smell the sweat of its tribe, glory in its victories, and weep at its defeats. And like every other Baggie, what I've been told of the past stirs me to envision a cold day in 1950 as the March winds blew fiercely across the pitch and the highest-ever derby league crowd of 60,945 jammed the ground to witness a 1-1 draw against the Wolves.

For the sheer delight of seeing your face, I go back and take you with me to that high ground, and in the moment, we let ourselves go, standing as one with the fans in the massive arena and like a mighty roll of thunder and in unison, begin to shuffle our feet, then stomp to the beat of the deafening music. With arms raised, we clap our hands and roar in deep-throated passion while bouncing up and down. The warriors are about to enter the pitch, and they respond to one thing—the ensuing battle and the cheers of hordes of bloodthirsty troops dressed in navy and white stripes, our tribal colours. With a wild imagination, we return to medieval times, to the days of the Priest and the Warrior, of the English hero, *Beowulf*, and remember the Vikings with swords drawn, shields in hand, moving and swaying as the chanting begins. The music blares, crescendos, intimidates as *The Liquidator* booms through the gigantic speakers. The time has come to enrage the opponent and archenemy. The longest professional rivalry in football history—in the world—is the Albion and the Wolves, and there is a conjured hatred for the Wanderers in this cauldron of a ground.

The contest is on. The crowd roars. It's a goal! The Albion score! And with arms raised and hands clapping, West Brom fans jump and like a reenactment from the medieval past, begin to bounce and shout: "Boing! Boing!—Boing! Boing!" Contradictorily powered by foul language spewing from every lip, and in stark contrast to the peaceful verse, the fans thunder loud and deep, the twenty-third Psalm . . .

> *The Lord's my Shepherd,*
> *I'll not want:*
> *He makes me down to lie*
> *In pastures green; he leadeth me*
> *The quiet waters by.*

"The West Brom (clap, clap, clap). The West Brom (clap, clap, clap)."

I've since attempted to understand the connection—the boiling cauldron, the hate, the rage—with the Psalm. Obviously, the Lord's on the side of West Brom Albion! Consumed with pride, as always, I scan the Hawthorns. These are my brothers in arms, my kinsmen, my tribe. The dynamic is intense; the upsurge is raucous, and it doesn't cease until the battle ends and the last bloke is off the pitch.

A hatred for the gold and black is in my blood. I came by it honestly. Guess we could have been more cordial, but Albion later on and not so affectionately called the Wolves ground the Custard Bowl. Mind you and if you can believe this, I was never a thug as were some of the fans from both sides. It was not so much personal with me. It was purely tribal. That is, until the day of my fourteenth birthday. That was the day it became personal.

On a blustery Saturday afternoon in March, I walked to the station and took the double-decker bus seven miles to the Custard Bowl. I was wearing my brown leather bomber jacket, the navy and white Albion stripes on my scarf by no means hidden from plain view. Nevertheless, I tucked the scarf inside my jacket as we got closer to Wolverhampton. That particular day was one to remember. Chippy Clark scored the goal that declared the Wolves the losers, and the noise that rose up from that pit of a south bank was brilliant: "Olbeyun, Olbeyun, Olbeyun!" It went on forever. Tempted to believe it could be no louder, I was forced to recant, and on a scale that runs from zero for the least perceptible sound to a hundred and thirty for sound that causes pain, that day I was more aware than ever it was at its apex with every excruciating decibel music to my aching ears.

With a big smile on my face, I set out for the bus station, feeling good. We seared the Wolves 1-0. On my fourteenth birthday, at that. It had been hot in the cauldron what with all the excitement, but the mid-March wind was chilly. I kept my bomber jacket fastened tight, my beloved striped scarf well hidden. I was in the middle of Wolverhampton town center, for heaven sake, little skinheads and old geezers on the rampage looking for trouble in the shape of Albion fans. Walking out of Molineux that day, their fans were overlooking, spitting, throwing bricks and stones in barbaric fashion. My ears rang as those Wolves fans began to chant: "Wanderers! Wanderers! We hate Olbeyun! We hate Olbeyun!" Those were voices I had not wanted to hear, especially after such a sweet victory.

And then one of them shouted, "Look lads, here's one! Yowm Olbeyun, ay ya mert?"

Before I could attempt an answer, a couple of young skins slid into me on their Doc Marten boots, skimming low to the ground and coming in for a crash landing on top of me, sliding made easier with about ten drawing pins stuck in the sole of their boots. Their Levis were rolled up as were the sleeves of their Ben Sherman shirts; and to further identify the less than fashionable rogues, a scarf dangled, tied to a dirty wrist.

They nailed me with those hurtful Doc Martens, hissing and spitting out insults and throwing blows to my body parts faster that I could react. Those bloody skinhead Wolves fans kicked me in my sides, and might have left me for dead for all they knew or cared. Guess they were hoping they could take us down one at a time, but it never happened. Neither did they discourage me from supporting my tribe. It did quite the opposite. Until that day, I thought I could not have loved Albion more. Somehow, I did.

That afternoon I lay there face down on the street, writhing in pain, but with a smirk on my face, for we had won. Albion had won the game. I would recover, but my young blood boiled with hatred for those Wolves. I groaned as I rolled over and struggled to my feet, hoping no bones were broken, then I decided it didn't matter. I was going to see my girlfriend, Lesley Chell, if I had to limp or crawl to get there. I met her later that evening at *The Rec Rave* on Gillity Village South Walsall (the posh part of town). I was bruised but happy.

To understand me, you need to understand my passion. If you're going to read my story you need to know that *soccer* is *football* or *footy*. For practically every nation on earth football is a huge part of life. It's not a sport like baseball. You don't watch it like NASCAR, and you're not a fan, because fans are fanatics. Football is a family institution, the gathering of people who don't necessarily have to know one another to share a deep love, a passion. In England a child of seven can tell you the subtle nuances on the pitch, give you stats, stats they learned from their grandfather, or the local newspaper, or the telly. It's a community, neighbours. The way things ought to be.

Someone once said this to ex-Liverpool Boss, Bill Shankly, and I've never forgotten it: "To some, football is a matter of life and death." His response: "No, it's much more important than that!"

A true supporter might say, "We'll follow our club through thick and thin." Albion fans take it a step farther like Frank Skinner, comedian and devoted Albion fan: "We'll follow Albion through thin and thinner!" for *it's Albion till I die.*

Did you ever pick up a book, read it and think, "What am I supposed to get out of this?" It's not as though I felt I had a story. If you sit down for a minute, you can imagine that you have a story and you may be right about it. But do you do it every day? Is there a fire in your belly that causes you to wake morning by morning with that fire ablaze? That's what this is. It isn't an ember, it isn't even a hot coal; it's an open flame that I cannot extinguish, nor do I want to, neither can I explain it. Maybe we've all been told a lie. Maybe the Machiavellian brainwash got on all of us, but there's another way; it doesn't have to be dog eat dog. You don't have to raise your voice, crack a whip, step on someone, engage fear. You can, if you have the greater desire, teach someone how to do a thing so well that you give them your passion. You can light their fire and then stand proudly alongside them while they show the world what they've learned about team, power, success. About heart, about life.

This is my passion. As far back as I can remember. But there's a poignant storyline that clashes with this charismatic spirit of mine. I'll tell that part first, as it never ceases to vie for prominence in my thoughts, taking me to the depths at the most inopportune times. But that's part of who I am.

For the first time in my life, I'll pull to the frontal lobe of my brain the things that have been too painful for me to say, much less record on paper. Things that need to be said, some of them having never been spoken. I never intend to erase the bittersweet memories; but I will say them in hopes of relieving the pain in my chest. At least I'm counting on that. I'm a man. An Englishman. But I've learned that real men do weep. Maybe not enough. I still have a lot of tears inside me from years gone by.

I hasten to say, despite the sad memories, my life is intensely meaningful, and I know I am where I should be, at least for the present, though an entire continent away from my birthplace and my beloved children. "You are where you are meant to be" is a beautiful line written by, Jon Anderson of *Yes*. I didn't realize how meaningful the music of *Yes* was for many years. Now, I cling to the words as if they were written to me.

If I could sum up my life and finish my story in this first chapter it would be in the words of my dear friend and colleague, Al Soricelli, just a few weeks ago as this book is being written. He wrote me this affecting message: "God has given you a gift to translate a beautiful game and deliver it to kids of all levels and abilities. In doing so you are improving lives and opening doors that otherwise would not be opened. Soccer is your ministry. Execute it well and lead your charges to Christ via the beautiful game. It doesn't get any better than that!"

Paul André Gibbons

This is my story—*Gibbo's Story*. Not just about football, but about life with hopes dashed and dreams realized. With immense heartache all crammed into fifty-plus years, and with the higher ground of happiness and joy that have supplanted the most unpleasant of times. If I have a song to sing, it's the brazen declaration of West Brom Albion:—*The Lord's my Shepherd*.

Chapter 2
MY ENGLAND

*It's a spot of tea at the appointed time,
announced in the poshest English accent.
It's medieval buildings; it's blimey; it's bloke; it's Baggies.
It's Albion till I die. Forever.*

I'm proud to be English. That is—like England used to be. Like it must be once again if it is to survive. Enoch Powell was a Conservative Minister of Parliament for Wolverhampton during an unsettling time in England's history. He delivered a daring and controversial speech to the Annual General Meeting of the West Midlands Area Conservative Political Centre in Birmingham on April 20, 1968. I was fourteen years old and remember little about that day, having my own teenage thoughts and dreams. For me, there were things to be happy about, even though I did experience the scourging of the bloody Wolves fans just a month before. I was beside myself with excitement, for WBA, which you know by now is West Brom Albion, were preparing to play in the Football Association (FA) cup final in May of that year. We won 1-0 with a scorching left-foot goal by Jeff Astle.

But for Enoch Powell, it was a wrinkled brow. I've since read his speech and it rings in my ears today. He dared to stand up for what he believed was right concerning a real problem coming down for England. He said as much in the so-called *Rivers of Blood* speech. That speech went like this: "As I look ahead, I am filled with foreboding. Like the Roman, I seem to see 'the River Tiber foaming with much blood'. That tragic and intractable phenomenon which we watch with horror on the other side of the Atlantic but which there is interwoven with the history and existence of The States itself, is coming upon us here by our own volition and our own neglect. Indeed, it has all but come. In numerical terms, it will be of

Paul André Gibbons

American proportions long before the end of the century. Only resolute and urgent action will avert it even now."

It may be too late forever. That I fear. Powell was offering critical advice, clearly contemplated, clearly communicated, but arrogantly refused by the powers that be. He was dismissed from the Shadow Cabinet for his controversial speech in opposition to mass Commonwealth immigration to Britain, paying the price for taking a stand for what he believed and against what he knew England would face. Obviously, America has been too proud to learn from history—their own and that of England.

⚽

Through the eons, my country has been categorically contradictory. On the one hand, lighted by democracy; on the other, dimmed by class oppression. But there may have been method to madness. There's much to be said for institution, and I have always loved the pomp and ceremony that sets England apart from other countries. There is nothing that sends chills up a spine like the days, weeks, and indeed the closing moments of *The Proms*, with the last magical night, a time when everything turns truly British, Union Jacks proudly flying everywhere, the music resonating in the parks, the pubs, and the prisons in that common instant when all of the British Isles are one. Hyde Park, filled with all the accents of Great Britain, linked live to the Royal Albert Hall and the grand orchestra, the crowds joining to sing along—*Rule Britannia, Jerusalem, Land of Hope and Glory, God Save the Queen*, and on that final evening with arms crossed, holding hands and swaying as one, throngs of British singing *Auld Lang Syne* in voices raspy from weeks of sustained use.

But I cannot forget the beautiful tradition and unwavering reality of coal pits and rising smog of earthy industry that have always joined hands with the Monarchy to keep the balance. The green hills and valleys beckon souls to come and live and play in the pleasant land that birthed the *Magna Carta* and the *King James Bible*. We're a nation of punk rockers and footy fans who live one generation behind another, and we never expect that part to change. It's pubs and shops, factory workers and financial traders. It's a spot of tea at the appointed time, announced in the *poshest* English accent. It's medieval buildings, it's blimey, it's bloke, it's Baggies. It's *Albion till I die*. Forever.

Forever? I believe Enoch Powell was afraid we were losing our *forever spirit*. He was concerned for England and what he saw coming that aligned with what was already happening in the United States. He was not wrong. I have now observed both sides of the Atlantic myself. My dad was such a left winger because of his concern for the men in the Labour Movement. I believe he was right at the time. I know he meant well, that he never expected a welfare state. Key word for him was the *working* class. He had a strong work ethic himself. But things changed in England. Just like they have in America. I've watched both countries digress in some respects reaping the harvest planted many years ago, nurtured by outside forces bent on affecting these two great countries with, among other social issues, illegal immigration unchecked and borders unsecured.

Maybe that's why I love football so much—I love it for many reasons—but I see the work and play ethic that transcends politics and class oppression. That is, in the young people who play the beautiful game, and yes, parents who stick with the stuff, leaving aside personal and political ambitions. There's always a fly in the ointment, but in my wildest imagination, I would never have believed I would one day experience the ugly intervention of politics into the game for which I've spent my life. I'll explain later.

Chapter 3
BLACK COUNTRY

*I was born on St. Patrick's Day, March 17, 1954.
The year West Brom Albion won the FA Cup.*

The *Domesday Book* traces West Bromwich as far back as 1086; its meaning is the little village on the heath of broom, broom being a particular type of bush. Perhaps like the bush used to make the broom upon which Harry Potter would fly in years to come. Only kidding! About Harry's brush broom, that is. From the twelfth century it was actually a Benedictine community called Broomwich Heath, and by 1727, it was a coaching stop between London and Shrewsbury. That's long about the time it started to grow, this town I call home.

I was born Paul André Gibbons on St. Patrick's Day, March 17, 1954—the year West Brom Albion won the FA Cup—to Dorothy Rita and John Samuel Woodall Gibbons in West Bromwich (pronounced *brommige* with a silent "w"), in Staffordshire as it was known before it became the West Midlands of England about five miles northeast of Birmingham on the London-to-Birkenhead Road, originally built by the Romans. To put it historically—an *Old Roman Road*. I had always thought my dad had a double barrel name, Woodall-Gibbons, but was duly informed by one of my relatives, who is into the family tree, that it was apparently a trend to have a mother's maiden name as a middle name. It happened that my grandmother's maiden name was Woodall, and it was passed down to my father.

You already know how much I love this town—famous for its football club, West Brom Albion, founded in 1878. Ten years later in 1888, WBA became one of the twelve founder members of the Football League, the first professional football league ever in the world. They played at a stadium near the town centre until they moved to the Hawthorns on Birmingham

Road in 1900, where they remain to this day. They were my team when I lived there. Still are. The Baggies are my heroes. We are, in England, very tribal in the way we follow our hometown football teams, and I have never been an exception to that rule.

The Black Country where I lived was the birthplace of the Industrial Revolution. It was Queen Victoria who, in a visit, saw the dusty grey grime and smoke and named it the Black Country. Appropriate then, for there was black gold beneath the earth's crust, though in its raw form it was more depressive than lucrative, the atmosphere dull, drab, and gloomy. Yes, coal and limestone were beneath. And running water. All the components needed to participate in a period of time that helped industrialize the world. Black Country folk were, and indeed still are, earthy; life typically consisted of residence in a little house, a wife and mum who made nails, took in laundry, and hauled the kids off to school whilst her husband worked in the foundry. At the close of a hard day in the hot chambers of iron pounding, thirsty he was, and it was off to the pub for a drink pulled from the draft at the bar, right out of the cellar at just fifty-six degrees. In those days, water was not the healthiest drink. In fact, it was often polluted, not meant to drink. But the beer—it was fermented and processed. You might say healthy in comparison to the alternative. And a good excuse it was to drink the amber nectar instead.

"Bitter!" or "Mild!" was their shout. "And some black pudding or pork scratchings!"

Black pudding, now a delicacy, is black sausage made of congealed pig's blood, and pork scratchings are pork rinds to the Americans, simply crispy pork skins with the fat rendered out in a huge iron pot. The Americans use a wash pot. Another delicacy from Black Country fayre when I was a lad was sheep's brains on toast (enjoyed at home only, not in the pubs). I could easily spread my own. I know, sounds like something straight out of *Beowulf*. But you've got to get into the spirit of all things medieval.

My roots are steeped in Black Country tradition, something I'm proud of. I've been in The States for many years, but my accent is still thick. I should say—my accents, for the Black Country has many, sometimes varying from town to town, but all true Black Country people can speak easily in three accents—broad, posh, and la-di-da. Broad you'd speak (spake) at home (at'um); posh is a sort of neutral Midlands-ish voice using standard grammar that can be understood by outsiders; and la-di-da is a sardonic imitation of upper-class pronunciations, as near the Queen's English as possible. We put i's after o's a lot. The accent is unique, like a language all its own. J.R.R. Tolkien—Americans know him as a writer of high fantasy novels; the Brits know him as a philologist and professor at Oxford University—was born in South Africa; however, he and his mother returned to England when his father died. Tolkien was raised up in my country, the West Midlands in Birmingham. He considered the dialect of Middle English to be his own native language. "I am a West-Midlander by blood," he once said, "and took to early West-Midland Middle English as a known tongue as soon as I set eyes on it."

To a lot of people, it's a tongue hard to understand. We who know it say it's just plain comfortable and we've loved it *ever since we set eyes on it.*

What's not to understand about a little lady from Bloxwich who, in the manner of the English language, would look down at her snotty nosed child, who in between taking *sups of her warm tay in a little babby bottle, would spake and Mum would correct her.* "I've tode yow before, it ay ay, it's ain't!" What she means is, "You shouldn't say ay. You should say ain't." (Ay means ain't and isn't). In her case it was from one piece of bad grammar to another. Though, no doubt, Tolkien would approve.

There's a band called *The Troggs*, an English group with loads of kids following. They did a song called *Wild Thing*. Once we were on vacation for two weeks in Gothenburg, Sweden, walking through the fun park when we heard the band. The lead singer's name was Reg Presley. I came up behind him and in Black Country accent, I said, "Reg, can I get your autograph, please?" He turned around and gave me the autograph, recognizing by the accent I was from the West Midlands of England. There's just something about the Black Country dialect that can get you in the door!

Speaking of talking posh . . . at one time, the most popular television programme in England was *Blind Date*. Believe it or not, I was once on the programme. It was, of course, a blind date for the girl who would be choosing from one of three of us. The girl was tall, her height even more noticeable because of the bouffant hair, and she kept saying to the producers: "He cahn't be taller than I." I was obviously not as tall as she was even without the big hair, and to top that, she spoke the la-di-da. The other two guys (who were tall, of course) were speaking her dialect, so I just got comfortable in my seat and, off the cuff and unrehearsed, I leaned back and laid on the thick broad accent of the Black Country, of course with no effort. She liked it—they all do! I got the date, even though she was a foot taller than *I*. When we returned the next week, I brought two roses, one for the tall girl and one for Cilla Black. Everybody in England knows Cilla Black. She was the popular host of *Blind Date* and a celebrity singer. Fantastic lady! She liked the rose!

Black Country folk are fiercely proud of their heritage, distant cousins to the Geordies (supporters of King George). In that respect, is it the Viking link, I wonder? The Vikings first landed in the Newcastle area and found their way down to the Woden's Borough, now the town of Wednesbury, and the hard dialect, a huge part of that tradition, will never go away. As the locals always say, "It's bostin—*ay it?*" And, my American friends, that means *the best*.

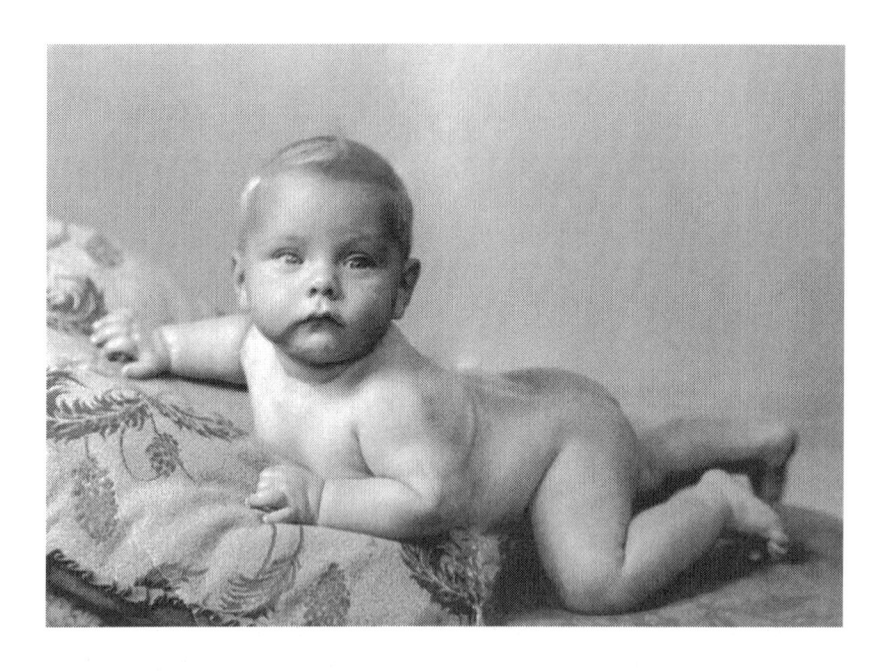

Baby Gibbo
I was born Paul André Gibbons
on St. Patrick's Day, March 17, 1954.
The year West Brom Albion won the FA Cup.

Chapter 4
The Watering Trough

He was all out for the working class.
A hard worker himself, he knew the woes.

We lived in the pub my father managed. The Watering Trough. *The Truff*, it was called. In Walsall (pronounced *Wor-sull* by the locals). I'll give a bit of history on the ancient little town of Walsall. It dates back to the eleventh century, but is generally first mentioned as a settlement in 1159, located on the hill by the Parish Church which I will mention later. Bloxwich, a town whose name suggests a pre-Conquest origin was in the same parish. This is also of significance to me, and I will tell about that later, as well. Most of the parish lay within Cannock Forest. By the fourteenth century, mining and iron-working had begun, and in 1540, Walsall was a little market town with a park, blacksmiths, bit-makers, and pits of coal, lime, and ironstone. Horse transportation was expedient, hence the necessity for producing horse furniture and for leather-working and rope-making. It's different now in the twenty-first century, but many of the old landmarks and trappings are there. The wonderful medieval buildings, the rich heritage, and certainly the accents remain. In years gone by, The Truff was a stop for stage-coaches with a twofold purpose. It was a place for them to take refreshment and a hostelry literally with a watering trough and a place to feed and bed down the horses for the evening.

Our bedrooms and bath were on the third floor. The kitchen and the living rooms were on the second floor. Yes, I said living rooms. We had two of them—one where we watched the telly; the other was the *best room*—with the big light. And the pub was on the first floor.

The pub was a way of life for my family. I loved the social expression it allowed, for when I was a lad, I didn't have the presence of mind to know the somewhat questionable side of it. I could walk through the different rooms that made up The Truff, wearing different hats so to speak—hats I had fabricated, sometimes with accents to coincide, for there was a different crowd in every room. People from all walks of life. I was good at interviewing the patrons. My personality fit right in with whatever was going on in the moment. I could as well speak with the CEO of a large corporation like Mr. Ackers of Ackers & Jarrett, or Chris Butler of Butler Aluminium. I played for their youth football team and later at age fifteen, for the Butler Aluminium men's team. I could converse with Bruce George, a local MP (Member of Parliament), and members of the Labour Party, who liked to frequent The Truff. My dad promoted the Labour Party. He was all out for the working class. A hard worker himself, he knew the woes. I take after him in many respects, protective of the underdog, always putting myself in their shoes, being one with them. I met Robert Plant, who was later with Led Zeppelin, at my dad's pub. I heard his first single when he was with *The Listen*—called *You'd Better Run* and got it autographed by the artist himself. I renewed acquaintance with Robert at West Brom Albion and later in Atlanta.

And there were the soccer players right off the field. I could mingle with the athletes, the social class or the normal working class. It mattered not to me. I was just enjoying life, flaunting my youthful abilities and accents, totally uninhibited in a world I had created.

When I was growing up, the pubs in England were much like the Wi-Fi cafés in America, places where friends met, where couples went to chat, a place for the practice of socializing. It was in the pub that I learned to mingle with people, expand my horizons, where I began to understand cultural nuances. I could tell you in a minute what a member of the hard working class was going to order. A pint of *mild* or *bitter* and *a crusty chaise and onion cob*—thick slices of cheese and onion on crusty bread from Ditchfield's Bakery, which I fetched myself from up the road.

Chapter 5
A Bucket of French Frogs

In no time and at Roland's directions
I had frog legs cooking in the olive oil and garlic
with a little butter added.

I was always glad for the occasion to speak French, and at every opportunity, I honed my skills. We spent holidays in France. Mom and Dad and my sister, Heather, and I. We would load up our camping gear, and drive all day across England through the Marble Arch via London to arrive at the English Channel at Dover, where we took the ferry across. The White Cliffs loomed behind, and then faded into the distance as we neared the shores of France. Come morning, I rose early, dressed and ran to the local market place in search of the bakery to order bread.

"Bonjour monsieur—dame—du pain s'il vous plait."

It was big stuff for *moi*—an eight-year-old English boy—trekking to the *boulangerie* alone and, in my best French accent, ordering bread. It gave me confidence.

Once we made a convoy of cars across France—Dad, Mom, Heather and I, Aunt Rene, Uncle Joe (Unk), and the cousins, Rob and Pat Marsh and the delectable Jenny who was to become Rob's *Hyacinth Bucket* (pronounced *bouquet*, of course) in years to come. We stopped, got out of the cars, and set up the blue camping gaz stove. The blue camping gaz stoves are famous all over Europe. We needed a cup of tea. And we needed to satisfy our hunger with French baguette, butter (melted in the back of the car), fresh tomatoes, and warm soggy corned beef from a can. While the family waited for tea, I walked into the forest to check things out. Picnickers lined the long Napoleonic road (originally designed to shade Napoleon's troops), and the poplar trees offered shade to me on that hot summer day. I was about eight years old, wandering in the forest some ten yards from a big cat when Dad and Unk came looking for me. I thought that was a right big cuddly cat I saw. Actually it was some sort of wild mountain cat. Dad and Unk were rescuing me from my audacious self! I shudder to think of how foolish that was. But at eight years of age, my lust for adventure and love for wild animals overpowered any sense of danger.

Once, much later, we camped at St. Julian des Landes with Aunt Rene, Unk, Rob and Jenny, who was now his wife. We couldn't sleep that first night for all the clicking out there in the dark. We had no idea what it was until morning when we could see. It was hundreds of land crabs. They were everywhere. Looked to me like biblical proportions, a plague.

At the campsite there was this local French guy called Roland. He wanted to go fishing and I was game. At the end of his hook, he attached a little red cloth. "What do you plan to catch with that?" I asked, doubtful of any pending success.

"You'll see," he replied, and led me down a beaten path familiar only to him, I supposed.

He turned down a country lane and continued the trek into a little field surrounded by hedges and trees to a murky pond. It was green as pea soup. I trailed along directly behind him with my own thoughts.

"There'll be no trout in there," I said.

I couldn't see his face, but he must have grinned at my pessimism as he went about the task of dropping his hook with the little red cloth attached, into the water, and proceeded to bob it up and down, popping the top of the water until a frog grabbed the hook. Within half an hour we were walking back to camp, and I was carrying a bucket o' frogs. We got out the blue camping gaz stove, the frying pan, a bit of garlic and some olive oil. Or was it butter? My best guess is that it was both.

Roland showed me how to *take care* of the frogs. He held one by the legs, laid him face down, and with the blunt side of the camping knife, he whacked the frog on the head rendering him unconscious. He turned him over and with the sharp side of the knife, sliced his legs off and threw the body, belly, and head into the bucket. Then he peeled the pajamas off (the skin). In no time and at Roland's directions I had frog legs cooking in the olive oil and garlic with a little butter added. They tasted just like chicken. Everything tastes like chicken. Ever notice that? Actually, they tasted just like frog legs. Delectable.

We went into the town to a café which was a butcher, baker, candlestick maker, post office. A commissary of sorts where you could get a brandy and coffee and anything else you wanted. On the way back to camp, a rabbit ran out into the road. My dad turned to miss him, and when we looked behind us, every car was turning to miss something that was not even there. The rabbit had long since fled into the woods. People are funny, including us! Had BBC been filming, we would have fit directly into the latest episode of *Last of the Summer Wine*.

Le Nauzan Beach near Royan is the most beautiful place on earth. Heather and I thought so. We could stay all day by the sea, swimming and playing on the rocks, looking for little crabs. I can still smell the salty air; and the sweet woodsy fragrance of a sauna reminds me of the balsam trees in France. We drank Orangina, a delightful fruit drink in pear-shaped bottles, and we sat under the pine trees having tomato, ham and cheese on French bread followed by some fresh peaches. Rob Marsh and I played babifut (foosball in America) and table tennis. Rob was champion of the local table tennis competition. Always my hero, he could do no wrong.

The French have a wonderful way of life. Everyone gets up early, and at noon, they all stop to eat and relax, a daily ritual that takes two hours out of their day. We drove down to Saujon, a little village by a river town centre with beautiful trees and boulevards, stopped to eat at a sidewalk café with birds twittering and French people chattering. That was fun, but my idea of a meal in France was at a little farm house with earthy food prepared by earthy people—*potage du pomme de terre*—soup of apples of the ground (potatoes). Potato soup dipped with a big ladle, but it tasted twice as good spoken in French. I loved that.

The town of Cognac is on the river, Le Charente. Built right on the bank, it is an old medieval city where the French make brandy and where cognac vineyards grow as far as the eye can see. Black mildew, caused by moisture constantly forming in the making of brandy has dripped from the sides of the houses for decades. There is an earthy, mossy smell that lingers with me when I think of Cognac on the River. We visited the top floor of an old stone building that had wood floors and wood tables. The place served about twelve courses. It was like the last supper, a fabulous meal that took three hours to consume. We gave it our best. *Bostin!*

Quite a few miles from Cognac is the town of La Rochelle, famous for its old harbour. Dad took me down to a little boat restaurant where we ordered fresh lobster and crab. When we were in France, eating was always an adventure with my dad. He took the ferries, the old roads, to the chateaux overlooking the rivers, always down the leafy paths to obscure places where the French people preferred to eat. None of those tourist places for him.

Travel was half the adventure. The only bad part about vacationing with Dad was that, from time to time, he saw fit to spit out the window. Once it went out one window and into the other. Sick! For I was always sitting on his side and in the back seat. I still gag at the thought of something so nasty hurtling my way at seventy miles per hour!

Vacations had a way of ending abruptly and, once again, it was back to pub life in Walsall with hopeful thoughts of next year and another splendid adventure somewhere in Europe waiting in the wings.

Aunt Rene, Heather and I on the ferry from Dover to Calais

*Mom, Heather, Aunt Rene and I
standing beside the yellow Triumph Herald,
on our travels through France.
Such grand holidays with the family!*

*Dad, Aunt Rene, Heather, and I
inspecting the grapes in the vineyards
Southwest France*

Heather and I camping in Royan, France

One of many bullfights in Spain.
Heather, Pat, moi, Peter Cashmore, and Rob

Chapter 6
Just Two Blokes

We would sit at the table in the big kitchen
just two blokes, having roast beef on crusty bread,
the windows open across the back,
gauzy white curtains blowing mysteriously in the night wind.

Mitchell's and Butler's Brewery owned the pubs in the West Midlands. They came around from time to time, and I got to know them.

"As soon as you get married, you can have a pub of your own," they told me.

"No," I said. "I don't want to bring my family up in a pub."

"Yes, and why not?"

"Well, sir, I have no desire to be a publican. I aspire to do other things. Not that I mind the way I've been raised, I just crave something different, perhaps another lifestyle for my own family. I need a change. Another direction. A real home life."

I never knew what a regular home was, with a mom and dad who had nine to five jobs. I guess I was breaking tradition, but at that point in my life, it didn't matter to me, for I was already thinking ahead, knowing there might well be something else in my future. I was either going to be an art teacher, a footy, or . . . or well, a rock star.

Before I left the nest, we lived in five different pubs. Never lived in a house until I married. Always over a pub, I think five of them before I turned nineteen. There was The Bell in Wednesbury and The Corner House in West Bromwich which is no longer standing. It was the headquarters for the Supporters Club for WBA. I went on stage a couple of times in front of Ronnie Allen, doing a fine impersonation of Elvis or Adam Faith, Cliff Richard or Lonnie Donnegan. Ronnie Allen was an international English football player and manager, a professional footballer for nineteen years.

Once he brought home a couple of wine-filled bull fight statues from a trip to Bilbao, Spain, which I still have. Don Howe and Bobby Robson also frequented the Supporters Club. I'll never forget Bobby Robson who was later knighted. A great man. Rest in peace, Sir Bobby.

Then, of course, there was The Watering Trough and next The Bell—a different Bell—on Birmingham Road in Walsall, of which I have fond memories. Famous Albion and England players still practice next door. They often came in for lunch. Having my heroes in my pub excited me no end. Willie Johnston, Bryan Robson. And Asa Hartford, who was named after Al (Asa) Jolson, frequented The Bell.

And, I can't forget The Elephant and Castle in Wednesbury, where one year Father Christmas gave me a three wheeler bike. I tried to ride it down the second floor stairs without a happy landing.

The pub consumed my family seven days a week, with not much time for anything else, certainly no promise of a spiritual life except at school. My mom and dad worked Saturdays and Sundays, too. But no depth of Christianity for me. There was not enough time in a day, and quite frankly, I never gave it much thought. No time to develop the spirituality that I didn't know lay deep within.

There was a lot to learn about owning or running a pub, for they were governed by the *Magna Carta*, the content of which declared the rules for the country as it concerned the drinking and serving of drinks. Getting served beer in public places meant each drink had to be measured and the proper portions served. It was constitutional, so to speak. And Dad had to know the laws that governed the pubs, the serving of drink, some of which might have been medieval, still they were the law and he was constrained to abide. If the drinking culture in the USA and England alike were examined, no doubt there would be fewer drunks on the streets of both countries, and if the governments spent less time quibbling over calories and obesity and more on drunkenness . . . well just maybe . . .

I don't know what year The Watering Trough was built. I just know it was old. A three story flat-front brick with a cellar, built right on the busy Road A34. It was a grand old building. The walls inside the pub were paneled and there were several rooms; a trendy black lounge where some famous people gathered—as you know, Robert Plant, a little later to become lead singer with *Led Zeppelin*, and Ozzy Osbourne of *Black Sabbath* fame and the lads from Judas Priest also. There was a room for smokers, where the old gentlemen would go; and a snug bar and lounge with a bit *posher* seats, more private where a man and his wife might enjoy sharing an evening in a quieter atmosphere. Come to think of it, smoking was allowed anywhere in the pub; and centuries of inhaling and exhaling, depositing vast amounts of tar and nicotine upon the walls, ceilings, and fixtures layer upon layer, rendered a ghastly shade of yellow that accumulated year after year after year. Not a shade of yellow Martha Stewart would have chosen.

My dad served lunch of such things as gammon, egg 'n chips. The aroma of ham steak cooking on the grill from our rooms above is with me still. The pub itself smelled old and musty; such was unique to the pub, enhanced by the aroma of hot sandwiches and diminished by the smell of warm beer unless, of course, one savored the smell of the *bitter* or *mild*.

We had the best music in town with all of my *Zeppelin*, *Cream*, and *Hendrix* singles ending up on my dad's pub jukebox. We listened to Santana's *Soul Sacrifice*, Sonja Kristina and Curved Air's *Vivaldi*. *Soul Sacrifice* and *Vivaldi* were Dad's favourites.

The barrels of beer arrived by truck once a week, the draymen routinely sliding them on big ropes one at a time down the steps to the floor of the cellar. Dad kept the place in immaculate condition, especially the pipes, for the beer was drafted through those pipes to the pub on the ground floor. He served a fine beer. The musty smell of damp and old mixed with the beer was unique to the cellar. Out back there was a glass covered place for empty bottles ready for the draymen to pick up on certain days, and outside toilets were available for our patrons.

A balcony overlooked the yard where we played football, and below the balcony was a greenhouse where I kept my pet hedgehog. He . . . well, my hedgehog had lice as, of course, they all did, and I was bent on ridding him of the pesky problem. I got a bucket of warm water and some bleach and proceeded to scrub him. It was an act of kindness, though the poor varmint died anyway; I was grieved while reasoning with myself that at least he died clean, for I had bleached him to death.

At night I used to sneak downstairs for a hot sandwich with my dad. Or sometimes late at night he would cook in our kitchen on the second floor. The mouth-watering aroma of a slab of tongue or a big side of beef would waft through my room and wake me. I loved being with my dad. He was loads of fun and a hard worker, though he always had time for me late at night when everyone else was sleeping. We would sit at the table in the big kitchen just two blokes, having roast beef on crusty bread, the windows open across the back of the kitchen and gauzy white curtains blowing in the night wind. Those were good times for me. And when my dad thought it was time to get some sleep, he would send me up the stairs to bed. I remember holding to the hand rail, smooth from years of traipsing up and down those stairs. Such a handsome piece of wood with my DNA all over it. And such great remembrances of Dad sitting at the table until his day finally ended and he climbed the same stairs to Mom.

If memory serves me, there was a fireplace in every room. Much needed during the five months of winter every year. When I was younger, I would trudge to the third floor at night to a bath near freezing until Mom would add a kettle of hot water from the stove, making it bearable. Quite warm if she added two. Ahh! Getting out to a towel warmed at the stove, and putting on layers of flannel, I would run to my bed and pull the quilts to my neck. Even with all the cover I could still draw in a breath and when I exhaled, watch the air around me turn frosty white. The windows, glass and lead, were all iced up not just on the outside but on the inside.

I was (still am) two years older than my sister, Heather (we called her *Zezza*). We were pretty independent while Mom and Dad were running the business. We got ourselves up in the morning, walloped down a bit of breakfast of toast and jam, dressed, and walked to school. After school each day, we rushed home to what should have been homework for both of us. Heather always did hers. I was not so diligent, only allowing myself enough to get by. I had better to do. But at exactly four o'clock in the afternoon, I was perched upon one arm of the sofa, Heather on the other, ready to ride with the Lone Ranger, and when the music broke, we were off to the Wild West, to the buttes and tabled rocks and wonders of another continent on our makeshift horses, all to the tune of *The William Tell Overture*.

Mom had tea on the table at exactly four thirty. Of course, tea is dinner in England. Dad always watched the news on BBC at quarter to six, when we were duly prompted to change the channel for the time being. Dad opened the pub at six o'clock, so our lives were always predictable beginning with afternoon tea. Come to think about it, so were my evenings, which were consumed with sports. Seven to nine, without fail, it was 5 v 5 soccer or some other sport mostly at Blue Coat Church of England School's gym club. Or I was outside running three or four miles. As we got older, Heather and I usually got ourselves ready for bed. There was nothing wrong with that. We were learning to be self-reliant.

Little did I know at the time it would serve me well in the not-too-distant future.

By law Dad had to close the pub by eleven at night. Sometimes on a Friday night, after closing, I would sneak downstairs and socialize with Dad and his friends who sometimes stayed for some good fayre, which we called *afters*. I would go to *The Barbeque* chip shop, next door to *Ditchfield's* to get chips for everybody. My favourite was a quarter chicken n' chips, with bread n' butter to make *Chip Butties* and maybe a couple of halves of Worthington E (a bitter). My dad could count on me. I knew exactly what to get.

Our traditional Sunday afternoon meal was roast beef with carrots, roasted potatoes, cabbage, and gravy. Afterwards, the big question was, "What's for puddin' Mom?" She would hand me a tin of Mandarin oranges; I'd pour some cream over and take a slice of bread, buttered and cut in quarters for dipping. Nobody dips bread like that anymore. It was just for *the times*. A lot of the traditions of England came from the War years when families had to serve what was available. Good thing for us that *out of necessity came delicacy*, for those were great meals. One of our favourites was oxtail stew. Dad prepared it, of course, and there was nothing better. He added a pig's foot, pearl barley, loads of vegetables like potatoes, carrots, onions, and leeks. The pig's foot was mostly for flavour, and he would remove it from the pot when the stew was ready. He ate the pig's foot himself—not us—though we scuffled for the delectable oxtail, and by the time the meal was over, our lips and fingers were stuck together from sucking out the marrow.

*Mom, Heather, Tiger and moi at the Watering Trough, 1963.
One year later Mom would not be on the picture.*

Chapter 7
One Sad Day

... I moved away from the wall in my room
toward the third floor windows that faced the street
and watched with my face pressed to the glass as the driver
turned on the siren and pulled away from the curb ...

I have substantial memories a couple of years prior to turning ten. Before that would be those conjured from what I've been told or from photos so poignant as to stir remembrance whether it is there or not. But after age ten, things changed. Dramatically. While only allotted a short time in which to get the job done, my mom shaped my childhood in ways inexpressible and then she slipped away. She was beautiful. Small, with dark hair and blue eyes. My best memory of Mom is from pictures, mostly black and white, and I near panicked when I couldn't remember what colour her eyes were. And then I found out. Aunt Rene told me they were blue. I have my mother's eyes. She was really quite fragile when I think about it, and young—always young in my memory. She was loving, but with an intense look in her eyes. Best described as Ingrid Bergman eyes. I never took pleasure in being around elderly people back then, even now. I suppose because of how I tenaciously resolved to remember my mom. I have my own image of her and her mystical smile, one that is pressed indelibly on my consciousness.

My mother died on June 17, 1964.
　In Hallam Hospital in West Bromwich, England.
　The hospital where she gave birth to me just ten years before.

I always thought it was a hospital in Walsall until February of 2010 when I saw a copy of her death certificate for the first time. It had been forty-six years.

Everything changed because of what happened that warm Saturday morning. The images in my head rocked my world for the longest time. Even now when I speak of it my chest tightens, the tears start, and I want to turn back the clock. And I force myself to remember.

It was early June, summertime in England, flowers blooming in window boxes, foxgloves and honeysuckle scattered about the countryside in spades and the hawthorns were in full white bloom, raising hope that every garden would soon be brilliant with the colour of summer. A wonderful time of year in the West Midlands. But in this particular year and for me—not by any stretch of the imagination. Darkness was about to settle all over my young world.

About eleven that morning, I overheard Dad talking on the phone. In those days we had one phone which we hardly ever used. The old white chubby device was locked away in Dad's office. I don't remember using it once. If we wanted to contact our mates, we would make verbal arrangements at school earlier in the day, or just pop 'round their house on the off-chance we would find them home. Who knew we would ever need mobile phones, computers, or texting devices?

Dad was ordering an ambulance. I tried hard to block out the rest of his conversation. He was calling that ambulance for my mother. I knew she was ill, but I didn't know to what extent. I don't even know if Dad knew to what extent. Although thinking back, he must have known, but my dad was very good at keeping things from Heather and me.

My mind was racing with thoughts of Mom and Dad. I was young, but I knew well enough about how much they loved each other, and if anything ever happened to her, Dad—well, I didn't know if he would make it through. I thought of all the things they had told us of their lives together. They were Harley riders, apt to just pick up and ride away if only for the day. This, of course, was before pub life when they had weekends and evenings free. And it was before Harley riding became so trendy. Guess you might say they were Harley riders before riding was cool. Back in the late forties, early fifties. How many people had even heard of a Harley in England at that time? I believe they biked around Cornwall, even lived there for a while. And off they would ride to France and Germany just after the War.

It was nothing for my dad to stoop and tie my mom's shoe. He was always doing the little things for her. A gentle touch, holding her hand. And they loved ballroom dancing. They were the West Midlands Latin American Ballroom Champions. They used to go dancing together with Mom's sister and her husband, Aunt Rene and Uncle Joe. My mom and dad were very close, and I could see Dad was struggling with what was taking place.

I didn't have the nerve to go into Mom's room, though I had seen her face earlier that morning and I knew she was sick. I was shaking scared, didn't want to see her being carted off to the hospital in an ambulance. I stood in the door of my room waiting while Dad rushed down the two flights of stairs to the pub below. I could hear sounds of life down there. A man laughing with gusto. Why didn't he stop laughing? Any other time, it would have been a welcomed sound. But not right now. And smoke. I could smell tobacco smoke mixed with beer and the smells from the grill where my dad had been preparing lunch the day before, not today. It was making me sick. The aroma I had always savoured was now unpleasant to me. I was relating those smells to my mom's illness, and I was nauseated.

A few minutes passed and I heard footsteps on the stairs again. It was my dad. He was running up the steps ahead of the men who were bringing a stretcher. They went into Mom's room and I jerked back into my own room, not wanting to see what was going on, tears chasing down my cheeks, knowing they would soon take her away. I heard the shuffling of feet, but no sound from my mother. My beautiful mother, whom I loved better than life. What was happening to her? Why didn't I have the nerve to just go in there and ask her? Why would my feet not move me in that direction? It was as though my shoes were filled with lead. Something was taking place that I couldn't grasp.

The man in the pub below was still laughing. A guttural cheeky sound. I wanted to cover my ears or scream out for him to stop, though I'm sure he meant no disrespect. He just didn't know. When the men came out of my mother's room, there was the metallic smell of blood. No doubt, she was hemorrhaging. I could hear movement as they brought her out of her room. She used to wear a little blue nightgown. Maybe she was wearing that, and the sheets on the stretcher were pure white. I can't remember if there was crimson on those white sheets, or if I imagined it from what I was told. I probe my brain to remember some things. I couldn't watch the final scene of that painful moment.

Dad stepped into my room. I could see he was a wreck; his face was pale, like all the blood had drained. My own head was spinning. He stammered and then spoke, "Son, do you want to step out and say goodbye to your mom?"

"No," I said. I think my dad was taken aback at my abrupt answer. So was I.

And that was it. There was no discussion, and thinking back, I know my dad had not the presence of mind to discuss anything. He was worried about Mom, but he was also concerned about Heather and me, trying to think ahead. Thinking the worst. "Will I have to live the rest of my life without my beloved Dot? What will I do about my children?"

As I struggle to remember things, it comes to me that I cannot visualize where Heather was at that moment.

Dad turned and left with the men. And I turned my face toward the wall and choked back the tears. The wall—that wall that was saturated with wonderful childhood memories of Mom and Dad and Heather. The wall—covered in dark grey paper, summing up the day, reflecting the mood of what was going on around me. Over the grey papered walls from floor to ceiling and some on the ceiling were Albion photos and posters, and there in the corner was the red blinking light I had gotten from one of the road works. (After forty-six years I finally owned up to theft! From Walsall Council Road Works Department, and I say, "Sorry lads.")

Though all those things were familiar to me, I felt like I was in a strange place. Like I didn't belong anywhere. My whole world was turning upside down. Mom must have been lying on that stretcher lifeless, for she never called out to me. I assumed she couldn't speak a word, and my dad was so distraught. Knowing how she must have been feeling, I wondered if Mom had fears of the worst. Fears of leaving us. Fears of dying. Right now I would give anything to know *what* my mother was thinking that day, and I would give anything to see her face again.

They started down the stairs with her, and I stood as still as possible, peeking around the doorframe, listening to the shuffle of feet as they gingerly carried her down. When they reached the bottom of the stairs, the laughing stopped. I heard the heavy wood door shut behind them, a deafening sound before stark silence settled over the pub. Silence as thick as miasma over the pond where I fished as a boy. The entourage was gone. Such a final word, *gone*. What I didn't know at that moment was that there would be no more lilting laughter at my childish tales and Heather's blithering chatter about her day at school.

I hated myself for it, but I just couldn't say goodbye. I couldn't speak a word. In that moment things were changing and I didn't like the way I felt. I knew something was happening; she was going away from me. I never visited her in the hospital. Not once, and I don't even remember how long she was there. I wanted to remember my mom as she was. Carefree, soft and happy, gliding and sliding and dancing around our home with her cotton dress touching her thin white legs, her dark hair brushed back and fastened with a comb, humming a tune while she prepared tea early of an evening. She was resolute. Permanent. At least I thought she was.

Reluctantly, somewhat like a robot, I moved away from the wall in my room, gravitated toward the third floor window that faced the street, and watched with my face pressed to the glass as the driver turned on the siren and pulled away from the curb and out into the street. I couldn't see her, but I knew Mom was lying on a stretcher in that ambulance, and Dad was right beside her, no doubt holding her hand. Crying. I was suddenly overcome with grief, having withheld my emotions as long as possible. I leaned into the window and followed the ambulance until it was out of sight, tears falling like rain onto the sill. I slid to the floor and cried until I could cry no more.

Chapter 8
ON HADRIAN'S WALL

My thoughts were granted reprieve for a time, but when the jaunt on Hadrian's Wall was over, the Enemy was still there.

Mom's only sister, Irene (we called her Aunt Rene) apparently knew Mom was seriously ill. She and Uncle Joe came for Heather and me and took us away to Scotland for ten days or so, probably the best thing for the time being, for I was so affected by Mom's illness. I remember some things about this time in my life, apparently impacted by what I experienced. Aunt Rene and Unk bought me a kilt. I romped the Scottish hills wearing it proudly. I walked Hadrian's Wall, sword drawn—well, I imagined I had one; it was probably just a stick—thinking about the glory days of the Romans who left this treasure from one of the world's greatest civilizations. Hadrian's Wall rivals the Taj Mahal for worldly chattels, and I walked upon it, battling Roman soldiers and any other enemy that came my way with my imaginary sword. I was angry. Mom was sick and in the hospital. I had thoughts that I may never see her again. The Roman wall that separates England from Scotland—the Wall North of England—was my battlefield that day, and I aimed to take out all my frustrations on the Enemy Death, on the forces of evil that were taking my mom.

⚽

Aunt Rene and Unk did everything they could to get our minds off Mom, wanting us to enjoy that trip. They took us to a place called *Gretna Green*, a village in the South of Scotland, near the mouth of the River Esk, the first village in Scotland that followed the old coaching route from London to Edinburgh. It was where the famous runaway marriages were first recognized in 1753 and where mock marriages have been performed for centuries. Aunt Rene, Unk, Heather and I stood at the old Blacksmith Shop *over the anvil* with a mock wedding party as a couple feigned a marriage ceremony. In ages past, it was possible for boys to marry at age fourteen and girls at age twelve without parental consent. Times changed and so did the law, but the attraction is still there, history whispering tales of marriage ceremonies for the young performed down the centuries. The anvil remains as a symbol of times past and true love confirmed. Happier times, perhaps. Carefree.

My thoughts were granted reprieve for a time, but when the jaunt on Hadrian's Wall was over, the Enemy was still there. And the mock marriage sufficed for distraction for thirty minutes then I was, once again, consumed by what could be happening to Mom.

We visited the Cave of Robert the Bruce. An ancient legend lingers that Robert I, King of Scots, battled the King of England, and after his defeat at the hands of the Comynes and the incarceration of his family that followed, Bruce hid himself in a cave on a deserted island. Downhearted, he watched as a spider sought to spin a web. Each time the spider failed, it simply started over again. Inspired by this, Bruce returned to inflict a series of defeats on the English, as a result winning more supporters and victory at last. The tale explains the adage, *if at first you don't succeed, try and try again.*

I remember looking down on a pool with salmon swimming in clear water by Robert the Bruce's Cave. We stayed in a lovely little B 'n B alongside picturesque Loch Lomond and its Castle. I've always loved medieval history, and with a good imagination, I walked straight into the era of the First War of Scottish Independence when William Wallace opposed King Edward I of England (Longshanks) and his cruel laws. Sad and bloody story. But later came Robert the Bruce. Happy ending. I remember years later watching the beginning of *Braveheart* and thinking, "I hate the cruel English." I was always sticking up for the little guy, a theme that runs through my life, I guess. Reminds me of Neil Ashton, one of my mates at school. Everybody picked on him. I stepped in, played the part of William Wallace, and fought for him, pleased to do so.

My mind goes blank on a lot of what happened in the next few days, and quite like Heather—until now—I've been reluctant to speak of my mother's illness, for many years even refusing to acknowledge some of it, specifically what happened that June morning in 1964. The hurt is still there, but just voicing it and stretching my memory on purpose and thinking about what might have been, has helped unleash the reluctance.

We returned to Walsall and our home at the pub. To my dad. I'm unclear on the timing. Looking back, it was a quiet Sunday evening, in the best room, the one with the big light, on the second floor. I opened the door and saw Dad standing at the far end of the room. I'll never forget the look on his face. After all the Scottish distractions, I was still not ready to hear what he had to say. I remember Aunt Rene and Unk being there. And Heather. Dad sat us down and told us while we were all together.

"Mom's gone," he said, choking back tears. "She's—"

"You mean—?"

"Yes, son. She's gone. We've lost her."

Dad sat staring at the floor, rubbing his hands together scarcely able to speak. He swallowed hard. It was impossible for any of us to give mental validity to what was happening.

He said, "This is the worst day of my life. Not sure what to do."

And then my dad broke down and cried so hard it scared me. His young wife was gone. Forever. But selfishly speaking, that had no real meaning to me in the moment, for no one counted but me. She was my mother, and I was ten years old, for heaven sake. I needed my mother. I had to figure out how in the world I would get on without her. Everywhere I looked there were memories. Her face was ever before me, and I had not even said good-bye. I had to live with that.

And yes, I was angry at God. I had just one question, and I pled to know, "Why? Why? Why did you take Mom?" I stared at the door, begging God to tell me, "Why doesn't she walk through that door right now?" I didn't realize until later that I was talking to an omniscient God of whom I knew little, but who knew me well. He was the one who knew the end of the story and who would see me through this trial, though I didn't know at the time how that could be possible nor that it was his plan to help me.

I didn't go to my mom's funeral. I just couldn't. I never wanted to remember her any way but the way I had always known her. Young and beautiful and soft . . . just . . . just my Mom.

Heather and I went to live with Aunt Rene and Unk and with our cousins, Patsy Diddle and Rob at 20 Bernard Street in West Bromwich, just a few miles from Dad. I don't really know why. Guess everybody concerned thought it should happen that way. Mom was like salt and light. The neutralizer. Our balance in life. And Dad may have thought living at the pub without Mom would be less than healthy for Heather and me. Aunt Rene was next best to having Mom. I loved *ma tante*.

Living in a regular two up, two down house was novel. And there was a garden, one side for flowers and one side for vegetables, separated by irregular broken concrete slabs. There was even an outside clothesline. It was a pleasant place, minus a very important amenity we were accustomed to. There were no inside facilities. We had to go outside between the house and the garden. Not fun in the wintertime with a solid block of ice that had accumulated . . . well, you know where . . . that posed a huge problem, even worse at night when it was both cold and pitch black. We didn't have tissue, but Aunt Rene (or was it Unk?) nailed torn strips of newspaper to the wall of our outside facility for convenience. We had a choice—either the *Express and Star* or the *Evening Mail*, both evening newspapers, so the supply was plentiful. *Express and Star* was the paper for real Black Country folk. *The Evening Mail* was for Brummies (Aston Villa and Brum fans. *Brum* is short for Birmingham).

Living there at Bernard Street was different from what we had been used to, but we were none the worse because of it. All these things—the good, the bad, and the in-between gave me perspective. If I didn't know where I had been—how would I recognize that where I was going was better? At any rate, I knew I had to make the best of life in order to move forward. I was willing to go the mile, especially with Aunt Rene and Unk, Patsy and Rob. I hope I thanked them properly.

West Bromwich was only about seven miles from Walsall. We stayed in our same schools, although it was no longer possible to walk. After all those years I had to ask Aunt Rene how we got to school and back. She drove us. Guess life *did* move on in spite of the heartache and my lapse of memory.

I do remember spending as much time in the gym as I was allowed, playing squash alone with my soccer ball, slamming it against each wall with anger and purpose, running, driving, calling my own shots, anything to quell the anguish. I needed to win the battle against my circumstances. I had to work hard just to survive the constant ache in my heart, and in so doing, I developed a passion for winning.

On Friday nights I went with Rob to get the fish 'n chips. Before you all ask—yes, in real grease-proof paper and wrapped up in *Express and Star*. Or was it *The Evening Mail?* Those newspapers were handy for a multitude of uses.

Little insignificant memories stayed with me, such as the insurance man coming by regular as clockwork to pick up Aunt Rene's premium. He always marked her book and then marked his own book, proof that she had paid for the month. Unk would be in the kitchen in his white vest—undershirt to Americans, or commonly known on both sides of the pond as *a wife beater* (remember Onslow on *Keeping Up Appearances?*) getting ready to go up and visit the Labour Club. We all went, but before we left there was yet another ritual. He would tell us kids, "Scrub your neck!" I often wondered why scrubbing the neck was so much more important than scrubbing all the other body parts.

We arrived at the Labour Club where the hard-working blokes looked forward to a night out with their families and friends. There was a Snooker Room, a snug, and the main room, with tables and chairs arranged around a dance floor, the stage set and waiting for *the turns*—people who would get up and take a turn at singing. In my memories I hear the clinking of glasses, music playing over loud voices, people having fun just being out together, taking a turn at singing the pop songs of the old folks' era. *A kiss is just a kiss; a sigh is just a sigh . . .* backed by the sounds of the big bands and orchestras. Lip-sinking to the music of *Cliff Richard and The Shadows*, *The Beatles*, and *Cilla Black*. A little *Tom Jones* and the tunes of the sixties that had successfully made it to the Top Twenty charts by then, and some nostalgic songs maybe. I was eleven years old. It was only 1965. We had a ways to go before *Zeppelin* and *Black Sabbath*.

We stayed a couple of years with Aunt Rene and Unk before returning to Dad. I have some recollection of those two years, but I was still trying to get over my mom being gone. I thought I may have stayed for, say, a couple of weeks throughout the summer, but two years? How? I do know that my cousin, Rob Marsh, became my hero. He was there when I needed him and I learned that he would always be there for me, one of the most comforting of thoughts.

While living in Bernard Street in that little terraced house with Aunt Rene and Unk and my cousins, most nights twenty to thirty kids gathered to play footy in the streets. We painted goalposts on brick walls in someone's garage. Most of the kids were older, and I was used to getting knocked about by mostly grownup lads. Rob was seventeen, and although they never made me feel like I was a nuisance, I must have been one, for I spent hours on end playing with Rob and his mates.

The year I returned to my father, I played my first proper game.

Imagine me. That was the year I knew without a doubt I had a passion for football. I was in senior school, twelve years old, and I was asked to play for the school team. It was on a Saturday morning. I was a "fusty" at senior school, and we had a game that morning in Bloxwich, on Field Road if memory serves me correctly.

I left The Watering Trough at nine o'clock in the morning, traipsed through the streets with my *togga* boots tied around my neck, off to the bus station, took the one to Bloxwich, got off and walked onto the field to meet my teammates. We put on our famous royal blue silk shorts and canvass-like shirts of blue and white quarters. The shirts were like a tent, heavy; and if it rained they were unbearably weighty. On our chest was the famous "Blue Coat" badge. By half time I was crying tears of passion, begging the teacher, "Put me in goal—anything." The second half I went in goal. It was pathetic. We lost the game 15-0. Every time we took a goal kick, it went straight to our opponent and they scored. After that game the teacher made me captain and centre forward, such was my burning passion for this game. I never looked back after that one game. It made me fight even harder for the underdog, not for me, but for the team, the cause.

Gretna Green, Scotland.
Aunt, Unk, Heather and I
June, 1964.
Where the heartache began.

My bastion—the soccer ball
Bernard Street, West Bromwich.
Healing.

Chapter 9
BLUE COAT C OF E AND ART COLLEGE

With every stroke I felt myself partaking of his suffering,
though in no way to the extent.
I looked down on that picture, on his agony.

Within a couple of years, I was back with a vengeance. I was always popular with the kids at school, and at twelve and thirteen, more so than ever. I had a fan club. The senior girls all fancied me no end. They teased me so much it was difficult not to blush. They liked my blonde hair, blue eyes, and the crooked smile that was bound to escape my sometimes melancholy spirit, at some point breaking through to the mischievous side that propelled me in my teenage years. They liked rock stars and soccer players, and I could head in either direction.

The counter culture offered me everything I could dream of, but with temporary fulfillment. I tried the long hair, attitude, *The Who, Zeppelin, Marc Bolan, Carnaby Street*. The rebellious scene that was so me. I dressed different from everyone else, and when the fads came and went, I still had my own style, influenced obviously but I kept my own image, easily identifiable. However, when my mates, Robbo and Hurky, went into skinhead mode, I stubbornly declined.

I spent a lot of time in two trendy clothes shops that opened up in Ablewell Street, of all places a few doors up from The Truff. One was called *The Trend*. The other one was called *The Poor Millionaire*. One of my favourite bands at the time was *The Move* from Brum—Ace Kefford, Trevor Burton, Roy Wood, Carl Wayne, and Bev Bevan. When they were invited to the grand opening of those trendy shops, I met those lads. *I Can Hear the Grass Grow* and *Night of Fear* were two of their first singles but *Flowers in the Rain* was their most familiar, which happened to be the first record played on the new *Radio One*. I later got to know Bev Bevan on an airplane flight from England to Atlanta. Even though he was a Wolves fan and he knew I was Albion, he gave me his card and invited me to go and watch *ELOii* in Atlanta. I still have the card. Nice lad.

Times were changing and I would not be left behind. I attempted to be the things I had never been and to do the things I'd never done. The things my mother would have helped me through. But she was gone. My dad was a fine man who loved us very much, but he was not my mom. At least I was picky about the girls, always comparing them to Mom. She was my ideal girl. This is still a problem for me. A petite brunette wins over a tall blonde any day!

I said I had no spiritual connection. We didn't go to church except for weddings and funerals, but St. Matthew's Parish Church was situated directly behind the pub where we lived. It is told that in the Sixteenth Century during the Civil War and the time of Henry VIII there were tunnels built that led from St. Matthews Church to The Watering Trough and the Monks used the tunnels as a hiding place during the Civil War and the Reformation. St. Matthews is made of stone; for me there was no spiritual link whatsoever, the vicar himself, like stone, boring. It was a medieval church, a big turn off to a young lad like me.

I did have a connection to St. Matthews, of sorts. We tobogganed on the hill in front of the church in the wintertime when it snowed. A splendid ride from the door of the church to the street below. And I attended the famous Blue Coat Church of England School at Walsall for all three schools—infant, junior, and senior. Richard Theodosius was my R.K. teacher in the senior school, a great teacher of religion. He opened our fertile minds to events that happened in the Bible. His thesis was that God gave us a brain so we can reason. "Do you think the Burning Bush was literally burning? Or was it the appearance of a strong sunset?" Such were the questions he would ask to stir our thinking. The man had a great mind. He was a thinker himself, one who rationalized everything. I liked him a lot. He later was the vicar at my marriage in Bloxwich at my request. But we mostly studied particulars about the Church of England—religious history, theology, and philosophy. It was my first experience with the concept of no absolutes. I'm absolutely more intelligent now!

From middle school my teachers were grooming me to become *head boy* of the senior school, the status dating back from an old institute in England with prefects, one where the head boy wore Oxford-Cambridge cap and uniform. I was a take-charge kid, and that was exactly what one of my teachers wrote across my grade card. *Born Leader.* I didn't get head boy. I was pleasantly rebellious, playing both parts quite well.

Two of my teachers, understanding my potential, pushed me toward the arts. Mr. Howard and Mr. Selway, both from Wales. They took all of us to new levels of learning. And my music teacher, Mr. Peter Morris, an Albion fan, was a great instructor. I took the A-level art exam at senior school, and one of my drawings is in Walsall History Museum and one is in the Blue Coat School. I graduated at age seventeen, could have left at sixteen; but I stayed on for an extra year to gain more knowledge, take more exams, and because I loved it. It turned out that staying was to my advantage. I needed the opportunity to mature.

My mates and I hitchhiked to Wales and spent several weeks every summer. Some of our old haunts were Oxwich on the Gower Peninsula, Abermule near Newtown, and Ambleside in the Lake District. Such great times we had. Amongst those who travelled were Blogsey, Spaz, Hurky, Robbo, Jim (Paul Oakley), Tony Hall (who got no nickname, well he did, but I can't mention it in this book), Stephen Flowers (Weed), David Croft (for obvious reasons we called him Bucket because he always looked *pale*) and me, Gibbo. That needs no explanation, right?

Amongst the other nicknames were Milko (Michael Wilkins, a very skillful footballer), Snail (Steve Neal), Spew (Steven Hewitt, God rest his soul), Satch (Steven Satchwell), Ash (Neil Ashton). By now, you know that England is big on nicknames.

On one of the trips to Oxwich, we all set out in twos. The tent would be arriving in parts. Before everyone arrived, we proceeded to set up our tent in the sand dunes, only to find out half of it was missing and we would have to make do. Nothing fazed us. We were boys and full of mischief. We had managed to sneak a bottle of cider along and we all got tipsy that first night, seven of us in one tent, thinking of every way in the world to make each other giggle. Like a bunch of girls, we were! We would take a couple

Paul André Gibbons

of swigs of cider and die laughing. We were the Oxwich Boys, camping in the sand dunes of South Wales, part of the Mumbles area, the peninsula, having the time of our lives.

One of the lads said, "There's a dew (pronounced *jew* in our dialect) on the tent." And another said in reply, "Tell him to get off then!" That was it. We all laughed until we cried and then fell asleep exhausted. What a summer to remember!

We were living at The Bell Inn when I entered Art College in Walsall. Every morning I would catch the 118 Midland Red Double Decker Bus, and head for the college, arriving early enough to cadge a fag off someone. I liked to smoke silk cut. My mate, Robbo, smoked No. 6. I looked forward to going every day, liked wearing the trendy clothes, looking cool. I always took my favorite snack, Twix. They were cold from the refrigerator just the way I liked them, hard to bite, but so tasty. And Walker's Crisps, plain or chicken, the best crisps in the world. Add to that a cup of tea or coffee. Now, that is a nice combination, ay it? A fag, a Twix, Walker's Crisps, and a drink.

I was always glad to see my muckas, Robbo, Slobba, Pedge, Jim (Oakley), and the beautiful Linda Turner. I really fancied her; she was so beautiful, so natural. She wore a smock, jeans, and clogs; and she had curly hair. I had to look at her with wishful thinking. It was hard for me to see my first girlfriend, Lesley Chell, with someone else, but it was best for both of us. We were getting on with life, leaving behind a first love. Her older brother, Robert, was a Wolves fan. He was not allowed to say the name around me! I liked playing Subbuteo with him and his mates. They were clever lads, went to Queen Mary's School, and frequented The Truff. For a time, I stayed in touch with Lesley's mom and dad, Betty and Norman, who were lovely people. He worked in a top job at Goodyear, or was it Dunlop? And he qualified himself to sail the world single-handedly. I heard Lesley married, moved to Dover and has four children.

My foundation courses were fine arts, sculpture, printing, design, and graphics. Looking back I have to say my best subject was design. I did well, was a quick study because I had the creative within. I was enjoying learning as much as the extra-curricular activities. That year we had a chance at booking an up-and-coming band called *Pink Floyd* for the Christmas "do" for £600, an opportunity missed and later regretted.

Living at The Bell was a nice experience for me. I had my own little quarters, a room I called my studio. A place to draw and paint as long and often as I wanted. I had a print of Salvador Dali's *Crucifixion of Christ* and a hard board about four feet by three feet. One night I got out my linseed oil based paints and started painting Dali's depiction of Christ on that board. I couldn't stop. It overtook me. Consumed me. It was as if the red-wine colours of the oil paints were part of the blood of Christ mixed with the water, the sweat. With every stroke I felt myself partaking of his suffering, though in no way to the extent. I was looking down on that picture, on his agony. I painted hard until two or three o'clock some mornings, only stopping because I was totally exhausted.

When I think back, most of my paintings were of a religious nature. I did another piece for my A-level art class, the profile of a nun lying down. And another I did from memory, part of Leonardo da Vinci's Virgin of the Rocks, a beautiful depiction of John the Baptist and his mother meeting up with Mary and her son, Jesus, and worshipping him as Christ the Saviour. I still have that.

But I was not on a good track yet, still trying to find my way since my mother died, still not knowing what I was going to do with my life, and still trying my best to enjoy the weirdness that was out there and available to a young bloke tentative about the future.

Chapter 10
CHELLY BABY

*The night I came back from Paris
with Hurky and Dad after camping in
Boise de Boulogne for a week in October,
I got off the 33 bus in Bloxwich Town Centre
and ran all the way to Bell Lane.*

This journey through life cannot go on without mention of my first-ever love.

Lesley Chell and I were high school sweethearts in the truest sense of the word. I was one year older than Les, our birthdates one day apart. I had been at high school a year when we first met. Her natural beauty lingers in my memory. She needed no makeup, her skin near perfect. Her face was like Sandro Botticelli's *Birth of Venus* so much so that I have to wonder whether Sandro was family with his surname pronounced Botti*chelli*. Funny, this has always been one of my favourite paintings and he, one of my favourite artists. And the Chell nose—there is something about a flared nose that does me. Her mom possessed the same loveliness, a Roman nose at its best. Lesley had lips soft and innocent; and beautiful hair, a mass of bouncing curls, not unlike my own, framed the lovely face that always boasted a smile

I look back in time and think of Mr. Joe Sturrock, who was headmaster at the senior school. He loved Lesley. Not too keen on *me*, he would talk to her privately about *us*. I knew he cared for her, just wanting to protect her from the likes of me. He couldn't know my heart, how I felt about her.

Indeed, my hair was getting too long and he took me into his office one day and, in his old-fashioned Yorkshire accent, told me: "Gibbons! Gibbons, lad! You look like one of *The Who*!" Did he realize he gave me the biggest compliment ever? I loved Roger Daltry!

Lesley was little and cute. She loved riding horses. For me, it was football first, but as soon as I had done with footy, we were together. I spent a lot of time at her house at Bell Lane, Bloxwich. Doing homework. I used to love being in a real house with a real family all together at the same time. Her mom, Betty, was kind and loving. Looking back, I think maybe my own mom would have been like her. Norman, Lesley's dad, was a big man, an intriguing intellectual. He had a special room filled with books and maps. Only he was allowed to go into that room.

Lesley and I loved each other so honestly and truly. We even went with my family to France on a camping holiday. Everyone at Blue Coat talked about what a beautiful couple we were—Paul and Les. We were in the same "house" together at school, and we sat next to each other. We thought we were destined to be together the rest of our lives. I wish it had been true. But living in a pub, as I have mentioned, had its ugly side. Temptations for a fifteen year old lad were there, and my honesty killed the relationship. I have to wonder why I ever said anything. When I think about it, it was honesty disguised as stupidity.

The night I came back from Paris with Hurky and Dad after camping in Boise de Boulogne for a week in October, I got off the 33 bus in Bloxwich Town Centre and ran all the way to Bell Lane. As soon as she opened the door dressed in black, I knew. The look on her face told me she had something to say that was going to devastate me. She was working at a Debenhams in Walsall when she got asked out on a date by the Glen Johnson look-alike, Dave Clarke. For those of you who are interested and not up on English *footy*, Glen Johnson is a fullback for both Liverpool and the National team. I was off school for a week, so heartbroken. November 17 is a sad day for me, the official day of the break-up. *The Long and Winding Road* by the Beatles whom she adored, especially John, will always open up another crack in my heart. I like to think of happier songs like *My Girl* and Led Zeppelin's *Thank You,* and one of her favourites, *Revolution*. I can hear her singing that now.

It killed me to see my girl with Dave Clarke. He used to wait for her at the school gates, a good-looking chap. We talked some after they broke up. He told me all she ever talked about was "her Paul." That first love is something special, even now, I can assure you. When we went to Art College together I used to see her and Steve Haynes, her new flame, walking down the marketplace together, curly hair bouncing in unison, scarves waving. I had to admit they did look good together.

Paul André Gibbons

Years passed, putting time and distance between us. Betty and Norman and I stayed in touch, especially after they met up with me on learning of my dad's death. They invited me to their home once knowing that Lesley, who no longer lived at home, was due for a visit and would be there on that particular day. "Wouldn't it be nice," they said, "if you were here with us when she arrives."

We all surprised Lesley. I was married by then, and my wife knew I was going to see her. Lesley and I went out and she drank me under the table. We ended up at a night club in Walsall listening to Tamla Motown songs, which of course, reminded us of how it used to be. I dropped her off outside her family's house and we both decided it was best for me to go sooner rather than later.

I have never heard from her since, even though her mom and dad wrote letters. I believe they went to Stafford then to a lovely place by the River Severn, Bridgnorth.

I can honestly say that in Sean Connery's version of *In My Life* (Lennon) I think of her when it says, *There is no one compares with you and in my life I love you more.*

Chapter 11
Outside Influences

*I was nineteen years old when I married Lyn
on September 22, 1973, in Bloxwich Church.*

Looking back, I know I should have stayed in Art College. I loved it. I left after the first year. I had it to do, though, for there were outside influences. And at the same time, I cut off my beautiful blonde locks that had so identified me at that time in my life. My best friend, Dave Hurst (Hurky), moved on to another college and later became an art teacher. I was proud for him, but that had been my big desire at one time. The days of our lives passed so quickly. Seems like yesterday we honed our skills and flaunted our talents at the Art College and now he's retired, spending lots of his time on a sailboat somewhere between France and England with his lovely wife, Adrienne.

I ended up getting a job with Albert Lloyd, who was the Manager of Britannic Insurance Company in West Bromwich. At age eighteen I was the youngest employee in the history of the company, and by the time I was twenty-one or twenty-two, I had made assistant manager.

Back to the outside influences.

It was whilst at Art College that I met Lynda. Lynda Ann Horton. I called her Lyn. She lived in Church Street, Bloxwich, and she worked in a bank. Her mother and dad, Ann and Arn, were lovely people.

I was dating a girl by the name of Lesley Washbrook at the time. I was supposed to meet Lyn one night and something came up. Maybe I was saying bye-bye to Lesley Washbrook. I can't remember; I just know

I couldn't get there. Next night I walked into Beer Keller at the Dirty Duck in Walsall, and there was Lyn. Beautiful girl. Brown wavy hair. She was small, the little yellow and blue polka dot short skirt with black tights fitting her to a tee. And she was wearing clogs, which added just the right amount of inches to her five foot something height. I was happy to be taller than she. With half a cider in her hand, she stamped her foot, angry because I didn't make the date. She looked at me and said in her little Bloxwich accent, four words, "You can sod off!" That's when I knew she was going to be my wife. For the first time a woman turned me down. I had stood her up and the little Sagi had spoken. Sagi as in Sagittarius. Nothing more mystical than that. Just Sagi (pronounced Sajji, I guess).

I was nineteen years old when I married Lyn on September 22, 1973, in Bloxwich Church. Richard Theodosius, my RK teacher in senior school, performed our ceremony. Lyn and I got ourselves a little rental in Long Meadow Road, a semi-detached house in Orchard Hills in the posh part of Walsall on the Sutton Road up towards Barr Beacon. The Beacon was significant, situated high on a hill. Significant because it was a favourite courting haunt for Lyn and me. And historically significant, as well, for when the *Spanish Armada* was set to invade England and the Spanish were coming, the English lit beacons all over England. (A story similar to America's *Paul Revere* and the lanterns in the North Church.) Looking westward from that site, you can see all of the Black Country and far in the distance, the extinct volcano called The Wrekin, and sometimes on a clear day, the foothills of Wales. Looking due East from Barr Beacon, the next natural land mass as the crow flies is the Steppes, a range of mountains in Russia. I thank my geography teacher, Mr. Phillips, for these bits of geographical trivia I've enjoyed through the years.

I have bittersweet memories of living in Long Meadow Road. We had a red setter named Kester. And another dog that died of a mental disorder. His name was Stay. So I would shout, "Here, Stay!" He would make a move then stop abruptly. The poor thing went crazy in the head. Kidding, of course.

I remember taking Kester for long walks on a country road through the fields with my wellies on (rain boots in America). We hiked for miles through meadows, over the gates, through the hedges. The walks were as much for me as they were for Kester, but what a dog! He was so well trained he would not get into his food until I gave him the word. One day I filled his bowl and walked away failing to give him permission to go for it. I was gone about an hour, and when I came back into the kitchen, there sat Kes, eye on his food, drooling, longing for that bowl, refusing to eat it until I said it was okay. Yes, I felt bad. But he got me back. One Sunday morning we laid a chicken out to thaw and left the house. When we returned, the whole thing was gone. Kes had walloped it down without disturbing the plate that lay empty on the counter.

Once Lyn and I had an argument. Not the first, nor the last. Actually, we were married for twelve years and only had one argument. It lasted twelve years, mind. Anyway, she picked up an orange and threw it at me. I ducked and the orange hit the French window. Glass flew everywhere and Lynn yelled, "It's your fault!"

"How's that?" I said, laughing at her.

"You ducked!"

We both laughed.

We did all the little weird things that young married couples do, tried our hand at socializing, deciding we should have a dinner party and invite some friends over. With our favourite music playing, we served a nice dinner to Hurky and Adrienne, Jim and Jackie, and had a glass of wine afterward. Lyn excused herself and went upstairs to the bathroom. When she didn't come back down for a while, I went to check on her. She was lying on the bed. I thought something was wrong and lay down beside her to find that she was simply taking a nap. The next thing I knew, morning had broken. I had fallen asleep myself, and our poor guests finally let themselves out, locking the door behind them. We read the note they left, "Thanks for a great evening!" Obviously, at that early stage in our marriage, we were so lacking the social graces.

We left that little rental when we bought our first house in Overdale Drive, Willenhall in the heart of Black Country. By the M6 motorway—at one time, local coal was used to fire the furnaces and the air pollution level was unequaled in the world, but the heavy industry that dominated came to an end in 1968 when some of the coal pits closed and clean air legislation prevailed. So, by the time we set up housekeeping in Willenhall, Black County was not as black as it once was. It was a sad day for Black Country when some of the large old factories closed. There was still plenty of pollution from the M6, the busiest section of Motorway in Europe and from the forges that were still left, but soon the old furnaces were dropped forever, the smell and smog vanishing with them.

We bought the house in Overdale Drive in sort of a magical moment. We saw the "For Sale" sign, knocked on the door, and long story short, we made an offer on the house that had inside walls of a chocolate colour, and soon it was ours. It was lovely, though we had little furniture. We took a big cardboard box and draped a cloth over it—our dining table. We always played our music; even now, I associate memories of that house with the English band from Oxford, *Supertramp*, for that was the music we played. We did change the chocolate painted walls for cork tiles. It was ours, and for once we could do as we pleased. We could see the embankment from our house of what used to be a railway track. The town had taken up the tracks and made a walking trail. Nice addition to the neighbourhood.

Lyn wasn't the best cook at first; she was learning, and it was not long before she was very good at it. In fact, she progressed to the point our friends, Jim and Jill, and I could say—"Lyn's a good cook!" You have to understand the situation to know why those words had to be spoken.

But—in the interim, I remember she made rhubarb crumble. It came out of the oven one inch thick and twelve inches long. Looked something like a fat ruler! She served it in strips instead of slices. And her apple pie—perfect if you like an inordinate amount of crust, though it was a bit scary looking, the pastry covering four big lumps. It must have run in the family, for one night when we were courting, I went to her mom and dad's house. Lyn has two sisters, Julie and Jenny. Jenny made cheese soup consisting of boiled water and cheese chunks. And that's exactly what we ate that Saturday night—water with gummy lumps. We watched the telly, a British comedy show called *Morecambe and Wise*. Could never forget the sketch with Glenda Jackson in Ernie Wise's production of *Antony and Cleopatra* and Glenda's immortal lines, ". . . men find me so attractive because of the beauty like what I have got . . ."!

Arn and I watched *Match of the Day*, highlights of Saturday's games in England. Football, of course. A couple of crusty ham cobs with a *noggin' o' chaise*, some crisps and maybe a pickled onion or two. Nothing better. Then Arn and I would partake in the tasting of a double diamond (a pale ale). Arn, a great bloke, would sometimes drop me home in his Ford Cortina, and we would have a couple of fags on the way. Don't forget, fags are cigarettes in England.

We had good times together. There's a little place on the West Coast of France called Royan. Lyn and I spent the first part of our honeymoon there, the last half in Paris. Philip de Foursenay and his wife, Suzanne, from Great Barr lived near the Place de Mexico. They had a daughter whose name was Nathalie. We stayed in their apartment in Paris, soon learning that when the French have a meal, oddly, you don't *just* sit and talk. You have to be part of the preparation. You might be starving, but two hours later, you are helping to serve up potatoes, peas and a roast beef. One thing I learned is that you have a bite of food, put your knife and fork down, have a sip of wine, talk awhile, and enjoy the meal totally. It takes three hours to eat a French meal in proper style—a full production.

*In Bloxwich Church
Richard Theodosius performed the ceremony.
The most beautiful bride in the world and a
nineteen-year-old Gibbo.*

Chapter 12
NATHALIE AND DANIEL

There's something particularly wonderful about bringing life into the world, and the joys my children have brought me somehow diminish the heartaches and disappointments that have come my way.

July 10, 1977 was the night Nathalie was born to us, that most beautiful night when I watched the miracle of birth for the first time. Dr. Khan helped us all the way through, the midwife doing most of the work. When Nathalie arrived, the midwife gave her to Lyn. Nathalie was such a content little baby girl, so happy to be with us. She lay in her small cot sighing until she fell asleep that night. She was cooing. The most beautiful sound I have ever heard.

She is my angel, now more than ever, with her blonde curly hair. When she was a little older, we got her a little short skirt and pink under pants. We called her Natty Batty Pink Pants. She was eighteen at the time. Nah! Just kidding. She was about four. She loved colourful clothes. All sorts of colours. She would have made a great living model for Bassett's *Liquorice Allsorts*. Nathalie has always been ahead of her time when it comes to fashion. She was wearing *Betsy Johnson* clothes when she was eight. She still dares to be different. I wonder where she gets the nerve.

When she was a little older than four, we bought her a Wonder Woman outfit, crown and all, and she would wear it outside. With her little blue wellies on to match, off she would run, singing *Wonder Woman* never forgetting the tune to the entire song, including the intro bit.

She had a white rabbit, which she would sneak out and feed until it became addicted to chocolate. After eight mints to be precise. Her rabbit only ate the best. One night we heard a commotion out back. The next morning we went outside to discover a tale of woe. Little tufts of white rabbit fur lay all over the garden. The fox had visited, and it was bye-bye bunny. Nathalie cried all day. And when her butterfly died, Grendel—she called my dad *Grendel*—helped her bury it in a matchbox.

When she was four years old, Nathalie was off to her little pre-school. One day, at about two o'clock in the afternoon, Lyn was home and just happened to look out the window. Across the road was Nathalie, marching home from school with her little blonde curls bouncing in the famous bunches. Lyn was frantic, but very calmly went outside and brought her safely across the road.

"What are you doing home? You're supposed to be at school. And how is it you've walked it alone?" she said.

Nathalie looked up at her mom and said, "No, I'm finished with school for the day. I'm done, Mum."

She had walked the distance alone on the street simply because she was *done* and happy to be home. She was always independent.

One Sunday Lyn cooked roast chicken and left it on a plate to cool on the counter. Nathalie took the plate and our two red setters, Kes and Jace, and went outside into the garden for a chicken picnic. Our roast chicken was gone in five minutes. She ate it with the dogs, just wanting to share. I can hear her saying, "A bit for you—a bit for me." There was something about our dogs and chickens—roasted or raw!

One evening at the dinner table Nathalie was upset, apparently at Lyn and me. She angrily picked up knife and fork and pounded them on the table, pointing at the two of us. She was about five years old, and for better words, she said in her loudest voice, a little posh—"You . . . you . . . you two are like a plate of dirt with . . . with a daisy growing out of the top."

We howled with laughter, thinking if that were the most said when someone is angry, it wouldn't be such a bad world would it, eh?

Then came Daniel Alistair. On September 12, 1980. Our firstborn son.

The births of my children each held something special, something unique, feelings that commenced at the top of my head filling me up with beautiful emotion. That's my best explanation, and that doesn't give it justice. There's something particularly wonderful about bringing life into the world, and the joys my children have brought me somehow diminish the heartaches and disappointments that have come my way. I'm left speechless at times when I think of my son, Daniel. And can it be that he's a grown man with three children of his own? My beautiful grandchildren. Maddison, The Poppy Monster, who calls me *Bibbo*. The twins, Coco and Lottie, so sweet.

I can still see Daniel in his room when we lived in Overdale Drive, standing on his cot, jumping up and down, singing his little made-up song to the top of his lungs. We were treated to renditions of "Ducka, Ducka, Da, Da" for hours—for free, too!

One night we were in a country pub having a meal. When the kids wanted something, I let them take the initiative to ask for it.

"Could I have another drink of Coke, please?" Daniel asked.

"Ask the waitress when she comes," I said.

It's no wonder my children are independent. I raised them that way. Even now, that's the way I coach kids. I try to teach my students and then set them free to make their own decisions and take care of their own problems. In soccer, it's called guided discovery. In real life—well, it could be disastrous!

One night just the three of us, Nathalie, Daniel and I, were having a meal together. We affectionately called Daniel *Sid*. His teachers did and his mates still do. Sid in England is not a trendy name. Maybe an old codger's name, like Stan, Wilf, Alf. Before Daniel was born, I would come in from work and ask Lyn, "How's little Sid?" tapping her swollen tummy. When he arrived, we gave him the nickname. I still call him that to this day.

Sitting at the table in the pub that night, Daniel asked, "Dad, can I go to the toilet, please?" I could see the door from where I sat, so I said, "Sure, son, go ahead. Hurry back." What seemed like an eternity, five minutes later, the door opened and there he stood, little pants and trousers to the floor, and Daniel shouting, "But dow, but dow, but dow, Dad—would you come wipe my bottom?" So much for teaching independence. I proceeded to slink under the table. Everybody in the pub witnessed the scene. The people stopped talking, the cutlery stopped cutler-ing. There was stark silence as I got up and walked across to my helpless innocent son. Those kinds of things were always happening to me with my kids. I could not have possibly deserved such.

On another occasion, we went to an Albion game—Nathalie, Daniel, Roggo (Ian Rogers) and I. Roggo was a youth player at Aston Villa and

Crystal Palace. He had tried out for the professionals but didn't get taken. He was a bit depressed. I said, "Roggo, come out and play for my team." He ended up playing for us on a Sunday morning. He said it was the best time he ever had. Roggo was a great player. A great bloke. I wonder what Roggo is doing today? His dad, John, was on Albion's books some time ago.

I must get back to the *Sid* story.

After watching the game, we went to the Beaufort Arms in Hamstead for a drink. Again, Daniel had to go to the toilet, but the restroom was closed. I didn't think it was for serious purposes, so I told him to scoot to the back of the pub and hurry back. But no, Daniel the Pooh strikes again! I waited a few minutes and went to check. There he was stooping against the wall, his back resting on the bricks—! What was it about that boy?

When he was a kid, Daniel called me *Stumpy*. Come to think about it, he still does. He recently reminded me of when I surprised him with some unexpected visits. Once when he was at high school, the first parents' night. Then when he was sixteen and it was a GCSE exam awards night at high school. When he was at University of Central England (Art College in Birmingham), I surprised him at his final graduation show. Just to see the look on his face when I showed up out of the blue was an everlasting joy to me. Being four thousand miles away from each other has not been easy. It still affects me. However, Daniel loves it.

I wouldn't take anything for being there for his graduation art show. It was a huge production, not just the showing of a painting. It was a walk-in piece where the viewer opened a door to an actual office, spoke to a real receptionist, sat down on real seats, had coffee, put their cups on a coffee table while looking through a Daniel Gibbons-designed magazine that described the company and its choices of the perfect baby for the couple—a futuristic mail-order baby, so to speak—whilst in the background a video was playing, informing the public about the company. With music, too (some *Yes* was in there!) and his guests walked away with a business card designed by Daniel. He had formed a real company. Such a brilliant man!

Daniel and Nathalie were splendid disco dancers. I used to ask them to show my friends what good dancers they were, and so as not to disappoint me, they duly obliged. How embarrassing that must have been for them. But to me it was a dad proud of his kids. What a *plonker*, they must have thought.

*Daddy Gibbons with Daniel and Nathalie
In Handsworth Wood*

Chapter 13
BUSTLEHOLME BOYS

The disappointment on his face and
the family's was dreadful. I was a cruel man.
It's very lonely being the head coach.

Dad left the pub business, and he often visited us. He loved his grandchildren, always brought them a pack of Smarties (sweets in a tube). In his Black Country accent, he would say, "Ee am, I've got some 'suck' for ya." In posh version, "Here you are. I have some sweets for you." Dad would pretend to be Grendel, chasing the kids through the house, growling, "I'm the one-eyed monster from the marshes." When Dad was not around, I had to be Grendel, chasing my kids and even Heather's Kayleigh and Tim through the house. Sometimes, when Lyn left the house, we were even more boisterous, running around, each of us with a cushion up our back, jumping about and pretending to be Quasi Modo. We looked like a family of Modos—Daddy Modo, Siddy Modo, and Natty Modo—such fun we had together.

My kids had a positive influence on me, even when they were very young. I had a smoking habit—that is, until Nathalie and Daniel came home from school one day with their "stop smoking" project. They got right to the message.

"Dad, we want you to live a long, long time. If you smoke, that means you're taking years off your life."

And that was it. If it was that important to them, it was that important to me. I stopped smoking that day. There was no "I'm quitting" or "I'm trying to stop." I conditioned my mind to say to my body, "I used to smoke." That worked.

When I coached the Bustleholme boys, Daniel was playing a year up on the team. He was ten or eleven at the time, a very good player. It was a good team. Looking back, I should have played him more. But the laws of the game dictated that we were allowed no rotating subs and it didn't work out so well. I was coaching at the Albion and we got to the Staffordshire Cup Final. The Cup Final! The U12 Bustleholme Boys were playing against our archrivals, mainly because most of the players were Wolves fans. The team was called the Lanehead Strollers, and Dave Hall was their coach. Willenhall, where they were based, was thick Wolves territory, and Bustleholme was in Albion territory. Dave also coached with me at the Albion.

We arranged for these kids to play the Cup Final at the Hawthorns. On hallowed turf. We played just before a Men's Cup Final. Daniel's grandparents and all the family were in the stands. It was a tight game; we won 3-2. Because of the rules we were only allowed to make one substitute. I never took my Daniel off the bench. That grieves me to this day. My own son never got to play at the Hawthorns. The disappointment on his face and the family's was dreadful. I was a cruel man. It's very lonely being the head coach. I had to do what was right for the team and in so doing I could not give special treatment to my own son. But looking back, we all read the rules in the book before we set out to play the games. In time, we would have plenty of other things to cheer about.

That incident affects me to this day; however, the rules have changed and I believe they allow rotating subs now in England. Funny enough, when I came over to coach in The States, they allowed rotating subs, something that was alien to the English coaches. I see the benefits of it now. The USA system was ahead of the English game in that regard, and that was twenty years ago. In some ways, the English think they rule the world when it comes to coaching soccer. I was one of those cocky coaches once. I have learned to be a better teacher over here. I have to be, as the kids in The States don't watch it on television as much, so it's a little like describing a newly discovered Picasso painting over the phone. It is abstract to them in every sense of the word. A coach has to pay attention to detail and try and paint pictures.

The best teacher is the game itself. I encourage players to watch as many games as they can on the telly, then at practice to have a chat about the game. When we were kids we would go and watch our local team (Albion in my case, of course); and then in the school playground and in the street, or back garden, we would imitate our heroes. "I Baggsie be Tony Brown," I can hear myself saying to my mates. We didn't realize that this basic learning tool would become a great teaching tool for coaches.

I coached at West Brom and at Bustleholme with a free-flowing, attacking, passing style of play, and even in the early days, I established a reputation for producing good soccer players and teams that were a pleasure to watch. It all stemmed from my love of the Dutch Coerver method, which was becoming evident at this time in my coaching career. One of the head people from the Birmingham Boys' League liked my method of coaching and invited me to be the Birmingham Boys' Manager (head coach). He was always searching for different methodology, such as the Swedish and Dutch ways of coaching. We were the first Birmingham Boys' team to beat local rival Walsall, and this became reason for them to offer me another year as coach, which had never been done before.

Speaking of the best teaching tools, when we were at Blue Coat Church of England School, we would always play 5 v 5 in the gym at every opportunity during P.E. and also at Gym Club a couple of evenings a week from seven to about nine. We played on a basketball court. The rules were simple; the ball could not go over head height, lest an indirect free kick be given to the other team; and nobody except the goalie could be inside the three point semi-circle, neither could he come out. We used two wooden benches, the flat part on which you would normally sit facing the field on its side and two rubber mats, green on one side and grey on the other, for the goalie to dive on. We shot at the flat face of the two benches, probably eighteen inches high and twelve feet long. (Two six-foot benches.) This taught us to keep our shots very low and to the corners. The best teaching aid ever, apart from soccer tennis, of course.

Later, when I was living in Peachtree City, Georgia, a mate of mine from Bloxwich, Ken McDonald, and I started talking about this. It culminated in the "Boing lo Goal," a Coerver type goal but only four feet high by twenty-four feet (or twelve, or sixteen for smaller kids). Kwik Goal helped me develop it. I really should have promoted it more. A project I still haven't given up on, maybe after this book is finished—

Something else, which I like to forget, happened when I brought a team to England from the USA. We landed in Manchester and drove down in rental vans. I was driving one of the vans, so I was without excuse. We had tickets to go to Wembley to watch England versus Mexico. I drove straight past the M6 junction to the exit and forgot to pick up my two lads. Yes, I said *forgot*. What sort of dad, eh? We laugh now, but what a pillock.

Back to Bustleholme.

I was coaching a game on a Sunday afternoon with Bustleholme Boys FC, just behind the flats when local Football Association coach, Ian Cooper, said to me, "All you are doing is giving *running commentary.*"

Ouch! I needed that critical instruction!

He helped me more than he'll ever know, by correcting my coaching style. I've never forgotten his sage advice, and what's even more important, I took it seriously. Shortly after that, I started to realize my own coaching style. The teacher was within and had always been. It would be either art or football. Remember, I was groomed in senior school and Art College to be an art teacher. The principles were the same; the opportunity, very different. I was beginning to teach my charges how to *play* the game not just to *win* the game. Some of those kids were the underdogs, and I dared not suppress the uniqueness of their individual personalities. I was teaching them to enjoy the game, to love the game.

Bustleholme boasted some famous players. Stevie Bull, Steve Lynex, David Burrows. Let's not forget the legend that is *Bucketman,* too. And my boys played for the Birmingham Boys League. I coached Bustleholme for two years, and in those years, I began to look at different aspects of coaching the game, with an even closer look at the Coerver method. I wanted to enhance the rough and tumble lads' game. Dave Martin of the Bustleholme Football Club wrote a letter concerning me. Here are excerpts from that letter:

> We are primarily a boys' football club that has progressed since 1975 from one U12 team to a present complement of seventeen teams. During that time quite a few parents have developed into excellent football coaches. Paul Gibbons is one of these and not only has he produced good quality football teams, but he has also developed his own coaching ability to the extent that he has had control of boys who

have been taken on at the West Bromwich Albion Football Club. His personality is second to none and his organizing ability first rate. He recently set up matches in Paris for his team. Only last November saw him invite a top Hungarian boys' team from the Ferencváros Club in Budapest. . . . This involved a lot of hard work and planning. I can honestly say that where soccer is concerned there is not a more confident person.

Bustleholme Boys
Unforgettable Days of Coaching and Teaching and Learning.

Chapter 14
To Lose a Love

There is a strangeness that grips me.
My adult children live on another continent.
Sometimes I think I squandered away the formidable years of
their lives, although that was not my intention.

We moved to a nice detached house in Handsworth Wood. I could see Albion's floodlights from my top bedroom window, a lovely sight. And just around the corner Albion owned a house which was used to accommodate some of the players. Bryan Robson lived there at one time. When I first saw Bryan play it was with my mate, Mark Gascoigne (Bamber), who ended up as assistant kitman at The Albion. We went to watch the intermediate league game, which was the league in those days for the youth players. Bamber and I were such Albion fans. We heard that Aston Villa had two kids, Bryan and Alan Little, and we were looking at the youth players to see who might have a good future. The league games were held at the Albion training ground at Spring Lane, aptly named, not for a nice spring day, but for the legacy of the Black Country. A lot of the factories made springs there.

We watched the game, during which I noticed this kid about fifteen years of age. I said to Bamber, "I don't know who that kid is, but one day he'll play for England."

That kid was Bryan Robson. He later became an Albion legend then moved to Manchester United and subsequently captain of England. Later, after Bryan left the house in Handsworth Wood, another Albion legend moved to that house—Cyril Regis. I got to know the big man a little, too.

We were a typical well-adjusted young family, enjoying life as best we knew how, key word being *young*, for we were so very young. Granted, there is nothing like young love, but did we have a lot to learn! I have to ponder if it is really good to marry at such an early age. Life was getting ready to teach us some lessons that we were not equipped to handle.

I loved my garden, used to spend hours getting all the twigs and rubbish out, cutting the grass with an old fashioned push mower, building bonfires, at peace with the world, my two red setters, Kes and Jace, beside me. On Saturdays I had practice with Bustleholme. When Albion were home, we watched their games, and on Sundays I played football, had the in-laws and my dad around, or washed the car.

We lived a couple of miles from Handsworth, which became heavily populated with tropical people, and a lot of the not-so-savoury characters used to come up to the posher part and rob people's houses. I came home one afternoon and saw two men casing the neighbourhood. Even saw them on someone's porch. When they saw me, they skedaddled, and I started to follow them, got the number on their license plate, and phoned the police. They asked a lot of questions, to which I replied, "I told you, I'm following them now, got the number of their license plates."

"Did you see them break into anyone's house?"

"No."

"We can't do anything unless you see them breaking the law. Leave it be. We'll handle it."

"Right," I said.

What they were actually saying was they would do nothing. I was out there doing their work for them and they were going to do nothing because their hands were tied. Not too encouraging. I thought, I'm doing your bloody job and you won't make an effort to do anything about it! I know—they didn't make the laws, they just enforced them. But these guys were there with intent to do mischief.

Nevertheless, we were happy. The kids liked their schools. New neighbours moved into the house directly behind ours, and it was not long before we got to know them. We became close friends, went on holiday in Spain together. The guy put up a little gate in the fence so we could all go in and out, visit each other conveniently, and have barbecues and the like.

Once we went on holiday with those friends to Anglesey, an island on the northwest of Wales where the Gulf Stream hits the East Coast of the British Isles. We all went out on the boat, the water choppy and bloody cold. So cold we had to wear wet suits, wondering all along why they are called wet suits when they're supposed to keep you dry. I was on the skis, got dumped about a mile out where everybody on shore looked like ants and where all I could hear was water lapping and, in my subconscious, the theme song from *Jaws*, when about twenty yards from me I saw a huge dark shadow. I thought it was a small thirty foot submarine, not of the yellow variety. And then part of that shadow, that submarine, came to the surface in the tell-tale shape of a fin. Luckily for me, the fin was going right to left. If ever the fin had come toward me . . . well, I don't know what I would have done. Meanwhile, my mate turned the boat around and came back for me. I climbed onto the back, and just like Abbott and Costello, if you can imagine, I was trying to speak but nothing was coming out but a raspy, shivering, stuttering version of "Loo loo loo. . . . look out there. It's a sh sh sh ssshhhaaarrrkkk!" I came to find out there was nothing to worry about. It was a thirty foot basking shark, supposedly harmless. All they do is swim along, open their enormous jaws, and swallow tons of plankton. When I think about it now, doesn't matter that they're harmless. Besides I didn't know it at the time. It might just as well have been a killer. I could have panicked and died of a heart attack, or been mistaken for a large wad of plankton, mulched down or swallowed whole by this harmless monster.

On another occasion when we vacationed in Spain with these friends, my mate and I went swimming in the bay—from one set of rocks to the other. I swam for the rocks, to the aluminium ladder set firmly so you can climb out, where a big octopus awaited me. I thought . . . every time I go into the water with *that* friend of mine, something dreadful happens.

⚽

And then as suddenly as the day I saw Lyn in that little pub and declared I would marry her, just as suddenly it all came crashing down. The longer I live, the more I realize I was to blame. I was responsible for my family.

But I never wanted to lose my wife. I loved her, loved our two beautiful children, and loved what we always had together. I was working hard just to keep a roof over our heads. And yes socializing, with assistant managers and managers alike, and it was mostly evening work, too. Lyn was staying at home with our children. Again, the fact that we were young and inexperienced didn't help matters, though unacceptable as an excuse for our inabilities to stick with the stuff for the duration. We allowed life to bombard our marriage. We drifted apart and for whatever reason, it belongs to Lyn and me alone. We worked through it, but it meant doing the hard part. We both tried. Just not hard enough, and we were both to blame for what happened next. We had a chance to move to another house in Willenhall, but our situation had digressed to the point of no return. I can only speak for myself, but I know I should have tried harder for the sake of my children, who needed both of us, together, always. They say hindsight is twenty-twenty, though cliché, a reality I should have embraced long before I got there.

Eventually Lyn went to stay with her mom and dad. We lost our house. Of the worldly goods that I possessed, I wanted my records and my chess set. But far above that, I wanted my kids. I couldn't stand the thoughts of being without them. I went to see Lyn at Ann and Arn's house with one last plea. I begged her to come back, told her I had a house ready for her to move into, that I was willing to start over and do the hard part for the sake of our children. But that didn't happen.

I wanted my kids to know how much I loved them and I wanted them to love me. Some years later, Lyn's father, who was a great bloke, told my children, his grandchildren: "Your daddy's a good man. He's a good man!" I needed that vote of confidence, but far more than that, I needed my family, for I didn't feel like the good man, and by then it was too late.

I have since changed my mind about divorce. It should never have been an option. I look back full of anger at myself for not being able to fix it. For not making it happen. I still beat myself up about things. Sometimes too much water rolls under the bridge and it is hard to fix things.

Lyn and I divorced after twelve years of marriage. I had a lot of adjusting to do. I had lost everything. Time and years have healed a lot of the hurt and pain, and I still love the mother of my children. We will always have that bond no matter what. I recently chatted with her between America and England via email. She said this.

Paul, do you remember how quick my labour was with Daniel? We only just managed to get to hospital on time (8.30), no time for pain killers or gas and air; I just climbed onto the delivery table and had him! He was born at 9:15 pm, probably only the quickest thing he has done in his life for one so laid back! Can you recall the time he decided to dive off the tree trunk into the rockery because he wanted to practice and ended up at hospital with concussion? And the time he shinnied up the rotary line, got entangled in the line and almost strangled himself! Why did we not invest in a camcorder to capture those times? When we are gone who will remember them?

Big love xx, Lyn

Looking back I see that my kids had to create their own happiness after Lyn and I split up. I'm glad they're happy now, at least to the degree possible under the circumstances. I reflect once again on the song of TobyMac, *I don't want to gain the whole world and lose my soul*. I'm trying to learn to make it my business to take into consideration the consequences for my own actions.

There is a strangeness that grips me. My adult children live on another continent. Sometimes I think I squandered away the formidable years of their lives, although that was not my intention. I struggle with that every day of my life. I often ponder what on earth I can do to recall those years and fill in the spaces, and I am reminded it is never too late to do it right, but I have also learned it is impossible to retrace my steps, to look back on yesterday as if I could change a single thing. I still have requirements on me, and I contemplate how I will deal with those things that may have been left undone. When I weigh up the fact that I may have, through the years, considered someone else's child (my many soccer children) before my own, I find myself awake in the small hours of the darkness. There is nothing more painful than sleepless nights.

It was not as if the heartaches had not mounted in those days prior to the break-up. When it rains, it pours, and the poignancy of the times was almost too much to bear. Lyn and I were still in the Handsworth Wood home when it happened. Suddenly and unexpectedly. Dad was fifty-nine years old when he died. Like Mom, much too young. And now they were both gone, leaving emptiness that beggars description. I was twenty-seven, again much too young.

I recall on a cold wintry day, snow fell in huge flakes across the West Midlands. My car wouldn't start and I needed Dad's help to get it going. I visualize him now helping me push that car in the driven snow. He suddenly grabbed his chest, but said it was nothing. Dad was like that. Tough. I should have known better. A few months later, he went to the doctor with chest pains. The doctor gave him a pill or two, I think the story goes. And six hours later he had a heart attack and died. I suffer with guilt about that, wishing I had not sought his help to push the car on that cold, snowy day.

I kept losing people out of my life, and it was painful. So painful.

*True Love on an Iberian Island—Paul and Lynda.
Nathalie and Daniel, playing in the sand.*

A Young Daniel
Royan Harbour

Chapter 15
ORIGINAL MOCUMENTARY

*I was laughing so hysterically that
tears were rolling down my cheeks.
From the angle, the man couldn't see that his mate was gone.*

Terry Pettiford and I worked together at Hambro Life in Walsall. Great bloke, Terry! We went for Chinese take-away in Walsall once, walked right up to the tall counter, dropped our trousers and stood there with a serious face ordering our food, whilst our girls were in the car cringing. Of course, those taking our orders knew nothing of it, for they couldn't see. But anyone coming from behind could see with no problem. Guess we were revolting. Was that the start of awkward comedy we now see in programmes like *The Office*? I wonder. Were Big Terry and I the forerunners?

We were in the Co-op Bank in Bridge Street in Walsall once, and two elderly ladies were talking to the teller. We heard them say, "So the bank is moving, eh?" Terry and I were behind them. We started moving from side to side, swaying. "Oh, yes," we said, "it is moving. Feels strange, doesn't it?"

Whilst in a Walsall Wood pub one night an old regular said, "Come over. Play dominos."

Terry and I, brilliant blokes that we were, sat down with the old guys having a pint of mild. They were watching me play dominos with fives and threes. We were putting matchsticks in the holes.

One said, "Watch this. A double six." I looked at my dominos, pretending not to know how to play and purposely put the domino down. I was on zero, so I never scored.

After a while, the old man shouted out, "A bloke in here can't score."

That kept going until all the pub knew about that dumb bloke who couldn't score one point at fives and threes. Terry knew what I was doing.

He doubled over, attempting to stifle the laughter. We never let on. It was so funny watching the reaction of the regulars. They don't know to this day.

We were in that same pub on another occasion, standing at the bar. Terry and I were watching a bloke talking to his mate who happened to be blind in one eye. Terry and I had no idea, of course. The conversation was going on, and in a pause, his mate innocently went to the restroom. The guy was still talking to him long after he was gone. Actually, he was talking to an empty space. We couldn't help ourselves. Terry being so kind hearted, pointed out to him by saying, "Excuse me, but your mate has gone!" Terry and I were laughing hysterically inside; tears were rolling down our cheeks. From the angle, the man couldn't see that his mate was gone. When he came back, they continued chatting, the guy never missing a beat of his conversation.

One night Terry was in a pub in Beechdale playing pool. His ball was blocked by an orange ball. He asked his opponent quite innocently and honestly, "Do you mind if I move that orange, mate? It's blocking my shot."

The guy replied, "Ar, of course, mert," not thinking that Terry would move it.

Terry said, "Ta, mate," moved it to the side, and played his shot.

Word soon got out to the rest of the pub. They all came out to see situation comedy at its best. Yes, Terry and I lay claim to being the founders of such. If it had not been that we were so entertaining, I could still feel guilty over all the brilliant laughter at someone else's expense.

I was in an Indian restaurant with a friend one night about seven thirty. In Walsall, down the road from The Truff. There were three other people in the place that night. It was quiet. We ordered food and whilst we waited to be served, I started whistling a tune. Softly. Nothing obnoxious or anything like that. The other three people were miles away from where we were sitting. I didn't even realize I was whistling.

The waiter came over and said to me, "Stop. Stop whistling. You're disturbing everyone in here."

"Have they complained?" I asked.

"No."

"Well, if no one's complaining, who complained? And since no one is complaining, why do I have to stop? There's no one in the place."

Guess I insulted him, and at the same time, I was annoying him with my whistling.

"Okay. If you want me to leave, I'll leave," I said.

"Yes, well, I'll have to ask you to leave then," he said.

My friend and I laughed, supposing we were on *Candid Camera*. We left. We might as well have been on *Candid Camera*, for when we stepped out, someone took a picture of me. A day or two later, I made the *Walsall Observer*. Great story for the *Observer*. And nice publicity for the restaurant.

Now, Jane, who abhors whistling except it be Bing Crosby in *Holiday Inn*, and who agreed with the waiter that ousted me, just asked me if I ever went back.

"No—it closed down after that! And I, who never got a letter of thanks for the publicity, must have gone down in history for whistling a tune for the smallest number of people ever. Or was it for the masterpiece photograph, *The Whistler*, which I believe Mr. Bean would have been delighted to unveil in the Royal National Gallery in London if only given occasion?"

Chapter 16
Coaching at The Albion

"Mate, we dow know hoo yow am,
unny that y'ove just cum back from America,
but yome the best coach since we 'ad Nobby Stiles!"

We all grew up in little villages, our roots aggressively planted in medieval history, the history of the Vikings. My name is from Viking extraction; Gibbons originally meant Gibson and in the Viking translation is *son of Gibb*. We recently learned that our family name has been present in the Black Country since the 1600s, with further research underway. Our football teams became our modern-day tribes, depending on the town of our birth. We wore their colours and supported them in every way, something that one generation has passed down to another. I need not say more having been born in West Bromwich. By now, you are familiar with my tribe.

It was my cousin, Rob Marsh, who first got me interested in coaching. He got me involved with Bustleholme first. I was captivated, something that did not surprise Rob because he knew how much I loved the game. My continued involvement substantiated what he must have thought would be a life calling for me. He asked me, "Paul, why don't you write a letter to Albion and introduce yourself to Norman Bodell?" I owe Rob a debt of gratitude for it. I've said it before, he's my hero.

I sent that letter, and the next thing I knew, Mr. Norman Bodell, head scout, called and asked me to meet him at The Hawthorns on Sunday morning at ten o'clock. Thanks to Rob and his encouragement, that meeting led to an invitation to coach at Albion's School of Excellence and also to coach the U17 team. In my first few practices, parents of budding pros came up to me and one of them said, "Mate, we dow know hoo yow am, unny that y'ove just cum back from America, but yome the best coach we've 'ad since Nobby Stiles!"

Now, that was a compliment, to say the least. Nobby Stiles was a fiercely committed ball-winner for England and Manchester United in his day. He was on the winning side in a World Cup and European Cup final. In 1968, Nobby returned to Wembley Stadium to help United defeat Benfica in Europe's premier club competition. He was a defensive midfielder, tactically speaking, the central figure of his team's set-up. He didn't always get recognized for his accomplishments, but his peers knew and appreciated his worth.

I've alluded to *Coerver* a couple of times, but it was about this time that I heard the name for the first time, in a strange *scouser* accent from a certain Mr. Dennis Mortimer, former Aston Villa captain and former manager of Redditch United, a non-league outfit, before moving into coaching and becoming assistant manager to Ossie Ardiles at West Bromwich Albion. He had just been on a course at Warwick University, and he started talking to me about this new Dutch way of thinking. That was in 1985. I got in touch with Coerver, and started studying the books about this revolutionary new method. I eventually persuaded Adrian Davis (a Coerver coach at Norwich and Chelsea) to come and spend a weekend with me, a couple of other coaches, and my U17 Albion team. That was the start of my love for this method.

The coaches at WBA were told by Manager Bobby Gould to play in a certain manner, basically finding the corner flags with long balls. This was okay if there were players enough to be successful at it. We tried it against our archenemies, the Wolves. We lost. The next time we played them it was a different game. I realized that we weren't the sort of team to throw long balls up to the corner flags and chase. We were a more technical team, so I asked them to pass the ball around on the deck. We started to play that kind of footy and became the most successful team at West Brom. More importantly, we thrashed the boys in Old Gold and Black! Never forget the passion between Albion and Wolves. Seven of my team were offered pro contracts, a record that may still stand. I put my neck on the chopping block for what I believed in. I wanted my U17 team to execute Albion's quality style of play.

I was beginning to develop expertise in recognizing winners, looking for certain skills and talent in a soccer player. I observed their techniques—the way they prepared their bodies, the way they ran, the way they turned, the things they said. I had to know they were taking on the image of a real footballer.

Sometime later when he was just under seventeen, one of my players for Atlanta Lightning, Junior de Souza, visited England with his dad and me. They were from Brazil. The Albion coaches called Junior's dad Senior. Nickname, of course. I took them to West Bromwich where Junior trained with the youth team, then with the reserves, and he also practiced with the first team. He played a game with U17s, very influential with all the Brazilian strokes and the Coerver moves I had taught him.

Two great blokes, two great coaches, John Trewick and Richard O'Kelly, watched Junior practice on Friday. That day, they asked Senior and me to join in on the staff game. It was great fun for me, the coaches against the U17s. John Trewick and Richard O'Kelly were coaches and ex-professionals. John played for Albion and Newcastle. Richard played for Walsall. We played opposite the Albion ground that day, and after the game we walked back to The Hawthorns, ending up in the manager's changing rooms.

There we were getting stripped off, chatting away. Before we went to the showers, we were having a cup of tea, still chatting like crazy, fast and furious with every other word foul and fit only for the dressing room, still stark naked with that cup of tea in hand, sharing USA soccer stories with Ronnie Allen, an Albion legend, God rest his soul, Allan Buckley, Albion manager at the time, great player for Walsall and great manager for Albion, and assistant Arthur Mann (RIP). I was connected to my home town team, WBA, having a grand old time reminiscing in Black Country and weird Nottingham accents with Albion legends and the boys from Brazil. It was the greatest most surreal moment. Smashing, and the funniest thing ever, having a cup of tea—naked? It would have been like meeting Bill Clinton in the Squash Club stark-bollocked naked. Surreal, indeed. Just happy no one spilt the hot tea!

Chapter 17
SEAN ANDRÉ

*I wouldn't have missed the birth and bonding with my baby
boy for all the tea in China—*

I had known Louise a long time. She was an old school acquaintance. There are some things that happen in life that don't quite make sense, and this may have been one of those times in my own life, but if for no other reason, our relationship rendered the most beautiful and wonderful child, just like my other two children. We were together six years when Louise found out she was pregnant. We never married.

Louise and I went on holiday in Tunisia in North Africa. We stayed at a holiday resort there. She was *with child*. This is a great descriptive and old fashioned phrase. So a woman that is not pregnant is *without child*? Or has she just mislaid one? Anyway, a sight to behold was Lulu sitting on top of a camel. We visited an old Tunisian walled city where part of *The Life of Brian* was filmed. One of my favourite films. The scenes I can recall are the ones where the Judean People's Front (or was it the People's Front of Judea?) painted graffiti on the wall, the prophet in the market, the spaceship and the town scene. I didn't think Mel Gibson's remake was half as funny.

Whilst taking a shortcut back to our car from the market, a couple of Arabs cornered us. We found out they wanted to buy Louise! I thought about it, but what could I do with two goats and a camel!

My son, Sean André was born November 27, 1988, making his grand entrance the day I was to take the final exam that would launch my career into the world of soccer. I had finished part of the requirement the day before, and the final was to be taken on December 27, 1988, under the observation of Ian Cooper, the local Football Association coach. I owe gratitude to Ian Cooper for allowing me to take the final exam the week following, and for giving me my first opportunity. I wouldn't have missed the birth and bonding with my baby boy for all the tea in China—football or no. Cooper later took my place at West Brom on my recommendation.

You might as well know on the front end that Sean got a couple of nicknames. Shorrrn and Seany Bear. He was named after my dad and me. Sean is Gaelic for John and, of course, the André bit is my middle name.

Sean was only little, about three or four years old, when Louise and I took him to the northern part of France on holiday. To the province of Picardy, which has a strong and proud heritage. We stayed at a campsite where in front of the tent was a football pitch. Fancy that. The young Sean and I loved it. He showed his interest and prowess for the game even at this age. We went out every day; I normally ended up in goal, of course. I would roll the ball out to my skinny lad, and he would run up and strike it beautifully. Most of the time we were using bare feet.

Here's a tip for a good soccer dad. If you do nothing else with a young son at this age, you will be teaching him how to strike the ball sweetly. Even if he doesn't hit it perfectly with ankle locked and toes tucked under, he will feel it. Sean was hitting the ball left and right—beautifully.

We stayed near the port where William the Conqueror set sail for England with his ships in 1066, the last time England was successfully invaded. I wonder how all of those native *Brits*—Anglo-Saxons—felt about it, eh? All of a sudden we were being ordered about by some French-speaking people, who had different ways to us, different food, different customs, a different language. They occupied towns and soon began to breed and multiply. Hmm, sounds familiar in 2011. Are we sure 1066 was the last time we were successfully invaded? Anyway moving swiftly on—

We had a wonderful time pottering about the countryside of Picardy for just a few days enjoying the people, the town. We weren't there to occupy, just to say hello. The weather in northern France is similar to that of England and, of course, you know I am now going to start to include liquid words like *plueting, ne pas du soleil, beaucoup de pluet, il fait froid*. Work those out for yourself. I know you have a little Français in you. Wet.

Damp. Rain. Cloudy. You get the drift, and it was down to these liquid elements that I saved my little Sean's life.

Lulu (I liked calling my little Geordie gal that) and I decided we needed to go swimming. The weather wasn't great. In fact, it was *pluet-ing*, so we found an indoor leisure and pleasure park with waves that allowed the comfortable way out. So off we went to our indoor paradise. We were in the pool for a while, me throwing Sean up in the air and sometimes even catching him! We swam and played around. Of course, adults being adults, we had to go upstairs to the café that overlooked everything and have a cup of *café au lait*. It really is not the best idea to order tea in France, because they have no concept of it at all; they are great at coffee so that's what we had and it was, as ever, bloody lovely. To say nothing of *croissant avec confectionne*. Lulu and I were in heaven. The ever-inquisitive and the ever-boing-ing Sean wanted to explore after he had a bite to eat, so we let him toddle off. We could see him with no problem. Or so we thought.

Lulu and I were chatting and doing nothing. We did that extremely well. In fact, we were expert at doing nothing, especially if a sausage sammo were involved. Sean was hovering around the Jacuzzi or hot tub, call it what you like. We took our eyes off the explorer for a minute. I looked down and couldn't see him. Louise followed my eyes with hers. We couldn't see him; but no time to panic. Louise is one of the most laid-back people ever born, by the way. I thought I spied him in the hot tub—not just in the hot tub, but I could see a mop of dark hair under the water. I got up, sprinted down the metal spiral staircase and shot over to the hot tub. I looked down and there was Sean's eyes staring at me from underneath the bubbling water. He held his hands up in the air for help. So I left him there. It was his own fault. Nah, just kidding. I grabbed hold of his scrawny arms and lifted him up into my arms. He let a big deep breath go that seemed to last for minutes. Brilliant! He looked at me then he squeezed me and I returned the squeeze. We didn't want to let go—ever. I can't imagine what Lulu was thinking as she was watching all this unfold. I will have that picture on my memory card in my brain forever. Sean looking up at me from under the water.

Lulu used to call me spindle arms, but that was nothing compared to our little Shorrrn. His bones were tied together with string. A little Orangutan I think is how Lulu described him; she even had a photo of one. He was a lovely kid, though. Only Lulu and I know how special.

We used to make tents using sheets round the back of the settee. That was our hideout. Lulu's black dog, Ziggy, thought he was a coffee table and would go stand facing the wall motionless for ages. We have laughed often about that. Sean had a friend who used to come and knock on the door and ask in his gruff voice, "Shorrrn—want to come round the Spar? Shorrrn, do ya? Is Ziggy there? I dow like Ziggy."

Shazad was a little Pakistani lad. He was much older than Sean, but he loved little Sean. "Not aday—amorra!" he would say.

Sean used to play *curbs* in the street with the neighbours, which included his cousins from down the road. He played a lot of footy in the street and on the field a couple of doors away from our house in Bewley Road, Willenhall. I would go with him and kick the ball at all angles and speeds. Sean would control it, and as fast as he could, he would accurately deliver the ball back to me. He was happy doing that. He was even happier when his hero and older brother, Daniel, became a David Beckham to him, a great role model, an inspiration, and most of all a best friend. Now, when we lads get together, it is total giggle time. When Nathalie is with us, it becomes too much for her. *Does her head in*, she says.

Sean is the funniest kid in the world. No, I mean it! He is Graham Stark, John Cleese, Sacha Baron Cohen, Peter Sellers, Russell Brand—all the stand-up blokes rolled into one. We just cor stop loffin!

Seriously, he is convinced he's a Geordie boy, though he was Black Country born and bred. He even does the best *arf-soaked* Black Country accent in the world. "Ee am, Dad" is his favourite. And "Aaar" is his best response (that's *yes* in real Brit lingo). I have to remind him he was born three hundred miles away from Seighton Le Sluce, The Spanish City, Colour Coates or any of those delightful sounding towns near his beloved Newcastle. His Mom and her family are all Geordies, so that's why he clings to it. I tease him, and always call him when *The Toon* have lost. He very rarely answers on that day! *Je vous demande pardon, Americain! The Toon* is Newcastle upon Tyne.

The lad got me hooked on two things, *The Da Vinci Code* and *Football Manager*. The first was and still is an amazingly thought-provoking book. The second is a footy game, where the player is the manager of a team who handles all the day-to-day side of running a club. You get hooked on it. It proved useful to a famous USA coach. Sean and I went to meet my mate TR (Thomas Rongen) in the Osceola Café one morning. We wanted to show him this game. One of the features is that you can search for real players. It gives a load of details about the player, his personality, his vital statistics, his mental and physical attributes. It even gives detail on his salary and whether or not he has dual nationality. TR was very interested in this feature. Sean being the expert showed him how to navigate. Within a minute or so Thomas had pulled up hundreds of players who were under the age of twenty and who had a USA passport. This stimulated TR into delving further. He was later known as the most prominent coach in the USA to have unearthed about four hundred players previously unknown. It was funny to see these two studying the programme. They were like two kids at Christmas playing with their new toy.

When I visit my lads in England, the scene normally ends up with all three of us on the couch, telly on, football programme playing, me in the middle, Sean on one side, Daniel on the other, laptop on my lap. (So that's why they call it laptop, eh?) Playing guess what? Yep. *Footy Manager*. Daniel and I have to wait ages once it's Sean's turn. He is so intense and thorough. It really is like getting lost in a good book or film.

Leaping was and still is Sean's favourite thing to do. If leaping were an Olympic sport, he would be world class. He would easily outdo England's Eddie the Eagle Edwards' stunning feats. How much can Sean leap? I can hear you all ask. Well, he can leap a lot. He would be folklore, a hero in all of England. People would stop him in the street and gasp. I can see them. Yes, speechless, they would stop, stare, and gasp!

In all seriousness, Sean was an athlete. It must stem from his Borneo origins. It gave him the opportunity to play and be captain of Aston Villa for a few years, his presence on the field, brilliant. He came and played with my team for a tourney or two, a great time for me, of course. The American lads stood and gasped also. They looked up to him. He was an example to them all. He could have walked into any Division One college. He knew all the Coerver moves and used them to such brilliant effect. That and his other magical powers helped him get a shirt at Villa.

When he was released by Villa, he was gutted, a messy operation I always thought and a bit harsh, too. He was really down. They let everyone go except one lad. I opened a door for him at my beloved Albion where he played for the U17 team, and he was only fourteen, remember. He was playing, did a Cruyff, turned his player inside out, passed a brilliant forty-yard *Beckhamesque* ball to the winger. Fantastic stuff, right? Nope, not according to Jaffy Tones, a coach I trusted, but he shouted out to my lad in a very derogatory manner, "Who do you think you are, son? David Beckham?"

Who was Jaffy's hero as a kid, I wondered? Kids always copy their heroes. That is the way we learn. It is typical of some coaches still in England. "Get stuck in, son!" That's how they were brought up, and so it carries on at some clubs even today. I hope they change and follow the ways of Barcelona, Spain. Johann Cruyff started all that with the *Dutch Total Football* way of playing. Coerver Coaching (yes, a Dutch method) encourages players like Sean. We wonder why England are never the powerhouse they should be? If they installed a method like Coerver at every league club and taught it at the early ages, it would make the hugest difference in the world. Jaffy did my son Daniel the same way at Bustleholme, especially when I brought a team over to play them. "Jaffy, I trusted you with my lads." And there was never a word of apology.

Sean now has a mate called "FPM" (he has lots of mates, but you know what I mean). Football Pitch Mitch is what it stands for. That comes from Sean's nephew. Mitch, by the way, pronounced with a lisp, *Mith*, is the nearest I can come up with. Mitch loves Chinese nosh and football. Yep, that is FPM.

Sean was with me in Clearwater, Florida, once and we decided to have an ice cream at Rita's. We sat outside and ate our sundries. Sean played saft and ate it like a retard. (How else can I describe him?) Ice cream was everywhere. It is the first time in my life when everything came out of me at the same time! I was hurting laughing! Tears, blood vessels bursting, I was being sick and my bum must have suddenly gone to sleep as it snored! I was hurting of lofta, wor I?

We like it best when I visit when we (Sean, Daniel, and I) play a game of footy at Wyndley Leisure Center in posh Sutton Coldfield. We played with Daniel's mates and Lucy's side of the family. It is brilliant when we are playing on the same pitch at the same time. Not necessarily at the same speed, mind—Sean at death speed; Daniel at crafty speed, and I, at no speed whatsoever! Up the pub later and we are *az appy az ze ippo!*

Sean André is attending Camberwell Art College in *sarf London, en it*. He has held numerous exhibitions. Iceland was one venue. He has his graduation show this summer, and I believe that when I finish my visit to Botswana, Durban, summer 2011, I fly into England just in time.

Lulu and I are proud of our lad. He graduated with a first. That means with honours!

Gibbo, Louise, and Sean André
Sarah, Jen, Nathalie, and Daniel

"Blind Date" at Newmarket Races
With Amanda
1986

Chapter 18
IBERIAN MOMENT

The sea breeze blowing across my sun-browned face...
Maybe one day. If not—in my dreams.

Mojácar is a mountain village in the southeast of Almeria in southern Spain, a place I long to be even now, warming myself on the white sandy beaches of the mystical Mediterranean Sea. My mate, Mick Cartwright, asked me to go and explore an opportunity with him, a business just getting set up to look after apartments and housing when the residents go away. I should have known any opportunity in a place that magical was too good to be true.

Originally inhabited by Romans and Moors, Mojácar still clings to its Moorish past with whitewashed, flat-roofed houses meandering down the mountainside sitting on Kasbah-like cobblestone alleys and narrow streets that mesh the picturesque adobe dwellings tight against the side of the hill. Like old Algiers, an enchanting place. Fresh spring water pumps and gurgles from the ground below and has for centuries. I kept noticing an iconic figure and found it interesting that Mojácar's long history of mixing cultures and religions had perpetuated the use of a little guy called Indalo, which is a sort of totem of a man stretching out his arms, holding a rainbow. It is said to bring protection and was painted on the fronts of the houses for that purpose and for good luck. It was an ancient practice, pulled forward and revived in the 1960s.

Whilst we were there, I spent some time with Keith Bradley, an ex-Aston Villa soccer player. We were asked to coach the local Mojácar football team. I stayed with a couple at a villa halfway up a mountain, a rough trek up the side where goats ran wild on a barren desert. In the fourteenth and fifteenth centuries it was one huge forest. King Philip of Spain needed the wood to build his Armada to battle Queen Elizabeth I of England. So down came all the trees to make a boat load of boats, and without regard to the eco system, it left the land barren. The spaghetti westerns were filmed near Mojácar. It was a cheap location for filming, a place that resembled the western USA. The films were produced and directed by Italians with Spanish and sometimes German involvement. The best known of the spaghetti westerns was *The Man With No Name* trilogy starring Clint Eastwood. Part of *Indiana Jones and the Last Crusade* was filmed near Mojácar. Whilst I was there, I was asked to be an extra, a German soldier, because of my blonde hair and blue eyes.

I am told a lot of English people live there now. Some years ago, the mayor, in an attempt to revive interest offered an incentive for people who had vacationed there to come back. So now a large percentage of the people are English, some scrupulous; some unscrupulous. I was once introduced to a person who, I was told later, was a member of the police force who fabricated evidence to get convictions of the Irish Birmingham bombers. That policeman was hiding in Mojácar. I met one of the West Midlands detectives England was looking for! Face to face. Nasty piece of work.

Before we could get anything finalized, Mick's father died, and he had to return to England. I stayed, exploring the possibilities of the business venture on my own, when I encountered an embarrassing situation. The partners in the business venture wanted me to run the business. Alone. They asked me to come back. I got the opportunity, but that caused a problem between Mick and me. And there was another dilemma. I was still with Sean's mother, Louise, at the time. I took the liberty of locating a beautiful cortija built of brick, a small farmhouse with its own orange grove for £35,000. I presented this idea to Louise and she said, "No, I want to stay here with my mom and dad."

So, it all fell through—soccer, film extra, and business venture.

Neil Ross, former Aston Villa footballer, whose son I coached, lives in Spain and always leaves the door open for me to come. In my mind's eye, the airplane lands on the tarmac and I deplane, the sea breeze blowing across my sun-browned face. I walk through the noisy bazaar on the cobbled streets. The sights and sounds and smells of Mojácar call to me. Maybe one day. If not—in my dreams.

Perhaps Sean's mother saved me from myself on this one. I know—all that glitters is not gold but when a place renders such enchantment, there are lessons hard learned; but better than that, good memories that tag along.

Chapter 19
COMING TO AMERICA

The giant oak trees canopied and locked branches from one side of the street to the other; and the Confederate jasmine climbed the white trellises, their fragrance sweet as sugar pie cooling on the back porch banister of some old pre-Civil War mansion.

It was another emotional time for me. Leaving my kids in England. Once when Sean was just a lad, he said to me: "Dad, cry and get all them tears out of you." If only that had been possible then, and if only it were possible now.

My ties to America were subtle at first. Dartmouth Park in West Brom. The Earl of Dartmouth visited America and brought back seeds. He planted them and huge trees still grow in Dartmouth Park, a reminder of England's connection to America. I walked in the shade of those trees years on end, never dreaming I would go there one day. I've driven past the Asbury House thousands of times. Francis Asbury was the first Methodist Bishop to America. He lived in West Bromwich. Well, Great Barr anyway, about two miles from the original West Bromwich, the Old Church at the top of Newton Road. The Wesleys preached in Wednesbury and West Brom in the market place. In hindsight these landmarks were my connection to America. When I think of the spiritual heritage that I neglected when I was in England, I wish I could recall the days. But no one cared enough to plant a seed in me much less water it. And I needed that. For I was no saint. Nowhere near. Life in a pub was like Sodom and Gomorrah at times. A proverbial den of iniquity. I saw things I should never have seen. Unspeakable things, so I'll not speak of them. It's neither in my best interest nor yours, my reader, that they be mentioned.

Even before my mother died, Heather and I were left to ourselves a lot of the time while Mom and Dad ran the pub. The days were long for them and we had to entertain ourselves. I knew what was expected of me and I made certain I followed the rules. But in my spare time, it was football. Like the rules of home, I knew the rules of the game, the subtle moves that would get me to the goal. It was in me. I would take that and much more to the USA.

I was working for a real estate company in England. Times were getting tough. The stock market was down. It wasn't looking good for me in business. I had been successful in soccer, and that was my first love. All signs pointed toward success in America. My dad admired two countries outside of England—France for their lifestyle, and America for the ability to make dreams happen. He always said, "Son, those Americans, they got it bloody right, eh?"

In 1990, when Sean was just two years old, I did a soccer camp with NASC (North American Soccer Camps). My first ports of call were Hazlet, New Jersey and Rockaway Township. Rockaway was the first camp. I stayed with a family, and on Sunday night we sat on the patio getting to know each other. My eyes were going funny on me. I kept getting flashes of lights flickering on and off. I thought I was losing it until one of the family members told me what it was. For the first time in my life I saw fireflies. The beautiful lightning jewels! The nice thing was that they never touched you. They just flitted about turning their lights off and on. Brilliant!

I took a Greyhound Bus from a station somewhere in New Jersey at 11:00 one night. I thought my life was in danger, as I had been warned about the Greyhounds, so I didn't venture toward the rear but sat up close to the driver. We were riding across country to Cleveland, Ohio, and I was experiencing fear like I did when I was a lad watching TV with Heather, shows like *Mystery and Imagination. Tales of the Unexpected. Hammer House of Horror*—films about Dracula. I was inadvertently psyching myself, for those creepy tales were filling up my thoughts. I wanted to fall asleep, but the sinister atmosphere wouldn't let me. I envisioned lady vampires, women with gauzy black dresses floating up to the windows, dark hair hanging down and blowing in the wind, fang teeth appearing through a wicked smile on a face that was pressed fast against the pane where I sat. I fell asleep on the bus during the night and around two-thirty that morning we stopped somewhere in the middle of America. The doors opened and up steps this family, all wearing black. Vampires! They were black bats with wings flapping everywhere. Up the stairs they came, rising towards me from the pit. Not vampires, but bats. A whole family of them. I was still dreaming. I shook myself, rubbed my eyes, but they were still coming aboard. Once they got on and settled down, I saw that they were regular people. They were neither vampires nor bats, but Amish people dressed in black from head to toe. I had never seen Amish people before. My first impressions in America were fireflies, six foot black bats, and a Greyhound ride from the *Hammer House of Horror* through territory unfamiliar to me, a spooky journey across Midwestern America! It's a wonder I ever returned!

I had been accustomed to the successful U17 Albion boy's team, and here in this first camp in the U.S. a guy by the name of Rich was in charge of a group of five-year-old kids. I nicknamed him Shep because of his sheepdog tendencies when rounding up the young kids when they went chasing after butterflies and such. He did a first rate job of corralling them, and we formed a great partnership. The games we played! *Duck, Duck, Goose?* What the heck was *Duck, Duck, Goose?* I had to talk to myself: "I just came from West Brom Albion. What am I doing here in America playing Duck, Duck, Bloody Goose?"

Everything about that camp was fun. We had the kids dress in funny get-ups and we did all kinds of things to capture their attention. I do it now with my younger kids at the camps. It makes us unique with them. I was learning some things that had never crossed my mind. Shep's job was to corral them. Mine was to coach them.

I was in The States for ten weeks on that first visit. June, July, and August. I came home to Sean and Louise and to no permanent job, so I resigned myself to whatever various jobs I could get.

In 1991, I went back to America. We did a camp at a place near Shreveport, Louisiana, where I had the honour of receiving the title of Honorary Mayor of the City of Natchitoches. But, on the other hand, while I was in New Orleans, I got mugged! Two women started to walk beside me, propositioning me. Quick hands or what? They took me for $20.00. We were advised to split our money up and put it in different pockets, not to keep it all together. This I did. We coaches visited Pat O'Brien's, a restaurant and bar in the heart of the French Quarter, famous for an open garden that had a fountain with fire in the middle. It was just after *Top Gun* was released, and of course, once I asked the hostess if I could borrow her microphone, the famous deep toned first line came crooning out . . . "You never close your eyes anymore . . ." I tell you, it was a great feeling when all the patrons joined in the singing with me and my backing group—*The Coaches*.

It was June 24, 1992, at 8:00 a.m. when I visited the U.S. Embassy at 5 Upper Grosvenor Street in London for final approval and interview before gaining my records for coming to America permanently. My son, Daniel, was with me, cheering me on, encouraging me to take my opportunity. What a bloke, Daniel! A strong boy—unbelievable, and so young. As I speak of it now, it seems worse than my mom dying. Stirs me to tears when I recall it. I'll never forget that poignant moment. I was torn between necessity and leaving my children behind. Daniel knew how I was feeling, and he did everything in his power to make me feel comfortable with my decision.

It was before daybreak that morning when I left. Louise got Sean out of his bed. It tormented me, made it twice as hard for me to leave. When coming to America would have been a dream to some, it was a nightmare to me for the simple reason I had to leave my kids. I cried so hard I couldn't answer Louise when she said, through tears of her own, "How can you leave him?"

She was right. How could I? I was thinking I was no good to my kids without a job. In 1990, when Sean was just two years old, I visited the U.S. for the first time with a clue that I should be there setting up a coaching opportunity—then I would come back to them. Now I had been offered two jobs. Nashville or Atlanta. The choice was mine. I had already said good-bye to Nathalie and Daniel who both lived with Lynda, and neither was she happy that I was leaving the kids. They were teenagers, and at a time when they needed me the most, I was not going to be there for them.

I walked out of the house where I had lived with Louise, the mother of my son, for several years. Beautiful, beautiful Sean André, just a babe in arms. It was not a good time for Louise and me; I had already determined it was time for me to leave. I remember it was pitch black that night. I took a taxi to the train station in Wolverhampton. I had to be there at four in the morning in order to take the train to London, where I would catch a flight to Atlanta. I left with Led Zeppelin's words ringing in my ears—*Made up my mind to make a new start, going to Georgia* (I know, it's California) *with an aching in my heart. Took my chances on a big jet plane. Never let them tell you that they're all the same.* I had a couple of bags, my papers, and fifty quid in my back pocket, given to me by Steve Joynes. Eight hours later I was on the other side of the ocean, confirming that nothing is impossible, at the same time wondering—what now? In the back of my mind I would bring my kids; we could all be reunited in America.

Shortly before I left for the U.S., I worked a month doing hard labour for Steve Joynes. I wanted to appreciate the life of a labourer, knowing I might well have that to do before long. I had no way of knowing what would happen when I arrived in America. I was attempting to keep my expectations realistic. My dad had spent a lifetime supporting the Labour Party in England. Through all kinds of weather, the miserable rain and cold, these men struggled to eke out a living. I wanted to live that life for at least a month before I left. Besides, I needed the money. I worked as a labourer, helping the more skilled brickies, plasterers, and woodworkers. I had never laid bricks in my life.

My boss, Ken Hodges, said to me: "Gibbo, I want four spots."

I thought, four spots? What's a spot? I was actually looking for four spots! I didn't know what he was talking about, but I obviously needed to know, so I got to it, swallowing my pride and asking, "What's a spot?"

"Four bricks with a hard board on top."

I said, "Why didn't you say that then?" I was laughing so hard. He laughed, too.

It was a table of sorts. He wanted a work table. I had never heard the labour lingo—not for brick-laying. I got a crash course, though, and at the end of the month, Steve Joynes said to me, "The lads have told me you've done a great job."

He paid me off and gave me an extra fifty quid which I took to America. I'll never forget him.

I stayed about forty miles south of Atlanta in a place called Newnan, a beautiful little antebellum town with all the pretty houses, those that Sherman evidently missed when he took his March to the Sea towards the end of the American Civil War. It was another world from that to which I was accustomed. Medieval places in England, buildings dating back to 1076. In Newnan the oldest homes dated back to before the Civil War in 1861, only a few years before WBA was formed. That seemed fairly new to me. I shared a flat with a friend, Kimberly Burgess. She had stayed a week with Louise and me in England, and she was gracious to let me stay temporarily. Her mother worked at a hair salon frequented by Alan Jackson's mother. I was exposed to lots of country music, but it was later that I learned to like it. I was invited to Jackson's wedding. Hindsight tells me I should have made other arrangements, but a soccer game kept me from going. Kimberly had some interesting acquaintances. She worked for a photographer named Bob Shapiro. *Fried Green Tomatoes* was filmed using Shapiro's house. I was getting a taste of the Deep South. People were very sweet. Very slow talking.

"Hey . . . Paawl . . ." They had a never ending drawl, which I liked. And I thought Paul was a one-syllable word. Silly me.

At the Post Office or other places about town, they would say, "Hey . . . How y' doin'? Not from around here, are y'?" I wondered how they knew.

I often took Kim's dog for walks, noticing people driving their Lincolns and pick-up trucks and Ford Crown Victorias. They would always slow down, wave, and yell, "Hello!" The people fascinated me. So did the cars.

The only exposure I had to American cars was my dad's 1966 gold Nash Rambler with the electric roof.

It was in Peachtree City, Georgia, that I bought my first American car—a *ve-hick-el*—the way Southerners say it, with a few extra syllables to the word. What I purchased was a boat! A gold and brown Crown Victoria, like the American police cars we watched on TV in England. I cruised everywhere in this second-hand boat for which I paid a good $1200. It had electric windows, electric seats, and cruise control. A regular dream mobile. When I went back to England for a visit, I left my car with some friends. It kept breaking down, stalling out, and they determined it needed a new battery. When they went to replace it, they found it was running on a boat battery. My boat was truly that. Needless to say, I got teased with no slack.

The azaleas and crepe myrtle grew thick as hops, and I've never seen a more beautiful place than Newnan, Georgia. The giant oak trees canopied and locked branches from one side of the street to the other, and the Confederate jasmine climbed the white trellises, their fragrance sweet as sugar pie cooling on the back porch banister of some old pre-Civil War mansion. I've always loved history. In junior school, we got bubblegum cards with U.S. Civil War Generals. We had mock battles, and I chose to be the Confederate generals, leader of the underdogs. I was always for the little kids who were suppressed by the bullies, something I couldn't abide. I wanted to lead them out, like my dad, with the same undying loyalty to the men in the pit—the Labour counselor, himself—of the true Labour Party. It was easy for me to fit into the South. In fact, I'm proud to be a Southerner now, y'all. I love that word!

I went for an interview with Lightning Soccer Club in Fayetteville about twenty miles south of Atlanta. I feel like talking slow even now as I reminisce. At the Fayetteville Indoor Center, Mr. Lemay gave me a few kids to work with to see how I would do. He was French, and after he had an opportunity to observe me, he said in his French accent that sounded a little like Peter Sellers, "Hey, you can coach!" He recommended me to Phil Neddo and Dave Chadwick who looked at my curriculum vitae.

The Boat!
The car I purchased in Newnan, Georgia
when first coming to America.
Wearing an Ossie Ardiles shirt.

Chapter 20
Backstage Passes

*I had my concert battle gear on—tatty jeans
and, of course, my favourite Albion shirt.
I walked toward the entrance
of the theatre where we scalped two tickets.*

I was coaching at *West Brom* when I noticed a new kid practicing with the U13 or 14 boys. I asked his name and he told me it was Logan. I glanced over toward the fence and there stood Robert Plant. I said, "Is that your dad?" to which he replied, "Yes." I went for a quick chat, of course. I hadn't seen Robert for a while and, as you know, he used to frequent my dad's pub in Walsall. The Watering Trough. I was a fan. Had his posters on my wall. I knew he was born in my town—West Bromwich in the West Midlands. While I was in Newnan, Georgia, working at the Lightning Soccer Club, I found out Robert was doing a *Fate of Nations* tour and happened to be in Atlanta that day. I asked my friend Kimberly Burgess if she would like to go; I told her I knew Robert Plant.

"Yeah, right."

She didn't believe me, of course. It was clear *Led Zeppelin* was still so big in The States. We drove to Atlanta, parked the car in the multi-story somewhere near the famous Fox Theatre. The *Fabulous Fox* they call it. A gorgeous building with Moorish design in Midtown Atlanta. The auditorium replicates an Arabian courtyard with a faux clear night sky with twinkling lights and moving clouds. It was really quite beautiful.

There are Fox theatres in other cities, but none of this unique Islamic and Egyptian design. Fox Theatre hosts performances by national touring companies of Broadway shows and is home of the Atlanta Ballet. It was a treat for both of us, and Kim still did not believe that I knew Robert Plant.

I had my concert battle gear on—tatty jeans and, of course, my favourite *Albion* shirt. I walked toward the entrance of the Theatre where we scalped two tickets. Quite a few people stood around on the corner where there were traffic signals, or as they say in France *du feu*, which means fire (red lights). I'm telling Kimberly: "I do know Robert Plant." And she's still telling me, "I don't believe you."

We were standing there on the corner in front of the Fox Theatre. The traffic lights were on red, and a white stretch limo pulled up and stopped. One of the windows came down and Robert Plant stuck his head out and shouted across to me: "You can take that bloody shirt off!" Of course, Kim was beside herself, jumping up and down like a kid at the fair, pulling at my sleeve, shouting. She was saying, "You do know Robert Plant!"

I gave Robert thumbs up and the lights were doused, no longer on fire. Guess someone threw water on them! The entourage moved on around to the side of the theatre.

After Ki-em, as they call her in the South with extra syllables, got up off the sidewalk, we proceeded to walk into the foyer of the hall. We spotted the merchandise tables where we stopped to look at the t-shirts (mine is still neatly folded away in a drawer for keepsake). Working the merchandise was a guy they called *Cod*. He proceeded to tell me he was a Millwall fan and started to tease me about Albion. I was talking to him, asking: "Any chance of going backstage and seeing Robert afterwards?" I told him my connections, that I had coached Robert's son at the Albion, and that I knew Robert from my dad's pub. Of course, Ki-em was getting excited. Cod left to find out, disappearing for about five minutes. As he was walking back across we could see him.

"Oh yeah, you know Robert Plant!" he said. He was teasing me.

"Oh, yeah. Never mind," I said.

Then he presented me with two backstage passes to see Robert after the performance. Concert was great. Robert had a little throw-away camera. He was taking photos of people in the audience, and we were sitting up close.

We got backstage, after passing through a security gate where most of the guards were English people. They kidded me about being an Albion fan. One of the band members was a Carlisle fan. We were motioned upstairs and told where to go. We walked into a room filled with press people. And a lot of girls, friends of the band members, were there. At one end of the room were tables loaded with ice and beer. Robert was getting one. He caught my eye, held up a beer and said, "You want one?"

Kim punched me in the ribs and said, "Robert Plant just yelled across the room at you—like he knows you!"

"Ki-em, I told you I do know him."

He walked over. We shook hands and talked. Kim is about four feet eleven inches tall. She was looking back and forth from me to Robert all wild-eyed while we talked football. I asked about Logan, who was playing at The Wolves School of Excellence. Robert used to play football for a little pub team near Kidderminster. He was a good soccer player, right winger. I once saw him play against my cousin, Rob Marsh, at Kidderminster. I felt like I had ties to the legend. His beautiful song, *Thank You*, was mine and Lesley Chell's song when we were dating.

Robert had to leave.

"I've got to call my brother," Kim said, dialing her phone. "You'll never guess who I just met." She was going on and on, chattering quite like a chipmunk if you can believe that about a drawling southern woman called Ki-em!

That was one of the best dates I've ever had, and when I've taken teams to England, from time to time, I've included a side trip to his local pub in Cookley near Kidderminster. Robert Plant's photo with his soccer team hangs on the wall in that pub.

⚽

Peachtree City is built around six lakes, with six golf courses meandering around the lakes. Golf cart paths are everywhere, under the main roads to the shops, through the woods. The homes in Peachtree City are enchanting—surrounded by dense undergrowth—wild plants and flowers of every species native to the South, and where I was staying, they were growing thick and out of control.

I got this idea I would get to the bottom of all that undergrowth, clean it out and make it look really great. So I machete'd my way through, hacking limbs, bushes, trees. Amongst my discoveries was an old 1953 American car of some make unfamiliar to me, an old wooden house, perhaps where the slaves lived who took care of the big house, and a plum orchard. I kept hacking away.

Mind you, no one bothered telling me about the killer that could be lying just beneath the surface of the earth in an old hollowed out tree trunk in this jungle of a ground. On the other hand, neither had I inquired about such. And then I hit it. Yes, I hit the web design, cracking the envelope surrounding the cells, stressing out all seven million of some *bald-faced hornets,* sending pieces of chewed up wood flying, angering the mother of all caste systems, causing the arrogant queen herself to threaten my very existence. They were swarming. I was sweating. Running—I was yelling like a lunatic, jerking my clothes off piece by piece, galloping across the grass towards the sanctuary of the house, pieces of clothing flying from my nude body parts as I sprinted onward, full speed ahead, a sight to behold, I know. What I didn't know was that the electrician had been called to make repairs and he was in the house. And what he didn't know was that I, the house guest, was in the jungle stirring up a hornets' nest. So I was running and yelling, and he was running and yelling. Only he was running from me, knowing I was a naked lunatic. I was outside not realizing the electrician was inside working, and he didn't realize I was outside breaking and entering the sacred ground of the hornets. I scared the poor man to death.

I couldn't remember the gentle rolling, friendly countryside of England ever being this hostile.

Chapter 21
TOBACCO TOWN

*After a few visits, I could order without looking at the menu
and in a civilized fashion with a straight face.
Hash browns—scattered and smothered,
covered, chunked and topped . . .*

I spent seven years in Peachtree City before I accepted the coaching opportunity near Nashville, Tennessee. I had done North America soccer camps there through the years.

All I had to do was whistle to get their attention. Every day for a week I noticed a guy was watching me from a distance. He was dressed in a suit and tie. At the end of the week I found out he was a local attorney whose son I was coaching. He said to me, "I've never seen anybody as good with the kids as you are." He and his lovely wife invited me to stay in their home during summer camps. It was that attorney who arranged for me to coach a club and high school in Tobacco Town on a permanent basis.

I was happy to be in Tobacco Town, Tennessee, where they had my favourite short order restaurant. I loved this place for three reasons—the food was great, the service outstanding, and it made me laugh. I walked into the local Waffle House one morning, absolutely cracking up because to order what I liked was a production. A bacon, egg and cheese sandwich with hash browns. My son, Daniel, was with me, and we were bent double by the time we gave our order. The waitress yelled out to the cook, who was standing three feet away. I jumped out of my seat! And I just had to ask, "Why are you shouting at him? Or better still, why not just pass him the order? Is he bloody deaf?"

We soon learned this was nothing unusual, that it was ritual at the Waffle House, and no one but the two of us thought anything about it, but really, we were enjoying ourselves no end. When it came to the hash browns, the waitress yelled, "Double flipped, flopped, blopped, splattered, and curved!" By then Daniel—who now does the best impersonation of a Waffle House town crier in the world—and I were afraid they were going to cart us out. After a few visits, I could order without looking at the menu and in a civilized fashion with a straight face. Hash browns, scattered and smothered, covered, chunked and topped—

When I think of laughter, I immediately think of the *Geordie Boys* from Newcastle. (Newcastle was on the Scottish border; they were called *Geordies* for they supported King George.) It was Lee Irving and Anthony Winter. I've always related the lads from Newcastle to the Black Country. Newcastle is one of the areas where the Vikings first landed. They explored England, eventually finding "The Midlands" by the river. Imagine a Viking going to the travel agent, "Rape and pillage for two weeks, last week in July, first week in August, please Miss!" Maybe that's the connection. And they have a dialect all their own.

These Geordie Boys came to America to coach, and met me in Whitehouse, Tennessee, at a shopping centre. There was a Piggly Wiggly in that centre, and we got the idea we would call ourselves the Giggly Wigglys. Primarily because we laughed about everything when we got together. We even had tee shirts made that read, *The Giggly-Wigglys on Tour* in honour of the store where we met.

I was driving in the hills of Tennessee near Whitehouse around election time with those same mates from England. We kept seeing signs that said *Vote for Smith*, *Vote for Henry*, and then there was one that said *Vote for Goats*. Obviously, a local politician's name. I said to my mates, laughing so hard I was crying, "Blimey! They're really struggling for candidates around here, ain't they?" We practically turned the car over with laughter at the expense of our lovely Hicksville friends.

Paul André Gibbons

In the small tobacco town near Nashville, there had been two soccer club coaches, one for juniors and seniors and one for freshmen and sophomores. The juniors and seniors were allowed to do as they pleased. The coaches were good, but the kids were spoiled rotten and showed little respect.

When I came, it mattered not to me their age or their social status. I intended to treat them all the same just like I'd always done. I had an idea of what they were doing, and I was happy when they initiated random drug testing. For everyone, coaches included. On Monday when the kids came in, the Athletic Director and the Sports Med picked three names randomly. One kid refused the testing. The reason was obvious. But there was a problem of even greater magnitude. The parents always came to their rescue. This was all new to me. I was brought up where if you got the cane at school, you got the cane at home. But in this case, the parent took the side of the kid, making life pretty difficult until we faced the problem and took care of it once and for all.

There is a generation gap when it comes to humour and discipline. In England, we were never *grounded.* Neither did we get our phones taken away. We didn't have phones, of course. We were whacked or sent to our rooms. The punishment we received had a lasting effect; we made a good attempt not to do it again. At school, if we were summoned to headmaster's room, we would stand on the black line for what seemed like an eternity, embarrassed. What we got, we usually deserved, and there were few repeat offences.

When the guilty party was exposed, it stirred up a hornets' nest. We were leaving on the bus, heading for Cookeville when a parent grabbed me around the neck and yelled, "What have you done?" I knew exactly what he was talking about. His son had been busted. I didn't react. It was show time. A couple of days later, they were all summoned to the school gym with the principal in charge. A great bloke, this principal. The underlying situation was a scheme, where if the majority of the juniors and seniors quit, the school would fire the coach. It backfired.

"Those of you who want to quit, stand against the wall," the principal said.

It was that simple. About a dozen of the boys took their places against the wall with the thought that if enough of them threatened to quit the team, I would be forced to leave.

"Is that your final decision?" Again, the principal never raised his voice.

They all said, "Yes."

"Then you're free to go."

The boys slogged away, muttering amongst themselves. I say, well done to those parents and players who devised this wicked scheme. What an end result, eh?

Great! I had about fifteen boys left, the cream of the crop, mostly freshmen and sophomores. Anytime the truth prevails, the cream rises to the top. Before I arrived in Tennessee, the club coach for the younger group had brought them up right, and they had benefited from the foundation he laid, as opposed to the other club coach, who would, after practice, take them down to the sto-ah (store), roll up naughty cigarettes with them, and open up a bottle of Crown Royal.

Those who chose to leave later regretted it. Some of them were college prospects, but when colleges inquired about one of them, I could only say, "He quit." However, their departure opened the door for opportunities for the good kids. We went to tremendous success.

I'm an American citizen and proud of it. I received citizenship at the Miami Convention Centre on Wednesday, December 15, 2004. Since that time, I've held dual citizenship with England and America, and I still love the country of my birth with a passion. But I have found some basic differences in the young people in America and those in England.

In many ways, English youth have an advantage. They are streetwise. And education is quite different. English kids enter high school at age eleven, and they are two to three years ahead of the Americans in maturity when they get to high school. When they enter senior school, they choose what subjects they will learn and study for the next four years; their choice is based on their bent. If they want to study the maths, they go in that direction. If it's the arts toward which they lean, they study the arts for four years. And they are expected to study on that path until graduation. By the time they finish, they know their stuff, and a strong measure of stability and responsibility helps them grow up a lot quicker.

The pubs are an institution in England. It was no big thing for me to sit at a table in my dad's pub. I was properly instructed. In America, it's a thrill for kids to go and secretly meet in a field or sneak around to someone's house when the parents are away, or in the trucks, doing upside down kegs, smoking a joint or two, then speeding off. This coupled with a driving test that borderlines pathetic, and we wonder why we have so many crosses and flowers by the side of the road for those young kids. They all like to see what they can get away with, and as a result, they often end up in trouble and with a police record like the young kid in Tobacco Town who was doing drugs.

In some areas, there's poor teaching in America, and kids get high marks regardless. The authorities in the public school system are under pressure to make the schools look good. They need high marks themselves to receive funding, and they make it happen one way or the other.

When I came to Tennessee, I knew my training methods were going to be different, somewhat based on my raising and my experience in England where we were expected to achieve. At Tobacco Town in the football locker room, all the coaches were there with their dip cups. The first thing they wanted to do was get me a Dixie cup so I could dip and spit with them. They showed me how to fill up my bottom lip. And I did. That lasted about two seconds when I spewed the dreadful stuff out all over the locker room. It was the worst taste ever. What a horrible, nasty habit! Yet the back pocket of half the population of Middle Tennessee boasted the imprint of a Skoal can.

The football coaches were a lovely bunch of lads, though, always asking me questions. "Do you scout teams?" They were curious to know how I operated as a coach.

I had to answer, "I concentrate on my team. If I can't tell that the fast left winger is causing my team problems in the first five minutes, I shouldn't be a coach."

I was out on the field one day, teaching this kid how to kick a ball. We practiced kicking over the goalpost. I placed the ball, took three steps back, two steps left, and then came in at an angle. Look up, look down. Strike the ball. I was knocking the ball thirty-five yards with a kick in bare feet. The coaches were so taken by my method they asked me to teach their football players how to kick.

They also asked, "What do you do on a game day?"

"I have the players show up in shirt and tie," I replied. "We all walk to Subway, spend an hour eating and bonding. We go back to school, and the players (not the coach, of course) take pillows and blankets, and sleep for an hour in the classroom."

"What?"

"That's right. And after an hour of complete rest, we have a very light practice. They're relaxed and ready for kick-off at seven o'clock."

The coaches were flabbergasted at my methods which, they had to admit, always worked.

I just had to get my digs in about another sport to this big black coach in T-Town—the basketball coach. I said, "You know why all these black kids wear the big baggy trousers?"

"No, why's that?" he said.

"It's because their knee-grows."

He howled with laughter—a great bloke with a great sense of humour himself!

The high school girls in Tennessee couldn't get the pronunciation of my town. I was trying to tell them where I was born and about my part of the world, explaining that the "W" is silent in West Bromwich.

They said, "Oh, is it Est Brom-witch?"

"No. The 'w' in Bromwich is silent. Like West *Brommidge*. Not *Est Bromwich*."

In their history, the T-Town girls had never beat Hendersonville. On the day of the game, I got the team together in a classroom and had them watch *Braveheart*. I did this with the boys' team, too, before a big game with the same dividends. When it was over, I said to them, "Now you know how it feels to have passion, to believe, to fight for the cause. That's what it's like when England plays Scotland or when the Albion and Wolves play. In the words of Robert the Bruce, "You have bled for Wallace, now go out and bleed for me." That's the passion I like to see in a footballer. That's how much it means to me. And for the first time, those T-Town girls won their game. I still remember those celebrations. Even the female vice principal gave me a peck on the cheek.

In England, there's always a first opportunity to get the rules straight. In my American classroom where I subbed on a regular basis, I gave the same first opportunity.

"Here are the rules. Get it right. If you want to go to sleep in the back of the class, just know that the couch in the principal's office is more comfortable because that's where you'll be taking your nap if you sleep in my class. And clever people don't pass their homework around, so here's what we'll do to avoid that. We'll do class work at our tables. I'll take it up. We're going to be honest in this class."

The principal liked that I always left the door open. We got more work done in one class hour than the others got done in a week. Sometimes I would take the last half hour and reward them with a video of Mr. Bean, an English comedian whose name was Rowan Atkinson. The kids looked forward to classes. Just before the bell, instead of waiting by the door, I had them sit at their desks with their arms folded. The one sitting up the straightest went first. The slouches were last, but they learned, and soon they were all enjoying the rewards of quality and hard work.

My philosophy concerning education came from my own experiences in England. Whether you are part of the government, or school administration, or an athlete, or of the working class, God in his infinite wisdom made us all different. In high school, no matter what year you were in, there were three classes. A, B, and C classes. I was in the A class for all subjects except maths, for which I was in B. However, I started in A and when I realized my struggle, I moved to B. I worked hard to get back to the A class.

In this country, we mix them all together. The kid at the back who aspires to learn nothing will do just that—learn nothing, and sitting at the back of the room, he is set to fail. Why not put the kid where he can excel? The best way to terminate a kid's ambitions and dreams is to put him at the back of the room with other non-achievers. I like to put them where they can do well with like-minded students.

Electives in America are ineffective. What's the point of an elective just to get a grade? If it hasn't to do with life purpose, it is of no benefit. A very feminine girl I know took a weight lifting class, something she could not do. She took it just to receive a grade. It profited her nothing. Why? Because she couldn't do it, and even if she could, it had no educational value to her whatsoever.

For years I've contended with parents who want their kid to score all the goals, thinking: "If my son's a striker, it will get him noticed for college."

Their philosophy shocked me. I had an eight year old whose father gave him $10.00 when he scored a goal. That reduces the game to selfishness, and soccer is the most unselfish game in the world apart from Rugby. Parents can easily do irreparable damage to players and teams by rewarding egotism. On the other hand, rewarding for winning a tackle, for passing to a teammate, or for making a great save builds character and team spirit and makes a lot more sense.

I just have to mention Lenny Greenbaum and Mike Steppling, a couple of soccer dads in Palm City, Florida, who did the best choreographed, in-sync sideline kicking-the-invisible-ball routine I have ever seen. I didn't know until they pointed out to me the consensus amongst American parents is that the best players play up front and the rubbish ones play at the back, and there I was playing their kids at the back sometimes. No wonder they didn't like me. Only joking. Evan Greenbaum turned out to be one of the best sweepers in Florida because he was a good player, not a rubbish one.

Sir Stanley Matthews, *the wizard on the wing*, famous English soccer player of the 1950s, said: "When I've got the ball, who's the most important player on the team?"

The answer to his own question, of course: "The players without the ball."

I ask my players, "How good a soccer player are you when you don't have the ball?" That's the question they need to be constantly seeking to answer.

A lot of American players think when they get the ball they look good dribbling, scoring. But anybody that knows anything about soccer can see a scrawny little fifteen-year old with so much potential for his heart, his passion, his willingness to open up doors for the other players, to give his all for his teammates, to work hard for the team—when he doesn't have the ball.

We can learn a lot from a certain Bryan Robson, who at his peak was dubbed the most complete midfield player in England. Indeed, in the world in a lot of opinion, including mine. I am, of course, biased. He inspired his teammates, represented his country in fine fashion, wearing the colours, aiming high, never giving in to criticism, but constantly seeking to take his game to a higher level, and in the process, leading the team not only on the pitch but behind the scenes.

Chapter 22
MISTRANSLATIONS

You wouldn't think there would be such cultural differences,
but when it comes to certain word usages . . .
well, the difference is there.

My first practice in Tennessee was interesting to say the least. I found that when a midfielder or defender won the ball, everybody else ran away. I chuckle when I think of that. I ask players now if the defender wins the ball what are they going to do, dribble or shoot? The answer should be neither. They're going to look to pass. I get all my players to play the ball *on the deck* (the floor). Brian Clough, a famous coach in England once said, "If God had wanted us to play the ball in the air all the time, he would have put grass on the clouds. He didn't, so let's play it on the deck."

Gibbo loves check-to's. This concept is easy to understand. I teach my players to check-to the ball instead of running away from it. I could never understand in 90-100 degree heat in Florida why kids want to chase around like *blue-arsed flies* (in America, headless chickens). The game in England is at a fast pace because it's bloody cold. We do it to keep warm.

Check-to is running toward the ball. It slows the game down so each player knows what's coming. They have to play at their feet. When it goes to the air, players only have a fifty-fifty chance. Check-to gives them time to think, to get into good positions. Even in free kicks I've seen coaches push everybody into the penalty area. It's then obvious what's going to happen next. The ball will be in the air. In the air! Defenders are normally favourites to get the ball. So I encourage getting one or two players in the box to check-to the ball, have it to their feet, and then play from there. Why would anybody *lump* (boot) the ball into a crowded area? For example, I ask a player, "Have you ever seen a bull fighter chase the bull? He draws the bull to him." I laugh when I visualize that.

While Daniel was with me in the U.S., he went to school in T-Town for a couple of months, found it embarrassingly easy and simple, nothing like the rigours of education in England. He was playing for my U18 club team. I have to say, one of the best inventions is *y'all* in the South. I love it! I don't know why that just popped up, but it's there now, and it's staying. Unless the publisher didn't print it for some reason, in which case I have just wasted a minute of my life writing this piece of rubbish!

We had a free kick about twenty yards from the edge of the box. We took the kick, and our big lanky forward, who was losing his hair by the minute, looked like a thirty-year-old, never mind eighteen! The ball was going toward him, and as he was trying to head it toward the opponent's goal, he accidentally got his hand into the way instead. So, it should have been a free kick to them, right? Wait for this one. You will love it! The referee got it completely wrong, the worst refereeing decision in the history of *footy*. He walked toward our penalty area, which, of course was some eighty yards away at the other end of the pitch and gave the other team the penalty for intentional hand ball in the box, y'all! (There it is again!) He red-carded our player in the process, too! There was nearly a riot. The referee didn't have a clue what was going on. "For," and I quote, "deliberate hand ball in the box." Right rule . . . wrong box! Daniel and I, in disbelief, doubled over with laughter.

Some things just don't translate properly. In the last five minutes of a boy's evening game against a top high school team, the floodlights on, grass kept like Wembley, was the best pitch I'd ever seen. We were winning, trying to run the clock down a bit. I told Jason Hollins to get the ball to the corner flag and put his foot on it. He did that okay—got the ball to the corner flag, waited a second or two, looked up, and kicked the crap out of it. He didn't understand. I literally meant for him to put his foot on top of the ball and shield it.

"What did you do that for?" I said.

"Because you told me to!" he replied.

Indeed, I had told him that! We just live and learn the proper translation of words from one continent to another, y'all. I love that word!

There were plenty of those mistranslations while I was in Tennessee. I was living and learning about these Americans. During shooting practice where the girls would shoot and miss and the balls would fly beyond the

Paul André Gibbons

goals, they would say, "Go and shag the ball beyond the goal." In England you just don't say the word *shagging*. It's quite another word for guess what? You got it. But the girls didn't know that. A perfectly usable word in America, but a not-so-good word in England. Another was when a couple of the girls said, "Let me show you how to trap the ball with my fanny." Well, in England a *fanny* is not exactly the back side, it's more the front bum. It, again, is not an appropriate word in England. That is, not by real ladies. You wouldn't think there would be such cultural differences, but when it comes to certain word usages . . . well, the differences are there.

For instance, when I hear a strapping big fireman is wearing suspenders I say, "He's wearing what?" I might be a bit embarrassed. For in England the stockings and suspenders belong to the women only, those you purchase at Victoria's Secret. Your suspenders we call braces. The images are there, but they don't always translate properly. Also, we don't express a need for *soccer uniforms*. If we think our players are wearing uniforms, we might say, "What for? Are they going to dress up as Japanese Admirals or what?" We call it a *soccer kit*.

I know, sounds funny to Americans. One of the funniest is when I was meeting someone, an American, for the first time. I told her I would be wearing a green jumper, jeans, and white pumps. She must have thought I was a cross dresser, but in England a jumper is a sweater and white pumps are white sneakers or tennis shoes. I would be wearing a green sweater, jeans, and white sneakers!

Chapter 23
THE WREN'S NEST

I watched them spread their wings and fly away.

I did a summer camp in Palm City, Florida, and blew them out of the water. Everybody was chanting: "Gibbo—Boing! Boing!" It was such a success that soccer dads, Allen Scott and Ed Hollowell, kept after me to move down. They tried to entice me by talking about the fantastic weather. Lots of sunshine. Beautiful beaches. "I'm not moving," I said, "but I am going to move my office down there." Who was I kidding?

The night before I physically moved to Florida, we finished practice and went to O'Charley's, more of a local place near Nashville, a favorite haunt of Reba McIntyre. She has a house and a horse farm in Gallatin. Every now and then I would see her at O'Charley's. That night, some of the girls' team came into the restaurant. Amongst them, Easha and Tanna, two of the soccer players. They were trying to get me fixed up with their mom, Renee.

"But I'm leaving for Florida tomorrow."

"Just one date," they begged.

"Okay, call her and we'll go out tonight."

I affectionately called her Wren. She fluttered about with her bossy little ways reminding me of that little bird. She said, "Okay. But what if I fall in love with you?"

"Don't worry," I said. "We're just going to see my mate, Chris, and his girlfriend, K.C."

Chris was one of my coaches. He played college soccer and then for Wichita Wings. I took him to England with me for a couple of weeks to have a trial at West Brom.

So we went down to Nashville that night. Chris was going to help me load up the moving van next morning. We had a fantastic time. Renee cried when I left, and said, "I fell in love with you. I told you I would."

I kept in touch with her and her mom, the lovely Shaz. Later Renee moved to Palm City. We bought a beautiful house together, and during this time she would be away for four days, back for three, which became her new lifestyle—a flighty, separate lifestyle that suited her personality. She was not anxious to settle down, especially to someone as tied to soccer as I was, and I could see from all the warning signs that she was drawn to her new way of living. I had helped her through a lot of hard times, but it was just a matter of time before she would leave.

Sure enough, on September 11, 2001, the infamous day in America and around the world, Renee interviewed with Southwest Airlines and got the job as a flight attendant. Appropriate. I encouraged my little Wren to go. To fly away. She was reluctant. But her new life took her to places like Las Vegas, nice hotels, cocktail fayre. You can imagine the rest. I loved her, so I let her fly away.

⚽

The house in Palm City had French doors that opened onto Jurassic Park. A preserve. When the hurricanes came in, the trees filtered the winds and protected the house. I loved living in this place. Loved the beautiful setting and all the birds and animals. Bobcats calmly walked past as I sat by the pool having lunch.

One time I had a chat with an otter down by the stream. We startled each other. He lay on his back telling me off in a real conversation. It was clack, clack, clack and as best he knew how, he told me to get out of his space.

One day I left the garage door open, and not too many days after, I heard a chirping sound. Two wrens had built a nest, and they were telling me it was their place now. Not just mine. I thought I had to leave the garage door open for their convenience to come and go as they pleased, when one day I was approached by the community security officer.

"You need to close the garage door," he said.

"But I can't. The wrens have built their nest. They must be free to go in and out."

He looked at me like I was nuts, rolled his eyes, and left. I watched the story unfold. The first baby wren dropped from the nest above to the fan on the floor. These were my little wrens. I had waited with the mother bird and I was there when they arrived. I watched them spread their wings and fly away. Kind of like when Renee left.

I was in heaven with all the animals and birds when I got to America in the first place. In Tennessee my apartment was surrounded by birds, astonishingly beautiful bluebirds. There are none in England, in spite of the song . . . *There'll be bluebirds over the White Cliffs of Dover* . . . From time to time, a snake would curl up on my patio and crawl up to the second floor balcony. One certain squirrel would lie down on my arm and nibble at the nuts I offered. Sometimes he would come in and scurry around the house. Yes, I now know I was asking for trouble, but I was attaching myself to these little animals. In my first apartment in Palm City, a lizard came in uninvited and sat on top of my clock radio to keep warm. His name was Eddie Lizard, named for one of my favourite English comedians, Eddie Izzard. I had friends visiting from England and sometimes the water had this horrible smell. They changed the name from Mallard Creek to—well you can imagine what kind of new name the creek got! Without a paddle, too!

I first lived in an apartment in Coquina Cove, used to go down to the lake in the late afternoon just before practice, and throw bread to the fish close to the bank. I noticed some frogs jump into the water from a bush close by, then a couple of startled doves humbly flew away. I kept throwing bread to the fish when suddenly a shiny black cable I had been watching started to move, turned and looked me in the eye like a cobra, then came at me. I wasn't exactly in the best running gear, wearing my favourite Adidas clogs. I just had to pick the black racer that was in a bad mood. Or was it a water moccasin protecting his territory? Beats me. I was learning how to cope with the indigenous critters, mostly the black racer that enjoyed getting into the pool, and slithering over to my patio. I would intelligently open the door, hose him down, and off he would go.

I have so many great memories about the time I came to the Sunshine State. Once I stopped for petrol somewhere in Florida and after pumping a tank, I chatted with the lady in the store. There was another customer behind me, a big guy who, when he heard me speak said, "Australia?"

I said without a pause, "No, mate! You're miles away. This is Florida!"

Poor guy, he was just being friendly and I had to spoil it for him. You know, I'll do whatever it takes to get a good laugh. It just comes naturally to me.

And then there was the time I was driving across the state from the East Coast to the West Coast and saw a sign that said, *Panther Crossing*, and thought to myself, how clever of these animals around here, they know where to cross the road.

I was happy to be on the East Coast of Florida where the little wrens built their nests in my garage, where the otters chatted with me beside the lake, and where the panthers crossed with or without a sign. I love this place.

When I think of coming to Palm City, I am reminded of the time I was doing camps in Cordova, Tennessee years before. A certain physio sent me to Campbell's Clinic, where I was told I would have to give up coaching because of the knee injury I sustained in England many years ago. He said if I continued I could become crippled.

If I had taken his advice I would have given up coaching because of that knee injury. In that case, I would never have come to Palm City. The dream could have disappeared and my life would be much different. Here's how that knee injury happened in England.

We were playing a game on a Wednesday afternoon (I remember it being a Wednesday league) with a mate, Bob Lockley, when a big thug came in to win the ball away from me with studs up. He went straight to my left kneecap. There were no cuts, no blood. But something happened inside my knee. I went to the physio, Tom Martin, who referred me to the Albion physio. He explained what happened. The kneecap floats and is tied together with nerve ends. The blow to my knee had split open all of those nerve ends.

I always played soccer like I live my life. All or nothing. If I could liken my game it would be to my hero, Bryan Robson. He was hard tackling, good passing, getting on the end of things in the box, leading by example. I was always captain of my team. That day when I took the blow to my knee and all the nerve ends split, I was devastated when I found out it would be two years before I could play again. But to be told later in Tennessee that I would never be able to coach soccer again was heart-breaking, not acceptable to me.

To describe the sensitive nature of the injury, if a dog happened to brush his tail against my knee, it was like an electric shock going through. Even now I've got torn meniscus in both my knees. Obviously I threw caution to the wind that day at Campbell's Clinic. There was no way I was going to voluntarily give up coaching.

When I came to the Treasure Coast of Florida from Tennessee, Ed Hollowell and Allen Scott, the founding fathers of our club in Palm City, asked me what I needed. "We want you to build the club from nothing, and whatever you require is what we're going to get for you," they said. "We're going to support you."

"I need some legs, a piece of grass, and a ball. And I want some uniforms for practice and an end of season banquet." I know! I had to conform to American usage with the *uniforms*. When in Rome . . . !

I got what I asked for. The first night of practice I had eighteen legs, a piece of grass, and a ball. It was going to be a daunting task, but I was happy. This was my calling, my profession. I started with two teams, and one of them got to the state cup final. This was never done before on the Treasure Coast. In the years that followed we went from two to five teams, then five teams to twelve. I had a group of people that supported me, and we got a reputation for skillful, good-to-watch soccer in no time.

I coached and taught my teams on the Treasure Coast for nine years when an opportunity presented itself for me to move to the Gulf Coast of Florida. My coaching reputation has always been impeccable, and they

Paul André Gibbons

wanted a piece of the action on that side of the State. I sold my house in Palm City, sadly on one hand. Not so sad on the other, for if I had not come to the West Coast to a place called Trinity, I would never have met the writer of my story.

Chapter 24
Picture on the Wall

He knew between him and the photograph of Lech Walesa sat
a man who simply desired citizenship
in a country where passions are fueled
in the warmth of moments like this.

It took about a year to get all the paperwork done and in order, but the day finally arrived. I drove to Miami early that December morning, on the way listening to local public radio as I often do, not that I'm getting old. I like to keep informed. I was brought up on the BBC, and NPR was the next best thing to it. Some habits are hard to break.

They happened to be talking about the U.S. Vice President, Dick Cheney, no relation to Lon, of course, and all sorts of stuff relating to the Senate, such as the fact that the President of the United States Senate is the country's Vice President, in this case, Cheney. How lucky for me! Little did I know this programme contained the answer to one of the questions to be asked at this soon-to-be-proven eventful day. It needs to stay, by the way—Public Radio needs to stay but pay its own bills without aid from the government.

I entered the building, feeling a bit weak in the knees, especially when I witnessed loads of people studying reams of documents. I sat quietly for a few minutes before I realised what they were doing. They were cramming for the final exam, which would be taking place in the next hour or so. On seeing a couple put their papers down, I scurried over quickly and boldly asked, "What are you doing?" They confirmed my worst fears. My attorney had not told me. They were looking at examples of some of the questions. I asked if I could have one of their copies to look through. Thinking back, this is how I used to study for my exams. Cram! All night. Nothing in advance. Cramming, I never let the papers slip my fingers over the next thirty minutes, which was the exact amount of time before someone called my name.

A grumpy old man motioned me into a huge office.

"Mr. Gibbons?"

And just so suddenly the enormous room turned to ice. The old man was cold, his demeanor detached. It was awkward for me. This is all planned, I told myself. A test of my fortitude. I shivered and sat down on a cold, hard chair opposite the old man.

I gave him all the documents he asked for, upon which he argued with me that there was one piece of paper missing. That I had not passed it over to him. The wooden desk that separated us—separated us! It was the bloody Berlin Wall! I chipped away at the ice on the wall and politely pointed out that under the nice manila folder was the document that was missing. He looked over his glasses and said, "Mr. Gibbons, I don't have that document." Cold.

I knew he had it, but I had to be tactful. I was beginning to believe my citizenship depended on it. Somehow I would be responsible for turning this thing around. He mumbled something under his breath when he found the piece of paper, as if to almost admit he had done something wrong, but not entirely.

I had to remain calm and polite with a smile. That was fairly easy for me, but this was stressful. I started to notice the wall behind his desk and the many black-framed photos that lined it. And then I discovered—amongst the famous people who posed with this man who sat across the Berlin Wall from me—one I recognised. It was Lech Walesa. I went for it. I had nothing to lose and everything to gain, so I said to him, "Can I ask you a question?"

He looked at me with a frown and said, "Yes."

The next five words changed everything.

"When did you meet Lech Walesa?"

Okay. Six words. Just checking to see if you're paying attention.

He was amazed that someone actually knew, cared about the great man.

"You know who Lech Walesa is?" he replied in shock.

By now I was forgetting the coldness of the hour and I responded with all the gusto within me. I had watched BBC through the years. I knew about Lech Walesa. He was a man like my father.

"Yes—I know who he is," I all but shouted. "The great Polish leader, an electrician by trade, who founded Solidarity, the Soviet Union's first independent trade union, and the man had no higher education."

I felt like a school boy, quoting from my world history book at the Blue Coat Church of England School. I sucked in a deep breath and watched the old man's countenance change. The room began to thaw as I exhaled and spoke from the fire in my belly about Lech Walesa. The chill of the experience turned to a spark of recognition of the man on the wall, an ember of hope burned within me, and my recollection of Lech Walesa melted the ice as I continued.

"He won the Nobel Peace Prize in the eighties and went on to become President of Poland. He was persecuted by the communist government, but as president, he transitioned Poland from a communist to a post-communist state. A great man, indeed."

The old man's frown turned upwards like the bark on a tree. He knew between him and the photograph of the great Polish leader sat an English bloke who simply desired citizenship in a country where passions are fueled in the warmth of moments like this.

At the end . . . he revealed his own fire, the passion that fueled him, and his mood changed completely. He proceeded to tell me how he met Lech Walesa, and only after he lifted his shirt did I realize the gravity of his incarceration in a Cuban prison. I could have put my thumb in the hole under the sternum.

I cleared my throat. "What's that, sir?"

"It's where I was shot and left for dead."

I was shaken when I saw the bullet hole. He had been tortured in that Cuban prison, but it was also there that he became a spy for the U.S. And later, he met Lech Walesa. Suddenly, I was honoured to be in the presence of this hero. Though in itself enough to convince me of the value of this country, I overheard another interview going on in the great room at the same time. An older Cuban man was seeking asylum. His daughter was translating for him. When asked the question, "Why do you seek asylum?" she said, "My father was tortured, beaten . . ."

I knew already, but I confirmed in those moments that day what America does for people. Two stories in the space of a couple of minutes—stories told in this room but likely never heard outside its walls. We get disparaged around the world, but the half has not been told about this great country—the *Little Eagle* with wings outspread. The *Lion's Whelp* ready to fight for its tired, its poor, its huddled masses.

The old man asked me for a couple of photos to complete the process and this time, it was my bad, y'all. My kids do not love that American phrase, but I have to admit, I've picked it up. I didn't have two photos. He said, "No matter. Go downstairs. There's a photo booth. Take your time. Bring two copies. And two coffees." He said to bring two coffees! We were the best of international friends, now. Lech Walesa saved Poland. This man saved the day for me. And BBC, thanks! A couple of questions later, he proudly announced, "Paul!"—it was no longer Mr. Gibbons—"I'm pleased to declare that you are a citizen of the United States of America!"

We stood up, shook hands. We hugged, and I said, "Thanks for everything you've done and God bless." We cried. We had connected, this grumpy old man and me. Lech Walesa had turned him proud to do this for me. I could tell by the warmth of his presence that he was proud I was a citizen. It was a poignant moment. Personal.

The cool December wind off the ocean blew against me as I made my way down to the car, reading the instructions on my passport, the changes and details of the swearing-in ceremony. Now my kids could come any time they liked. I thought of the time when Nathalie needed me. She needed to come to America, but it was before I got citizenship. I couldn't get her over here. They told me we would have to wait eight years. My daughter wanted to be with me. She needed me, and she was so excited about the possibility. So devastated when it fell through. We both were.

That interview gave me courage. It was not the ceremony, nor the flag waving, both grand experiences, but the meeting I had with the old man that made me want to give back to my country. My new country, for now I was privileged beyond mention to claim England *and* America as my own. Since then, I have found ways to give back, too numerous to tell.

One of the stock questions was: "What are the benefits?" The answer: "I can now travel on a U.S. passport." Not sure that's a huge benefit anymore with all that's going on in the world. I'm happy I still have my British passport and dual citizenship.

There's one thing for certain, the picture on the wall left indelible memories of the man who gave me an incredible *assist* that day in Miami, the day it all happened for me with American citizenship. I'm a blessed man!

Chapter 25
Best Moves—A "Footy" Bit

"I'll take any one of your players.
They have great ball skills in tight situations.
They have confidence, vision, and they are good sportsmen."

Whilst on the West Coast of Florida running my academy, as always, I used and will continue to use the Coerver method. Every kid has the same opportunity to learn from the same curriculum. Repetition of techniques builds skills. That produces and increases confidence.

The Coerver Method teaches individual skills within a small-sided game format, which is essential. If I could send one message, it would be to teach the individual skills. Play 1 v 1, 2 v 2 and then small-sided games. Within the small-sided game, make a rule that the ball cannot go over head height or knee height. Stick to that rule. If a novice coach (a dad coach) does nothing but that, he'll be successful. It is key.

The game is about maths and geometry. In a regular game of 11 v 11, if you see eight of the opposition on the left hand side of the field, simple maths (yes, I said *maths*, a shortened version of the word *mathematics*. Plural, right? Therefore by methods of deduction, it should be *maths*, not *math*!) tells you there are three on the other side. Common sense tells you where to pass the ball, on which side to attack. The geometry—when the ball is played below head height or knee height, the players have to get into direct line with the ball with no opposition players obstructing that line or pass the ball into open space, therefore the ball leads the player. Triangles and diamonds are formed.

One part of teaching Coerver is moves: changing direction; moves to beat a player; and stops and starts. Teaching these moves in realistic game situations gives the player a personality at an early age. In daily life, we are what we are based on what we do from day one—and then day after day after day. The same is true with soccer. Kids do the same thing over and over until it becomes part of their personality. Then a great thing happens: the reward is self-success. That becomes a very positive drug. He masters one move, goes home and tells Mom, "Look what I can do." Even from the kid that may not be very good at soccer to the best kid on the pitch, the effect is the same. They look forward to practice. They want more, and then their success is transferred to the home and the school. A team is as good as the individuals in it.

A lot of coaches in this country coach teams to win.

A totally erroneous concept, and my response to that concept is—give the coach his trophy at the beginning of the season and just go and play for the fun of it. His reward is with him. The piece is tangible with no intrinsic value.

If a kid cannot control a ball, then it doesn't matter what formation or tactics a *winning* coach teaches, it's not going to work. The game falls like a deck of cards.

One of the highest unsolicited compliments I've received was from a college coach who watched my team. "I'll take any one of your players," he said. "They have great ball skills in tight situations. They have confidence, vision, and they are sportsmen."

Vision.

He said *vision.*

When a player is not worried about what's happening with the ball at his feet, his eyes and brain are free to sort out different aspects of the game. For example, Thierry Henry (Arsenal—Barcelona and France) is so quick with his feet and his brain that he plays the game looking from above. He glides through the game like he's playing in slow motion.

A good practice is to do a lot of 1 v 2 situations—one player with the ball against two defenders. Tony Currie played for Sheffield United, Leeds United, and England. He was the master of this. And Zinadine Yazid Zidane ("Zizou"), French World Cup winning footballer, one of the game's all-time greats, is also an example of this kind of player. I call this exercise composure on the ball. I say to the kids, "We need to have a little bit of Mozart, Bach, Beethoven. You know, one of those *composures.*" Makes them laugh!

My philosophy was highlighted to me by two French guys, coaches at a professional club in France where Arsene Wenger grew up. I spent a week at Arsenal studying the Arsene Wenger method through Emma Hayes, who was at the time, head coach for the Arsenal Ladies. It was fascinating and rewarding because a lot of the stuff Arsene was doing I was mirroring here in sunny Florida.

The two French lads—Nicolas Mayer and Alexandre Tesevic—are soccer coaches at Racing Club de Strasbourg. (Nic is a Zoltan Gera look-alike, and Alex is a Ryan Giggs look-alike. Zoltan Gera plays for the Albion and Hungary. Ryan Giggs plays for Manchester United and Wales.)

Nic and Alex came over from France to learn the Coerver Method. They were two of my best students ever. They would rise early, by seven o'clock, and would be outside on the patio having *café au lait, du pain avec la confectionne*. Studying, writing notes on the Coerver Method. They interviewed me and even filmed me at practice. The thing that impressed them more than the Coerver Method was the way I taught it. They loved how I empowered the players from the age of eight in giving them responsibility to solve their own problems, letting them figure things out for themselves, not doing it for them.

Maybe it was not perfect, nor was it instantaneous as some coaches would like, but my players own the concept and it will stay with them for the long haul. Patience, observation, listening, silence. All of these elements are important during the learning experience.

Graham Whitehouse is a *guided discovery* coach. Graham and I are the area's two most successful coaches. Some self-appointed soccer experts on the Treasure Coast didn't understand this new method. They watched me as I sat on a ball observing my players during practice. They made it their business to confuse my methods with non-coaching. To an eye that was not trained, it would seem that way.

My response to them was: "Ask and observe all the players who are now playing college soccer about my methods."

Enough said.

The best teacher becomes the game itself and most of all the best teacher is the best student. Only with patience can the teacher-coach sit back and watch the kids figure it out based on what they've learned. Silence is key in this exercise. That way, it sticks. When that is understood, one student will tell the next. They learn from each other. This is how I learned as a kid in Bernard Street, West Bromwich. We used to go watch the Albion play on a Saturday, then on the playground and in our streets, we mimicked our heroes, copied their style. We didn't realize it at the time, but that was our best teacher. We had no street coach or playground coach. We just copied our heroes and organised our own games.

I received a note from Nic and Alex, whose native language is French. I treasure their message and I quote it exactly as they wrote it in broken English, though they *speak* English flawlessly. I hear the beautiful French accent now as I read this.

> Gibbo's coaching: one economical coaching. Our comings begins of an adventure, an hunger for knowledge Coervers method, which is number one in soccer world. We are now sure (convinced) of the positive impact of this teaching program, after what we have seen here in Florida. However a simple programme himself isn't enough. We have discovered more than a coaching method learning against this programme. Paul Gibbons give life and sense to this method. His approach, opening mind and experience reflect all values that a respectable educator must include. Our exchanges were fascinating, passionate, riches and stimulating. We are working together in the way to research contents more relevant. The evolution of soccer depends of this kind of meeting. We thank a lot Gibbo: the man, the educator, the coach, the philosopher, the friend.
>
> Our key words during travel: relationship, economical coaching, confidence, hungry for knowledge, skills, and pleasure.
>
> Nicolas Mayer, Alexandre Tesevic
> Coach Youth Academy RC Strasbourg, France.

Nic and Alex had said to me, "It's not just the Coerver method, but how you teach." That was good confirmation that my coaching style had evolved to a teaching method. There was no longer a need for shouting at players. Through the Coerver principles, I had advanced to where I understood that soccer is not a coach's game. It's a player's game where the coach should not be the "*vocal* focal point" as I put it.

An example is this: when a so-called *I'm-Great* English soccer coach came over to assist me in a tournament, I said to him after the game,

"You love the sound of your own voice." With a smile, of course, hoping I helped him realize what he was doing. He was that running commentator I used to be in England twenty-five years ago. Thanks again to Ian Cooper for pointing that out. I'm glad to say I took that constructive criticism to heart and I've progressed.

This *I'm-Great* soccer coach's style was coaching. Mine is teaching. This was a college showcase, and these were seventeen-year-old boys out there, not a U9 team playing a local league. In this game there was one point where my left-winger, Aubrey Ballad—who looked and played just like Peter Barnes of Manchester City, WBA, England, so much so that I nicknamed him Barnsey—was on the corner of the eighteen yard box with nobody in front of him, nothing but grass and a goalkeeper. The rest of the players, defenders and attackers alike, were congregated around the penalty spot and the six yard box waiting for the cross. The *I'm-Great* English coach told the player to cross the ball. He did as the coach told him. It was a quality cross but came to nothing.

I let it go for about thirty seconds, and then called over to Barnsey. As soon as I called his name, he automatically said, "Gibbo, yeah, I know."

I asked him, "What would *you* have done?"

He said, "I should have carried on with the ball into the empty grass and ended up with a shot."

I proceeded to tell the *I'm-Great* coach this: "A good coach—a great coach—would have wanted to find out the most important thing of all. What would the player's decision have been? Instead you blurted out your own decision. I would have wanted to know the player's decision, and so would the college coaches who were there to observe the players, not the coaches."

My point is—he made the coach's decision. Knowing my player as I did, he would have carried on to make the goal. The *I'm-Great* coach didn't like my observations. He threw down his toys and went home. Mind you, what would you expect from a twenty-three-year-old bloke who had only coached U11 boys back in England? He had only been in the U.S. for a matter of months, too. I was of the same mind early in my career. I thought I knew it all. He will learn, as I did. God bless him. One of my best "footy" buddies, Lloyd, will know what I'm talking about here. Lloyd Bayliss was the best manager I could have ever had by my side. Book two will tell you some great "Lloyd stories."

Here's an example. One night I had four 5 v 5 games going at the same time. All the hard work and discipline went into these players in the early days. I told them they knew the rules and conditions of the game, and then I let them go. Moms were coming to me, asking, "Are you okay, Gibbo?"

"Yes, of course. Why?" I said.

"Because, you hardly said a word at practice the other night."

I said, "Yeah, you're right. Know why? I didn't have to. The boys were magnificent."

As I've always said when Gibbo can sit down, relax and be quiet, it means the boys are doing the right things. They don't have to rely on the coach. They're thinking for themselves. My goal is for these kids to stand on their own two feet, something that will be helpful through life.

Once at a practice session with one of my coaches, I gave instruction for the players to solve.

"Get into four equal groups," I said, "in between the four cones."

Once again, patience kicked in for me. Patience and time to keep my mouth closed. It didn't matter, at that point, how long it took them to accomplish this simple task. But it was important for me to set the tone at the beginning of the session. The expectation was for them to think for themselves and solve the problem.

It had obviously been the experience of the high school coach standing next to me to take charge and enter into the problem-solving—to do the thinking for them. He started to tell them exactly where to stand.

I said to him, "No. Don't! I know you know the answer. Let them figure it out for themselves. If they aren't allowed to solve the simplest problems of the game, what chance do they have to be successful?"

Later on in a conditioned game, they were all bunched up. I stopped the play with my favorite whistle and said to the team in possession, "What should you be doing?"

As one, they all answered, "We should be spread out looking for space."

The fact was—they all knew the answer. The question was—why weren't they doing it?

It was a learning curve for the coach as well, shifting the emphasis to the players. It may take a little longer; certainly the learning experience is not as instantaneous as when a coach shouts out instructions, but in the long run what I am teaching the players will stay with them for the long haul. Will they still need to lean on the coach in ten year's time? Not my way; they become independent at the earliest age possible.

So . . . when people see me observing a session, sometimes whilst sitting quietly on a ball, it must not be construed as non-coaching. To the contrary, it is a far cry from a constant banter of play-by-play commentary delivered by so many coaches. Certainly a far cry from Bobby Knight—a great coach, nevertheless, always ranting, raving, shouting and throwing stuff.

When critics scrutinize me and determine that I'm "non-coaching," the truth lies in the players. How successful are they? Imagine a piano teacher ranting, raving, bullying the poor bored kid, telling him what to do on the keys and then shouting, "Move over. I'll do it myself."

Get the picture?

Certain onlookers and so-called experts observed my style and were so misguided in their perception. They forgot to look at the most important piece—the end product—a successful player. The proof is in the pudding. Someone once said, "Tellin' *ain't* sellin', is it?" Or in Black Country, "I've told you, it ay ay. It's ain't!"

Chapter 26
FULL CIRCLE

This has been an incredible and most fulfilling journey, one that is still in progress.

Proof solid that time tells all is reflected in a message I received from Allen Scott in 2008. I must share it. He entitled it *Eight Years of Fun*! I treasure every word.

> Gibbo,
>
> It has all come full circle. Spencer Scott, along with his younger brother Jake and best friend, brothers Jared and Evan Greenbaum, and with Danny and Josh Steppling attended the University of Central Florida soccer Camp the summer of 2000. Of course, the younger brothers were eight years old and the older boys Spencer, Jared and Josh were ten. With the boys being so young the dads decided to give the moms a break and take the boys to the one-week UCF soccer camp. Needless to say, the camp at that time was more about playing games and day care than any kind of serious soccer camp. The boys had fun being away with the dads and their friends but did not learn much in the way of soccer skills.
>
> After returning from the camp and a few cold beers at Palm City Grill the dads, including Lenny G, Mike S, Ed Hollowell, and I thought it would be a great idea to bring a soccer camp to our area. I think Lenny G. came up with the idea that he had read in a soccer magazine about this Coerver Coaching and thought that skill type was what we were looking for. Lenny even ordered the Coerver tapes and we dads all watched in amazement at the skill that these

young kids on the tapes had. I believe that Ed Hollowell contacted Mr. Paul Gibbons of Coerver Coaching Southeast then based in Tennessee to see if we could get him to travel down to Martin County to put on a Coerver camp.

Ed H. was able to convince Coerver Coach Paul Gibbons to come down with his coaches and put on a Coerver camp. Wow!! Coerver delivered. I think we had in excess of 100 kids turn up for this first Coerver camp and all the players and parents were amazed at what fun and how much skill and creativity the players learned in such a short time. Mission accomplished! We got to stay at home (no travel, no hotel expenses) and bring an incredible Coerver camp here to Martin County. Months later after another camp, we asked Coerver's Paul Gibbons what it would take to get Coerver Southeast to relocate to Martin County. After all we only had maybe two teams, a total of maybe thirty kids that were part of Treasure Coast United (TCU).

Somehow we convinced Coerver's Paul Gibbons to move down here and start a fresh new Club TCU and Coerver Academy. After doing two camps for us I think Paul fell in love with the kids and people here and felt incredibly welcome. Not to mention we have the nicest weather and beaches in the world!

Full Circle.

Here it is eight years later and Spencer Scott now plays for UCF Division One Men's Soccer.

This has been an incredible and most fulfilling journey, one that is still in progress. UCF's Head Coach Bryan Cunningham offered Spencer a roster spot after having watched him play. Cunningham's first notice of Spencer happened at the Norcross Nike Cup in Atlanta over two years ago. Since then Cunningham got to see Spencer play at various tournaments and games. Sun Bowl, Academy League games, etc. Spencer's own words. "I was never the biggest or fastest player." He still is not. (Dad's words.) The Coerver training within a team and club environment gave Spencer the skills and temperament to play at the college level. Spencer is comfortable on the ball (no panic). He has mastered many Coerver moves that give him space to take the ball into a positive and attacking position for his teammates. He has a work hard (positive) attitude at all times. I have never seen him argue with a coach, teammate or referee. Maybe only two yellow cards in his whole career.

Gibbo coached Spencer from the time he was ten years old. The past eight years have been incredible.

Weekly Coerver training (Gibbo and company).

Tournaments.

Camps.

Leagues.

England trip.

Incredible guest coaches—Thomas Rongen, Charlie Cooke, Albion Coaches, college coaches.

It is obvious that Gibbo loves the game and enjoys sharing his students with great coaches. I believe this environment is what gave Spencer the tools and background to excel.

As Spencer's dad I am incredibly proud of what my son has accomplished. I had no idea if he could play at the collegiate level? Never mind Division One. Remember—not the biggest or fastest player—not even close.

So far this year UCF is 4-3-0. Spencer started and played every minute in four games, and he played significant amounts of time in three games.

First game this year they played Penn State. Second game was against Ohio State. UCF lost in double OT 2-1. Spencer played every minute! Unreal for a kid from Martin County that is not the biggest or fastest on the team—not even close.

It really has been eight years of fun!

A proud dad,
Allen Scott

Chapter 27
PRINCESS OF GRASS

He can put a winning smile on a face, and I will always remember and cherish him as someone who did that for me.

Her name means *Princess of Grass*. Mark and Lori Stokes could have picked no better name for their daughter, Chloe, for she is truly supreme on the soccer field. She's twenty years old at this writing, a *footy player* in the true sense of the word, a Coerver coach, and a friend for life. She has a love and fervor for football that has surpassed any fears that tagged along as baggage in her quest for perfection of the beloved game. This is her story, too good to write in words other than her own.

> By the time I was nine years old, I was playing soccer on a recreational team called Hobe Sound on the Treasure Coast of Florida. It was that year my family met this wonderful guy by the name of Paul "Gibbo" Gibbons. He was the coach of a Club Team called Treasure Coast United (TCU). To say this coach had an impact on my life is an understatement. We always played against Gibbo and TCU. Rick Davis, head coach of Hobe Sound told me if I wanted to take my game to the next level, I should try out for TCU. But before I did, I participated in a soccer camp with Gibbo. I liked it from the beginning. Things started to happen, and my game came alive. Gibbo had passion, something I evidently lacked, and I wanted this same passion. I knew I had a natural gift from God, but Gibbo made me believe in that gift. He knew how to deal with me, looking far beyond my stubborn will to see the player within. He called it the true greatness in me.

"God tested me. She tested me," Gibbo would say concerning me.

We got into some heated discussions. He pulled me off more times than one and told me what was what. "This isn't all about you," he would say.

But he didn't give up on me. He changed my whole outlook. He gave all of himself to bring out the best in me, always seeing the greater potential, when I couldn't always see it myself, and I was obliged to do my best for this coach. I wanted him to be proud of what he was giving me.

There were times when I needed to shore up the team concept. I was so used to a different way of playing. I suppose the American way. He taught me English football.

"You have two touches," he would say. "Take a touch; play it to someone else."

That was his way of making sure I understood I was not the only player on the field. He was (still is) all about doing what's best for his players—the whole team—and I was a work in progress. His protégé. I had the desire, a true footy junky. Doesn't matter if I'm playing with or against, I have the driving desire to be the best out there. When I was twelve years old, he knew he had given me enough ammunition to flap my wings, take what he taught me to the outside world, and show it off to more people.

I had taken on a heavy schedule, spending four nights a week at practice with the boys, and with girls over three years older than I. And on top of that, I was going to Gibbo's striking practices just to get better. My consistency and perseverance paid off, for when I was driving age I had my father's blessing as well as Gibbo's to go down South to Ft. Lauderdale and play in better competition. Gibbo had said, "It's time to let her go." That meant I must drive to Ft. Lauderdale two nights a week, an hour one way.

I was playing for a high level team called Parkland Predators, but I was not getting challenged, so I took advantage of my best opportunities—Gibbo's practices in Palm City during the week and Ft. Lauderdale two nights a week.

I again confess my stubborn will. Gibbo and Dad ganged up on me at times for my one-way thinking. Those two knew what was best for me.

Dad would say, "Listen to Gibb."

Gibb would say, "Listen to your dad."

They always won out for they were right.

I'm still self-willed. Determined. But I had everything to play for—my coach.

"The method I taught fit Chloe better than any other player. She made it fit," Gibbo had said.

Thinking back, I see the error of my way. I never sat and listened to my coach at first. When I got on the field, I would simply ask my teammate, Katie Hughes. She always listened to the instructions. I wouldn't listen. Not because I was trying to be rude. I just wanted to play.

"What did he say, Katie?"

She would graciously give me the instructions and I would follow them. I think now how good it would have been if I had paid attention. It would have been from Gibbo's mouth to my own ears. When I think of what he endured until I could mature—well, it finally happened but not without pain and perseverance.

"One of the best things that ever happened for Chloe was becoming a teacher (a coach)." Gibbo knew me well.

I was fourteen when Gibb asked me to coach. It was in a camp at Halpatiokee Park in Stuart, Florida. My mom drove me, and I remember sitting in the car with her—crying. I was so scared. She tried to get between me and my fear until I could muster enough courage to get out of the car and face Gibbo who said, "You're going to be a great coach."

He wasted no time. "Set out lanes," he said, "ten paces apart." What? How? What does he mean? I was—I couldn't think. What to do? I was confused. I'm going to mess up big time, I thought. Wait! Oh, yes. With cones—remember? Just like Gibbo always does. Just do it! With the cones. "Man up," I told myself.

They (Mom, Dad, Gibbo) threw me in the deep end, and left me to swim—alone. I did it!

Gibbo describes Coerver Coaching as skills teaching. Principle-based skills teaching. His methods are entirely different from most. The key is building confidence, dispelling fear. At first, I thought Coerver was something that only a few could understand, only a few could master. But not so. Some incredible teachable moments take place. With Gibbo's methods, kids begin to understand self success, and like a respectable addiction, they want more. They begin to feel special. They become confident, learning individual skills within a team concept.

Principle-based learning teaches an athlete to become a soccer player. Sounds strange. But it's like this . . . an athlete may think he's arrived. But the greatest thing that can happen for the game is for an athlete to become a player. The thing that's killing the game is athletes—not players. Club soccer is primarily made up of athletes with few true footballers. When you are a player, you get up every morning with confidence, every day striving to get better, pressing forward to become a soccer player, not just an athlete. That's what Gibbo and my family wanted for me.

Coerver Coaching is a true way of life, more than just the fundamentals of soccer playing. Learning the Coerver way gives a player confidence off the field as well as on. It's not a narrow approach. It spills over, not only in the personal life of a player, but even to the fans. We can learn from a soccer fan. A true soccer fan is someone who has knowledge of the game. If a team plays good football but loses, it still feels good in the eyes of a real fan, for they know the difference. And when the game is over, whether the team has won or lost, it makes no difference. It's not about winning or losing. It's about playing the game with integrity. I used to think creativity was defined as one having certain talents—drawing, painting, other art forms. Talents and skills I didn't possess. I realized one day that I had that same creative in me. I couldn't paint a picture, but I could play soccer. Learning as I did from Gibbo and the Coerver method redefined the word creative for me. Now I understand the true meaning. It's all about the passion within and mustering the courage to release the inhibitions and let the creative take charge.

In February 2006, Dad and Gibbo took me to England. Gibb, Dad, and Mom thought I should be exposed to real soccer—football. I should try out for the Arsenal—the top ladies' team in the world. The Premier League. I'll tell you how that nearly scared me to death in a minute.

There were three tryouts—three cuts, and over one hundred girls had gathered from all over the world. Canada, France, Germany, Wales, and me, Chloe Stokes from little old Hobe Sound, a seaside village in southern Florida in the USA! I was the only one trying out from my country.

"She didn't just fit in," said Gibbo. "She took the game by the scruff of the neck! Not just her team—but the whole game!"

But I was petrified!

When the time came, I sat in the back seat of the car for a good ten minutes, Dad and Gibbo sitting in the front seat, probably rolling their eyes and heaving giant lungs full of air in disgusted sighs. We had traveled halfway around the world and I was stalling in the back seat of the car. Gibbo got out and opened my door and my dad literally pushed me out.

I walked the distance alone. Like a zombie, still scared stiff. When I got to the registration desk, I gave my name and received my number. I was wearing all white. I always wear white to a tryout. It's my signature uniform. At the registration, they were giving players Arsenal jerseys—colours to section them off on the field—yellow, red, and red current (maroon in America). My heart was pounding in my throat.

When I said my name and what position I played, they gave me a red current jersey—Arsenal's colour! It was a true Arsenal jersey. Their new jersey. My favorite one and that jersey fit me perfectly. It was made for me. My fears scattered. They suddenly and mysteriously vanished. For the first time, it felt right. Not many people ever have the opportunity to pull on an Arsenal jersey, and there I was wearing one that fit me to a tee and in their signature colour.

When I came out with that jersey on and Dad and Gibbo saw me, they both drew in a deep breath. They were so proud. At that point, it not only felt right. It was right! And when it was time to start, it all kicked in for me. I was so honoured to be there, and I was proud Dad and Gibbo were there with me and for me. I played my heart out—the best soccer I ever played. Gibbo and Dad agreed I stood out like a winner.

Somehow it was easy to play well. That was not my battle. My personal battle was the fear. But Gibbo had gotten me there. He made me shine. In another country. Some of the players didn't even speak my language. But when they told me, "You're really good!" they were all speaking my language!

We played little sections. The top coaches, four or five of them, were watching my game. They congregated on the sideline to check me out. I played like it didn't bother me. Can't remember if it did or not, I was so engrossed in the game.

Gibbo said, "It was an easy decision for the coaches to make."

This was the next highest level for me after the Parkland Predators in Ft. Lauderdale. I was the only American who went over and—I made it! I made the team. I was supposed to return for second tryouts in May, but they emailed me and said, "You don't need to come back. You're in!"

I was invited to play for the Arsenal Professional Women's Team and attend their soccer college!

I went back in 2007. Alone. I played not with the Academy kids, but alongside one of the top five players in the world, Kelly Smith from England. I played two games, scored, and gave two assists in the first game. I had a decision to make between going with the professional club and going to college in the States. Kelly Smith had chosen to spend four years at Seton Hall in America. That was fuel for my fire to come back to The States and enter college. When that is done, it will be soccer forever for me. To be accepted by Arsenal was extraordinarily challenging and fulfilling.

Gibbo is my hero. My coach. He's a man that will do whatever needs to be done to get you where you need to be, not only in soccer, but in all life situations. He is a principled man who teachers soccer while teaching life lessons. He can put a winning smile on a face, and I will always remember and cherish him as someone who did that for me.

He's a champ at the Coerver Method. It's not that he just understands soccer and how it's done (and he does), it is that he knows it and he knows how to teach it in the most effective method.

Gibbo always defends what he believes in and he will fight for that. Some up-and-comings say his way is old school, out of date. These are people who don't know soccer. They just play the game. They don't live it. The proof is in the success of the players he coaches and mentors, and I am living proof.

Personally, I think my dad has it right about Gibbo. "You think God brought a man from England and dropped him in our back yard for no reason?"

My dad was just doing his job as a Christian when he invited Gibb to go to church with us in Jenson Beach. He said, "You don't have to like it—just come!" And he did. I believe it changed his life—changed his way of thinking. There's a song Gibbo sings along with his radio tuned to JOY FM. The lyrics follow Scripture when they say—"What does it profit a man if he should gain the whole world and lose his own soul?"

Gibbo has given up a lot to do what he does for all his charges. His children and grandchildren are in England. His life and love will always be his children and the Black Country of the West Midlands. But he wakes up every morning and fights to make things right in his game, a gift most people don't possess, or at least they don't perform that gift as graciously as he does. He is the most unselfish man I know, with an abundance of love and compassion even for those who may at times have misunderstood him. But

Gibbo is an overcomer, to whom much has been given in the game of life and his calling. In the final analysis, it is always cream that rises to the top.

Chloe Stokes

Chapter 28
A Better Club. A Better Life

From practice sessions at the base of the bridge to tournaments across the country, there was never a dull moment with Gibbo.

Jane here! Facebook surely has its advantages, though a pain most of the time. I'm sure some of you will agree to that. But it served its usefulness well as I chatted back and forth with one of Gibbo's protégés, Chris Whelan from Jupiter, Florida. Chris is a student at The University of Florida in Gainesville, where he is an accounting major. This is one of Gibb's gazillion friends whom I've never met, but hope to someday. Sometimes you can know on paper when someone is full of energy and has that magnetic personality. Chris has it! I contacted him and something like two minutes later he wrote back and said, "I've already got a page and a half written. Quick, need some page requirements! He's after my heart. Now, if only Gibbo had been this conscientious for the entire writing of his story!

Chris wrote about Gibbo in terms of endearment.

> At the ripe age of thirteen, I was playing for a club soccer team called the Jupiter Sting, where the focus and drive were on winning and winning only. After several high level soccer camps and clinics, my father and I came to the decision that, if I were to continue on a path to soccer excellence we needed to find a club that focused more on development and team play than getting the win for the day. This better club happened to be located twenty minutes north of Jupiter. It was there that I met Paul "Gibbo" Gibbons for the first time, which I'll surely never forget.

Gibbo was Director of Coaching for Treasure Coast United (TCU), and a great one at that. I was nervous, but tenaciously tried out for the U13 boys' team. By the time the week of tryouts was over, I knew Gibbo was all he was cooked up to be! Personable and great with kids. I anxiously waited for my phone to ring, hoping to hear his voice with some good news for me. On a Friday afternoon, it happened. I struggled to understand the broad Black Country English accent, but when he said, "You've made the A Team for TCU, mate," I had no problem translating.

My journey with Gibbo began that day.

Over a seven year career with Gibbo's club, I gained a wealth of knowledge, invaluable advice, and memories that will last forever. From practice sessions at the base of the bridge to tournaments across the country, there was never a dull moment with Gibbo. And I could always count on him for a word of advice about football, about family life, or about anything else that mattered to me.

His charismatic determination spreads to any of those who know him—players, parents, and coaches alike, and his unsurpassed passion for football is contagious, touching everyone around him. I don't know a man who loves or knows the game better than Gibbo.

The more my father and I got to know Gibbo through practice sessions and games, the better we liked him. Far too many American soccer coaches only care about living in the glory of the moment. Not Gibbo! His genuine desire is to give his players an opportunity to be better than a win, not only on the pitch, but in life.

For the most part, my first year at TCU yielded losses, but Gibbo had the master plan that a lot of his players failed to see. He was looking five to ten years down the road while we watched the scoreboard. What he taught allowed me a different perspective, and I know I am a better player not only because of the moves and the plays and the methods he taught me, but because of the principles he instilled.

Gibbo is so effective in his coaching because of his persistence and true inner belief in his method—the Dutch

Coerver method. This method is all about skills development in young players, allowing them to gain confidence with the ball before moving on to more complex, difficult aspects of the game. Some parents saw fit to publicly (and privately for that matter) criticize Gibbo's method for their own means, but Gibbo pressed on, once again displaying his innate ability to plan for the long term rather than the present. And he did it with such class. At countless practices, players, including myself at times, just wanted to scrimmage, while Gibbo would lay out ten yard lanes where we would practice the Coerver moves against our wishes. But did we know? I bought into Gibbo's system early, so glad I did.

I recall countless games when he would be up on the sideline screaming his lungs out with phrases such as "Who ya markin?!" and "Keep it up stripes!" At times, I wanted nothing more than for Gibbo to stop talking and sit on the bench and watch, but like he has proven time and time again, he knew what he was doing. Every word from the sideline was designed to make us all better and to encourage us to play as a team. Sure, he looked tough during halftime talks from time to time, but it's because of his fiery passion that we all became better players and better people.

One thing he always used to tell me individually was, "Be accountable, Chris." On the field, off the field, with family, with coworkers, with anyone—he always preached to me that in whatever situation I find myself to be accountable, to own up to my team, my parents, my employer. He told me if I would do that, things would head in the right direction. To this day, I try to live by this principle of accountability.

In midseason after all the materials were picked up off the field, I'd always thank Gibbo before I left. After every training session, it was proper etiquette for all the players to shake the hands of the coaches as a sign of gratitude for the session. This is just a small example of Gibbo instilling maturity and dignity in his young players.

Then one day, something incredible happened. Session ended, and when I approached Gibbo to shake his hand, he asked me, "Chrissy Whissy, would you like to coach a camp with me up in Titusville, Florida?" Without hesitation, I accepted the invitation, although I was much more nervous than I acknowledged. I arrived at Gibbo's house the next day, bags in hand, not knowing what to expect. On the first day of camp, he instructed me to walk out five lanes, twenty yards by ten yards—a task that Gibbo did methodically and with no effort before every training session back home. I never realized such an easy-sounding task could be so complicated. My lanes were more crooked than you could imagine, and far off from the desired length. I brought the leftover cones back to Gibbo only to find him cracking up laughing at my mediocre attempt at making lanes. Even when in front of a huge group of players and parents waiting to be impressed by Gibbo's camp, he still found the heart to make me feel comfortable and laugh it off rather than get upset. He put me in charge of entertaining fifty young kids, while he effortlessly laid out the lanes like it was his job. I'm not going to lie; I was pretty embarrassed, yet impressed to see how automatic this was for him and how comfortable he made me feel in the responsibility he gave me.

Through this experience, I gained true insight to Gibbo as a fellow coach and I was taking it all in. He would be the first to agree that I was uptight and nervous when it came to announcing things to the group or taking charge as a trainer. At first, that is. After a week under his supervision, I was laughing and having a blast while running effective training sessions at the same time.

During those camps, I was getting a real taste of soccer coaching. We stayed in the homes with gracious host families. Several nights of the week, Gibbo, the other coaches, and I would eat at the host family's house where I learned things about Gibbo I'll never forget. I didn't know until then that he was a substitute history teacher. The more time I spent with Gibbo, the greater appreciation I had for what he does and how he conducts himself.

At every camp I coached with Gibbo, I observed his passion—that same passion he communicated to his own players back home at TCU. It was brilliant to see such an experienced and wise man like Gibbo, to whom football was not just a hobby or a sport but a way of life, share his passion with all those around him. His inborn love for the game was never placed on pause. That man can tell you every fact there is to know about West Bromwich Albion past and current.

Several years ago, I helped Gibbo move to the Gulf Coast of Florida. We loaded a moving truck with all his belongings and headed out with two other soccer coaches driving the truck. But in his little renowned red Jimmy truck it was just Gibbo and me for a good three hour ride. We laughed and enjoyed conversation—sometimes funny, sometimes serious—about any and everything. It was on this trip that I realized I wouldn't be seeing Gibbo twice a week for soccer practice anymore, and I could hear the nostalgia in his voice as well as my own. At last, we arrived same time as his moving truck, toted his things up three flights of stairs to his new apartment, and said our goodbyes until next time, whenever that would be. On the ride home, I was full of every remembrance of Gibbo and Coerver.

Of all of Gibbo's stories and quotes, and he has many, one in particular stays with me. "You get out of life what you put into it." This is a simple statement, yet accurate, a great life lesson from a giant of a man, one who has taught me to rethink a lot of my life. He was the reason for so many great things happening for me not only in soccer, but in my development as a person. I am proud to be a friend, player, fellow trainer, and football supporter of the legendary Paul "Gibbo" Gibbons.

Chris Whelan

Chapter 29
THE GREAT ESCAPE

I was getting close, and when I saw those players
in a practice game wearing Albion colours and stripes,
I knew I had arrived.

It was all hush-hush. But I knew!

Bamber, my old school mate, a true friend from the time we were six years old and then, assistant kitman for Albion, called me from England to tell me the Albion first team would be coming over to Orlando for mid-winter break and he had cleared it with Manager Bryan Robson and his assistant Nigel Pearson for me to join them as their guest for the day. I kept the secret. Didn't want to spoil the day. I knew if I told one person, the press and supporters (like me) would be all over it.

My thoughts raced back to the day Bamber and I watched with a keen eye as a young Bryan Robson played the intermediate league game at Spring Lane in the Black Country. It was the first time I ever laid eyes on him, and as I look back, I count it one of the highlights of my career—predicting that Bryan would one day play for England. He *did* play for England, representing his country on ninety occasions. He was the sixth and most capped England player of all time and has the eleventh highest goal scoring tally with twenty-six. Robbo captained his country sixty-five times. Only Bobby Moore and Billy Wright captained England on more occasions. It filled me up to think that I was about to be on my way to spend a day with West Bromwich Albion and the legendary Bryan Robson, thanks to my mate, Bamber Gascoigne.

I left the Treasure Coast that day, driving over to meet the lads, feeling like a schoolboy again with thoughts that it would be just like the days when Bamber and I used to watch Albion train when we were so very young. I thought about the possibility of Albion becoming the first Premier League club, the first top division team in fourteen years to avoid relegation, having been bottom of the table at Christmas Season 2004-2005. Robbo led the team to that "last-day" breakout. They call it *The Great Escape*. All the fans were singing the theme tune from the film *The Great Escape*. I'll never forget it.

I knew the venue well. They would be training where some of my Coerver Elite boys' teams have played a few tournaments in the past—Disney's Wide World of Sports, a lovely venue indeed. I arrived, got out of my car, and walked to the kiosk where Bamber had told me to check in.

The man behind the glass said, "Mr. Gibbons?"

I replied, "Yes."

"They're expecting you," he said.

It was one of those goose-bump occasions, and so I shivered as I made my way to the pitches, deep inside understanding the privilege that was about to be mine. I passed the indoor gym, which hosted volley ball and cheerleading, realizing for the first time why my lads were always keen on playing here. All those girls—

The baseball stadium was to the left, and in the distance I could just make out the medieval-type flags waving in the Florida breeze, telling me where the *footy* fields were. I was getting close, and when I saw those players in a practice game wearing Albion colours and stripes, I knew I had arrived. I could see Bamber in the distance, walking toward me. He put out a hand and said in his typical broad accent, "A doo, mucka." We shook hands and stood there watching our heroes play. Just like we used to all those years ago. We were school boys again. Living in another moment of glory.

I could see Robbo strutting his stuff amongst the players. There he was head coach, and he couldn't resist playing the game he loves so much, always leading by example, doing what comes naturally to him. He wasn't that skinny little fifteen-year-old Bamber and I first saw at Spring Lane that day so long ago, but he still played with all the flair of a football legend, such a stylish player even now.

After the game, Nigel Pearson came over and introduced himself, we talked for awhile, and then he introduced me to Robbo. We participated in a little photo op. I value that picture with Robbo to this day. He and I chatted briefly, I wished him the best for the season, then thanked him for including me on this one magnificent day, and I expressed my appreciation that Bamber had arranged for me to be there.

Bamber told me to meet him in the lobby of the Peabody where they were staying. He said, "I have a little gift for you from Robbo." And off he ran, disappearing into the elevator. In just a short time, he came back with a bundle in his hand. "Ee am, mucka," he said, handing it to me. Sweaty training gear all bundled up. I couldn't tell exactly what it was, but I had an idea he got it from Robbo. I thanked him and said, "That means a lot, mate." Bamber knew it did.

They all went for a meal, and I met them later. There I was standing, having a couple of beers with Robbo and the lads. They made me welcome. It was such a special day for me.

I traveled back to the Treasure Coast that night, arriving home around midnight. When I got home, I unraveled the parcel. It was Robbo's top, his shorts, and wait for it!—his Marks and Sparks (Spencers, we called it) XL black briefs. Talk about a personal gift! I still have them today and indeed I wear them, and for those that are reading and questioning—"Yes, I washed them first!"

*Memories of the Great Escape when Bryan Robson
led The Albion to that last-day breakout.
Picture taken Christmas, 2004.*

*Another unforgettable moment
Gibbo and Robbo
Disney Wide World of Sports
Orlando, Florida.*

Chapter 30
HEMAN, HORRORS, AND HILARITY

My eyes kept closing and I kept losing my equilibrium.
With numb fingers I groped for my eyelids
so I could prop them open.

A few years ago, I visited Costa Rica on holiday. I found the people of this country to be some of the happiest I've ever met. They live in little shacks. The towns are situated around a village green, and in the centre of the village is a soccer field. Around the soccer field is the church, little shops and cafés. It's all scruffy and dirty, but the lifestyle is thought-provoking and poignant. They love their families, they love soccer, and they love their church. Their community comes together around these three essentials. I learned a lot from those simple and wonderful people. It started on the beach one day as I watched a team in greens and yellows running along the water with chains wrapped around their waists, dragging anchors, a normal exposition of pre-season training, a picture of endurance, of resolve, of veracity. I felt proud to be a spectator on the beach that day. I noticed one kid in particular and asked the coach I was with, "How old is that kid?" to which he replied, "Fifteen."

Fifteen years old. I found out he walked five miles to practice every day, leaving a shack of a house, passing countless others on the journey. Walking, for he had nothing and lived amongst a people who have nothing. He walked the distance hoping, wishing for an opportunity to be the next Messi. Lionel Messi, an Argentinian footballer, is considered to be one of the best players of his generation. He plays for Barcelona, a club I admire and with whom I share kindred spirit and the same techniques for teaching and learning football at its best.

I realized then that those were the kids I would love to be coaching. Those who have nothing but big desires and great attitudes. The way it was in England thirty or forty years ago when a lad wanted to be a footballer. Not today when the kids want everything handed to them on a silver platter and with no questions asked.

Through some contacts I sat down with the FA coaches and spoke about bringing Coerver to Costa Rica. Talks went well. They had just returned from Canada and the U20 World Cup. All the newspapers were saying the Costa Rica teams were afraid to be aggressive. Afraid to lose, they played defensively. The cry was for the Costa Ricans to play with an attacking approach to the game. They desperately need the Coerver method. It could fit well with the FA. The talks are still on, and one day I hope to get to Costa Rica to bring Coerver methods to them in a big way.

Within a year of my visit to Costa Rica, I was in India. I had been in touch with a guy who was looking at ways to bring students from India to America for college or to England as football professionals. I did a couple of camps in New Delhi. Sean joined me from England, and I took another guy by the name of Nick Gates.

I should have known when I first looked at the plane schedule. West Palm Beach to Miami to Houston to Dubai to New Delhi. Talk about going the wrong way to get to the right place! I transferred and boarded the plane in Houston headed for Dubai to a sea of lovely people wearing saris and turbans. I was the only person on the airplane with blonde hair and blue eyes.

I once heard it said there are two kinds of people in this world. Smokers and non-smokers. The trick is to find out what you are and be that. I don't know if that's true or not, but I'm convinced there are two kinds of people who fly on an airplane—those who can sleep in flight and those who cannot. Those of us who cannot sleep on an airplane are cursed again when we land after endless sleepless hours and then the anticipated jetlag takes place. I stepped off the plane in New Delhi into that dreadful zone we all know as utter exhaustion. The flight from America was delayed by three hours, which meant Sean, who had traveled from London to New Delhi, had been sitting straight up in less than comfortable temporary seating, waiting for my arrival.

He looked like I felt, and as it turned out, so did the airport. It was under reconstruction and resembled a derelict's version of a Greyhound Bus Station in a Texas dust storm. I remember I felt like I was in the subway for some reason. Guess it was the makeshift passageways coupled with my fatigue and jetlag.

Now, to put this in perspective, the airport in Orlando, Florida, is so clean and hygienic and inviting that it is as if you are already on holiday at Disney before you get out of the airport. You could, if you were so a-mind, have a picnic on the terminal floor. Imagine the exact opposite in New Delhi the night we arrived. I'm told the airport was named the fourth best in the world just a few years before, but on this night I have to question that pronouncement. I know this sounds crazy, but I was thinking there was a toothless woman wandering around the near-empty airport terminal holding a bag with a live chicken inside, weird and strange sounds and smells emanating from that bag, and out on the street, the traffic was thicker than hops even in the middle of the night, with cows wandering in and out. Always cows wandering around. I have to question if the cow is so sacred, why does it smell? Why are they so thin? Doesn't anybody feed the cows? At any rate, whether in my imagination or for real, I remember being affected and nauseated by the dirty, dusty airport terminal. I was so terribly tired. And poor Sean had been sitting there waiting. Of course, he was waiting. Where would he go without me? He looked like a too-tired Zombie himself. And I *was* one.

I walked up to him and said, "Hello, Son."

Mind you, we hadn't seen each other in a long time, with a body of water, let's see, the size of the Atlantic Ocean separating us, and here we both show up in India and about all I could get out was "Hello, Son." And all he could say was "Hello, Dad." But that was enough.

On the inside we were excited to see each other, jumping up and down, embracing, chattering ten to the dozen with all the latest news. But on the outside, we were just two blokes who hadn't seen each other in heaven knows how long and who had missed each other dreadfully acting as if it were just another peaceful day in paradise. It would be a few hours before we could make up for lost time. We hardly knew our names, much less where we were. We had to get beyond the faux walls of this makeshift airport, past the cardboard cut-outs with advertisements in native language drawn and painted from top to bottom. I remember thinking Salvador Dali could have done no better with his double takes.

My mate, Hemanshu Chaturvedi, who organised the trip, waited outside the airport for our arrival. He had arranged a nice reception of people who had been waiting for hours. They put a "tiki" (red ink) on our faces and garlands of flowers about our necks as they greeted us. In fact, every time they greeted us. Was I rude or polite? I don't remember? I wanted so badly to crash right on the street, but there was no room. The cows and dogs had taken all the good spots.

Hemanshu knew Florida at IMG Academy in Bradenton, for awhile playing tennis there. He was an Olympic tennis player for India, a wonderful man of impeccable character. Heman, I called him, (I nicknamed his son *He Boy* and his daughter, I called *She Girl*) took our tired bodies to our resting place, where we crashed sometime around five o'clock that morning, knowing we had to get up early and face the day lagging. I was still on American time and my body was out of whack. There was no time for recovery, and just because we crashed didn't mean we were going to sleep. It was impossible. And my poor son looked like the ungrateful dead. We peeled off the socks, our dogs barking, lay down on our beds and watched wall-eyed as the sun rose over New Delhi, India from our windows. With little to no sleep, we hopped up early and tried our best to stand on our own two feet.

Heman had arranged for us to meet this very wealthy businessman at the end of that first day, and our hosts took us to a nice outdoor restaurant with a bit of a cabaret on stage. The gentleman we were meeting arrived with his wife and a bodyguard who was armed with a nine millimeter handgun. I could see the outline through his bright white suit. Suddenly I thought I was in Key West with Hemingway writing about an essentially good man who had gone bad, running contraband between Florida and Cuba . . . *To Have and Have Not*. Funny, I was feeling safe in the airport, in the college dorm where we were staying, but now, I was beginning to wonder. Here's a rich man that someone would obviously like to rob and kill, otherwise, why would his bodyguard be packing heat. On second thought, why would he have a bodyguard?

I was going and coming, dying from sleep deprivation and jetlag, hoping Sean was in better condition. The sun, which had not yet gone down, was cooking the back of my neck and I was wondering, "Is there an umbrella?" and the flies. Could someone scoop the cow manure? I shook my head and refocused, but to no avail. My eyes kept closing and I kept losing control of my equilibrium. Numb fingers groped for my eyelids so I could prop them open. And there were the mimes in tight black clothing, brown faces painted white. First time I've ever seen a brown-skinned mime, I thought. All over the restaurant, mimicking people. If one of them takes the opportunity to lie down on the ground, I'm going to lie down beside him. And if the rich man's guard shoots the mime—I'm going to fall with him and rest. The bullets, the mimes, Chaplin. And why was the Indian with the heat-packing bodyguard meeting with soccer coaches? I was sure they would tell me in due time. Had I been rested and clothed in my right mind, none of this would have fazed me. It wouldn't have mattered. I wouldn't even be talking about it now. For the first time in my life I could not have cared less that there were belly dancers on stage. And a guy dressed like Charlie Chaplin. An Indian Charlie Chaplin.

This is the dreadful part. Sean and I were so tired and desperately sleepy, we thought surely this is a *Cirque du Soleil* on acid only to find we were the ones hallucinating. Finally the sun slipped below the skyline, and the only thing I could think of was a bed, a fan blowing cool air about my wickedly tired body, and a pillow under my head. I could only assume Sean, who was sitting just inches from me was suffering from the same level of fatigue. We were like nodding dogs, falling asleep in place, catching ourselves before hitting the table, rubbing our eyes. They were talking about the plans. I knew they were talking about the plans, but I couldn't focus.

I was sitting too close to Sean to see his face, but simultaneously, we were doing everything in our power to stay awake. Just to keep our eyes from slowly going shut. We were twin androids without the slightest clue of what was taking place at the meeting, though we were sincerely trying.

The man with the bodyguard reached into his briefcase and pulled out an enormous set of architectural plans for a fabulous sports park he was going to build. Blinking successively for about thirty seconds, I could see that his wife was tall and thin with raven black hair. Her jewels were stunning, her pale gold sari scrumptious. She was a vision of beauty. But for some reason, my brain was a few clicks behind my sight. I needed to blink and rub my eyes again, needed to reach up there and with the toothpicks in someone's martini, prop my eyelids open. I couldn't help myself. I peered around so I could look Sean directly in the eye just in time to see a crooked smile besmirch his once handsome, now haggard, face. He saw it, too! I was not hallucinating this time. I looked again, and upon the nose of this vision of beauty was a big perfectly rounded drop, which fell out of her nostril. That must have been the third drip, but who's counting. She's dripping. I'm blinking. I wanted to look at Sean again, wanted to know if he had seen. Now it was dripping like a faucet. I wanted to stand up and yell in Punjabi, "Is there a plumber in the house?"

I was trying to listen to the conversation. I needed to know what was being said. "... soccer stadium..." *Drip.* "... money will come from..." *Drop.*

"Madam, how do you not know your napkin is soaking wet? Roto-Rooter!" I looked at Sean and turned away, hoping that I had not been speaking aloud. The seats were starting to shake, and Sean was holding on for dear life. I flew across the ocean for this? Cows are roaming loose everywhere, there's a dark brown Charlie Chaplin, a heat-packing bodyguard, some bloody belly dancers, a mime that could be cut down in his prime, and a nose in desperate need of—

"Could we have another Drano martini over here?"

Sean's leg was shaking. I stood to my feet, and with full throated voice, derived from jet-lagged reflexes, I blurted out, "Please excuse us!"

I grabbed Sean and we staggered to the restroom. Not from any drinks we might have had. We were on our last leg. We slammed the door behind us and grabbed each other, slumped over, fell to the floor and laughed our socks off.

"How does she not know?"

"I don't know that, Dad?"

"Is she gonna wipe her face with that napkin? It's already soaking wet."

"What? Is this common? That nose is running like a bull pawing in Pamplona!"

We were dying in the bathroom. Two English guys hanging onto each other bent double with laughter and Punjab walks in. What on earth must he have thought? We didn't make eye contact.

The miserable sensation of fighting sleep deprivation and fatigue that first night in New Delhi brought back a memory of Mr. Bean, one of England's funniest comedians, sitting in a quaint English church on a wooden pew trying his best to stay awake and entertain himself whilst the vicar drones on and on. Mr. Bean falls asleep, jumps awake, sticks his fingers up his eyelids to hold them open, rolls his eyes, turns his face inside out, and plays the part of a contortionist before he finally hits the floor on his knees and face, with feet pointing upward, stiff as a dead mackerel, then jumps awake and returns to his seat to finish off listening to the sermon whilst entertaining himself in sundry ways until the final "Hallelujah Chorus" is sung, hallelujah being the only word of the song he knew, and which he sang to the top of his lungs. There was just one event of our evening that topped Mr. Bean's antics in the pew. That was the wealthy man's wife with the drippy nose!

We walked back to our ride careful to avoid a bright white steed that galloped past us in the middle of the street. Surreal. That evening had been like having dinner at Salvador Dali's. With endless double takes. We hastened to our beds and attempted to overcome two days in Hades, provoked by jetlag, so we could begin to bask in Delhi delight, for tomorrow would be a new day.

Chapter 31
Namaste

*In Costa Rica, the phrase I treasured was
Pura Vida (wishing you the pure life).
In India, they use a similar word
—Namaste—a beautiful greeting
that means I bow to you.*

Sean André and I were staying in a gated college in one of the dorms. Finally recovering from jetlag and sleep deprivation, we walked outside for 'brecky' (breakfast of course), wondering if the day would be a continuation of the night before? We noticed loads of monkeys running around and playing like screeching little street kids up in the tall green trees, paying no attention to us whatsoever or the gates that secured the college. Our hosts picked us up and drove us to soccer sessions.

I've never seen such traffic and pollution (that is a subject all on its own, believe me) as there is in New Delhi. I told Heman, "This country could eliminate poverty in a stroke. There's no need for traffic lights. Take them down and replace them with roundabouts or islands as they say in America. Now that would be fun wouldn't it, eh? I can imagine the lads and Stig of 'Top Gear' getting their heads around a week in New Delhi traffic, masks compulsory, of course, the lads being the presenters of the brilliant TV programme in England. People are running the lights right and left as if they don't exist at all. And all those road markings? There should be no such things. These people go anywhere, inside, underneath, on top of you. You could save tons of rupees and help put an end to India's poverty by taking out all the markings and traffic lights."

Speaking of markings and roadways, in England and India, we call that part of the ground between the dual carriageway a central reservation.

In America, it's a median. Confusing to say the least, right? For in America if you were to speak of a central reservation, Jane says it might mean a place in the Midwest where Native Americans reside! (Strange place to pitch some wigwams though, in the middle of a road way, not much room and what about the bloody noise.) As Larry the Cable Guy says, "Don't care who you are, that's funny, right there."

Back to the dual carriageway. All of a sudden there were cyclists and even a car that didn't want to do a u turn, so he just drove down the "wrong way" anyway, heading straight for us poor souls, common practice on the motorways in India, hundreds of people walking or riding bicycles. It was a free-for-all, with camels and elephants sharing those same motorways. Seriously, elephants and camels. I can't imagine that happening on spaghetti junction in Brum.

One dark night while driving to Jaipur, the road was under construction and there was a detour. We moved to the detour lane, saw lights moving closer and closer to us, in the same lane. Holy Cow! (A great phrase to use whilst in India.) The cars were coming toward us. We just stopped and closed our eyes. I have never been so frightened, one could smell the fear from a long, long distance believe me. We survived the pitch black ordeal, or I wouldn't be writing this bit. Now as for Taxis, or "tuk tuks" as they are known—millions of tiny green and yellow things buzzing around like a swarm of crazy wasps (all wearing turbans of course)—they were everywhere, with less than an inch between the side view mirrors, horns hooting for no reason at all, in one grand concerted side show. We even saw an entire family on a motor bike, including baby perfectly content. I had a heavy desire to hang my head out the window and, with the contorted Mr. Bean, sing the *Hallelujah Chorus* to the top of my lungs, but no one would have heard me with all that din. (Or should that be *Gunga din*?)

In Costa Rica, the phrase I treasured was *Pura Vida,* which means *wishing you the pure life*. In India, they use a similar word—*Namaste*—a beautiful greeting that means *I bow to you*. These are gracious people, including the young ones.

Every morning we were up at five o'clock, out by six and at the schools by seven, greeted by students. As we walked through the hallways to the head mistress' office, the students dropped rose petals along the halls ahead of us, showing respect and giving honour for what we were bringing to them. We were English blokes coming to India via America and England to teach them soccer and their expressions of appreciation brought tears to our eyes.

Our hosts arranged a large assembly with the entire school present. We made speeches and were treated like David Beckham, probably the most well-known soccer player in the world. I was at the first ever game he played for the LA Galaxy against Chelsea, by the way. I've never seen a player have such an affect on a crowd.

Between eleven and twelve each day we had coaches' symposiums, and we held soccer camps in the evenings from five to nine. We ate dinner late in the evenings and went to bed around eleven or twelve, most nights getting only five hours of sleep. And in dry polluted heat to boot, grueling to say the least.

Kids in India have two passions in sport—cricket and soccer, cricket being number one by a mile. The young people were quite the colourful group, wearing their favourite team shirts, all familiar to us: Chelsea, Newcastle, Liverpool, and Manchester United. (Didn't see too many Rochdale shirts, mind.) They addressed us with intelligent conversation about soccer and their soccer heroes. We learned that English premiership through television has had a tremendous impact in India.

The people of India remind me of the original hippies mainly for the way they think. They love everybody. The women dress beautifully in their saris, and a visit to their schools is like going back fifty years, like schools were in England when kids wore uniforms and said, "yes sir" and "yes ma'am" to adults and teachers. Some even kissed my feet as a mark of total respect, incredibly humbling. The girls were respectful, wholesome, and innocent. They dressed properly and there was no talk of sex, no sex on TV. No one walked around in public with a drink of Tennants lager in one hand, and a barrage of filthy profanity in the other. No gangs of kids selling drugs. Teenagers are teenagers, but most of these young people are taught to wait until marriage for sex. They are old-fashioned in the best sense of the word, traditional, proper and most of all wholesome. There may be other parts of India that one could not say this about, but from what I witnessed, this was the case.

Our hosts took us to an orphanage, which was also a girls' school. We were invited to walk through and see how the girls live. Quite frankly, they are so well treated they don't know they are orphans. They are purposely not told. They were all dressed in traditional attire, and they sang and danced for us to the beat of bongo drums, performing in a most delightful fashion. I could tell they were smitten with Sean.

I asked the head mistress, "What's the age of the youngest orphan you've taken in?'

"One day old," she said. "Once a woman called and told us a baby had just been dropped into a dumpster. We picked her up immediately, the same day she was born. We took care of her, educated her, and loved her when nobody else wanted her." Tears filled my eyes when she told the story.

The head mistress invited us to go out on the floor and dance for the children, which she probably wanted to recant the moment we got out there. Why would she want us to dance? Did we look like we had talent?

I cleared my throat and said, "Sean can dance. I'll play the bongos."

Sean looked at me like I had lost my mind. I believed I *had* temporarily taken leave of my senses, for I could no more play the bongos than I could fly straight up. And Sean . . . I can hear you say . . . "What did *he* do?"

Quite frankly, I had no idea what Sean was going to do, especially to the beat of my drum. But that didn't matter. It was typical of me and my love for situation comedy.

I stepped over and got the bongos, sat down on the floor, and awkwardly adjusted my position. Too tall. Too short. Ah, finally just right. I started beating away, hoping my hidden talent would just show up. And what was Sean doing in preparation?

Good heavens! He was warming up with some bizarre gyrations first of the knees, then the elbows. I scanned the faces of the children out of the corner of my eye, trying to keep a semblance of rhythm. It was like sitting in a flower power office convention. They were giving indication of a little shock, a little getting into it. No, I said that wrong. It was total mortification. Embarrassment. But, of course—for us!

And then it happened. If you've ever seen the comedy programme in England a couple of years ago called *The Office* you will know exactly what dance Sean did. It was David Brent's famous Christmas Party Dance. The daftest, the most hideous thing you've ever seen. It was hilarious to us, but it scared the girls half to death. They jumped back in unison, sucking in a big gulp of air and clinging to each other for dear life, their beautiful dark brown eyes, already bigger than life, were getting bigger by the moment.

Sean, finished with his warm-up, was standing in a large space, and I was beating that drum in a sound similar to that of a flat tire flumping about on a gravel road full of pot holes. I kept thinking, is he going to dance? And suddenly it started. Just the knees. Everything was knees. Then he added the elbows until every part of his body was moving, running in place, one leg hiked and dangling, then the other. The worst version of the Hokey Kokey (Pokey in America) I've ever seen, and the more pieces of this so-called dance he put together, the more hilarious it became. I was beating faster, just trying to keep up, sweat rolling down my back thinking, "We'll never get out of this alive." Sean was now punching air. Was he swatting flies? Or grabbing them in mid air? He looked liked a strangled demented earwig on acid.

Finally he stopped, and in a futile effort not to further embarrass myself, I stopped beating that bongo, leaving the room in total silence, a bunch of lovely girls utterly exhausted just from watching, and the teacher clasping her hand over her mouth in disbelief. The puny and pathetic applause died a quick death and I dared to look on the faces of the children, who graciously broke into one gigantic grin, followed by giggles, however, still clinging to one another. That being done, we were off to a tour around the school, hoping to regain the ground we had just lost, yet finding it difficult to make eye contact with anyone but each other. We couldn't wait to get back to our dorm room so we could laugh our socks off—at ourselves!—wondering if we would ever be invited to dance again. I seriously doubted that.

Chapter 32
Bonanza

*We gathered up our purchases and started back
to our rooms at the college. It was not long
before we knew we were in leaf-bowl encumbrance,
chased by a laxative-injected mango.*

The second week we moved our soccer practice location next to the Commonwealth Stadium, which they were rebuilding at the time. It was not uncommon to see the women moving bricks on their heads and laying bricks dressed in their colourful saris, cheerfully doing their part to rebuild. We practiced on the outskirts of the stadium in a veritable dust bowl for the lack of grass. Sean and I had to squat low, trying to get below a cloud of the powdery stuff that was rising up, just to see the legs. And . . . so much was happening around us. People were running around the track; all sorts of games were going on. High jump, long jump. I said to Sean, "Good job they're not throwing the javelin tonight. We could lose our heads." Spoken none too soon, for the next night there they were—throwing javelin.

The food was fantastic, mind. Naan bread and curries by the spoonful or I should say leaf full. Morning, noon, and night. We ate breakfast and lunch at the college each day, like old colonial India. Service in the restaurants brought memories of how it might have been long ago in India with the snobs of the caste system. And there were some top of the list snobs by family name who were served first and best. The servers were still as they were in the 1800s, very polite and very subservient, indeed. I just wonder why the *snobs* treat them with so much disrespect. The caste system at its worst.

One day Sean and I took a *tuk-tuk* (took a *tuk-tuk* that's funny!) to Old Delhi, knowing we were once again making a terrible mistake. We had been warned that we could take a walk down the street and before arriving at the end we might have contracted the black plague, cholera, leprosy, terminal diarrhea or all of the above. The streets were filthy, people living in the gutters, excrement right on the streets. I started to heave, literally gagging at such dirt and disease—my God! And in the midst of all this, the Old Delhi Arabs were there selling their "fresh food" and wares.

All eyes were on Sean. He was wearing a purple wife beater shirt, his Russell Brand hair blowing in the breeze, with, if you can imagine this, a colourful sarong wrapped around the lower part of his body, and of course flip flops. The market street people thought he was a rock star or a famous soccer player, though I'm certain they couldn't believe he was wearing a woman's sarong. So wrong? Yes, so wrong! I thought he looked brilliant, and it was hard for me to keep from giggling out loud as people passed him staring. The funny part was his mom had bought the sarong while she was in Goa in the southern part of India, for herself—not for him. I guess he thought he would be right at home wearing this woman's skirt. He did look great in it, though, I have to admit.

I took my chances at getting some bargains, and we climbed a set of stairs, finally arriving in a labyrinth of cloth resembling Aladdin's Cave where the merchants were selling beautiful linen, silk scarves and native clothes. The deeper into the maze we ventured, the more we wondered if we would find our way out. Thank goodness the merchants were still with us, following close at our heels. They wanted to give us tea, sell us their wares, and by this time, we were happy to have the tea to calm our nerves. I imagined that nothing had changed through the centuries, and if I had ever dreamed of *Arabian Nights* it would have looked just like this.

Sean started to leave before we made our purchases. I tried to stop him. I wanted to get some things. He said, "No, let's go." Sean knew something I didn't know, and there was method in his madness. He knew how to barter. I didn't. And he knew if we tried to leave they would run after us, dropping their prices to practically nothing to get us to buy. It worked. We made purchases for a song and a dance, not Sean's funky chicken dance or whatever he was doing that day. We would have gotten no discount for that!

Once we bought their beautiful scarves at greatly reduced prices, we became good friends, part of the family. They loved us, especially Sean in the sarong. We had to join them for food, of which they were partaking in celebration of one of their gods. Not sure which, but I know this much—that god had a cast-iron stomach. They poured something with lots of curry into a leaf bowl and we dipped with the beautiful naan bread to the bottom of our leaf. Bloody bostin, wor it, ay? We were just two Black Country blokes doing everything the locals did. I felt like Anthony Bordain, feasting on warthog in Namibia—just eat it and take an ample supply of antibiotic later. The difference was—this food was outstanding, and Sean was sopping it down. Not that I wasn't.

We had taken all sorts of inoculations before going to India, people warning us we would get Delhi Belly, but hindsight is twenty-twenty. So . . . after eating the contents of the leaf bowl we bought two mangos from the street market. We peeled them and took large bites out of the most delicious, the sweetest fruit, juice running down our cheeks. We were happy. The little things in life, you know—

We gathered up our purchases and started back to our rooms at the college via a *tuk-tuk* again, we had the same driver that "tuk" us, and in fact he stayed with us all the way even during the shopping expedition. It was not long before we knew we were in leaf-bowl encumbrance, chased by a laxative-injected mango. If you can visualize this—Sean was blazing a trail to the restroom. Poor Sean, his bum was like the beginning of *Bonanza*. Remember the theme song, (bum boda bum boda bum boda bum bum) burning a hole in the middle of the map on the western plains of Nevada? That map was his bum! His little bum was on fire, that Bonanza theme song playing louder and more fiercely while the restroom door slammed behind him. Again. And again. I was in the adjoining room, laughing my socks off at the fireworks and noises, the screams and burning emanating from the other side, *Bonanza* still playing. Just like the famous toilet scene from "Dumb and Dumber." Then it hit me, both now laughing at one another. The last couple of days before I returned to my pristine and beautiful home on the Treasure Coast of Florida were vile. Something of biblical proportions laid into me. And for the last two days of our trip, Sean and I both were dog sick, taking it in turns to run to "the bog"! For fifteen days, it hit me. Fifteen days and fifteen pounds of weight loss I suffered because I had laughed and made fun of Sean André. I get the idea he had wished it on me. We were both suffering from Delhi Belly in stereo. Can you imagine the concerto coming from the latrine! I never wanted to eat at another "Delhi" again! *Kings of Leon* must have had us in mind when they wrote, *This Bum is on Fire*!

Chapter 33
BEAUTIFUL PEOPLE

The poor homeless and helpless, called the untouchables, are in the gutters dying. There is a shift it seems, although poverty is still ignored to the greater degree.

India is a nation of brilliant and lovely people. Its culture and heritage is a rich blend of the past and present and its globalization efforts rise to fascinating levels as its people vie in the marketplace as computer geniuses with a work ethic that never ceases to amaze the world. But there is a sadder side to India. A third of the global poor reside there. I saw both sides, realizing that the impact of the caste system still rigid in all areas of the country remains totally baffling. How will they make the transfer into the twenty-first century with such a weight around their neck, corruption at the top and even in local sport? Take a look at the shambles they call Gurgaon. An unorganised separatist infrastructure cannot be the best foundation on which to build.

⚽

Before we left India, we drove through little villages, working villages, with cows wandering everywhere, anywhere, always. The roads were dusty, the villages filthy. The dwellings with just a doorway for an entrance from a hard-packed dirt pathway boasted—yes, dirt floors. We saw women outside the entrances sweeping dirt floors, using a homemade broom, like a witch's broom. I thought, what's the purpose of all that sweeping? It's dirt anyway!

In the fields, women in saris were threshing wheat with an old sickle, just like it used to be done many years ago. To get to Monkey Temple, we climbed up a beautiful valley in a sharp ravine where we met a little family with a cobra and gave them some rupees for showing us the cobra. We walked the stone road to the village at the top of the mountain behind the main temple. The explorer in me had to know what was going on in the village. There we met ladies dressed in bright greens, yellows, reds, oranges. They were as cheerful and as colourful as they looked, putting their wash out to dry on bushes, then sitting around chattering and squawking like the parrots that were also decked out in their Sunday best. As usual, one of the ladies wanted to take Sean home with her. They couldn't speak English, but it was not difficult to understand what they wanted. They were lovely.

Those ladies dressed in colourful clothing chattering away were likely speaking Hindi or Punjabi. We would not have known the difference. Hindi is the official language of India and is widely used in the nation's capital of New Delhi. Since there are many universities and institutions of higher learning in New Delhi, its citizens understand the importance of being multi-lingual in a global community. The educated people speak proper English as well as their native languages in myriad dialects.

Monkey Palace, not unlike a lot of places we visited, was interesting to say the least, but I wanted to follow the example, get a broom and start sweeping. It could have been beautiful. To understand India, you must see the movie *Slum Dog Millionaire*. It's very true, although Heman might never agree with me. The poor homeless and helpless called *the untouchables* are in the gutters dying. There is a shift it seems, although poverty is still ignored to the greater degree.

In Old Delhi we visited a mosque opposite the Red Castle. Sean was given something for his shoulders. No bare skin allowed. We had to wonder about all the strange rules that came from somewhere, from someone. A group of Muslims looked at us with hatred we could feel, hatred of that particular group for the infidels. If looks could kill, we would all be dead as they put a jihad on us with their eyes when we took off our shoes and, out of ignorance of their rules, laid them right side up instead of right side down. The guide told us to turn them upside down. Again, what could be so significant about flip flops upside down or right side up?

The story of the building of the Taj Mahal could be perplexing to the ordinary person considering the contrast of the grandeur and splendour of this place with the utter poverty in the rest. It's a white marble mausoleum in Agra, northern India, completed in 1643 in memory of Mumtaz Mahal, the wife of Mughal Emperor Shah Jahan. It is considered the greatest example of Mughal architecture. It was quite possibly the most beautiful building I've ever seen.

I thought, "Why didn't you build it while she was living? She might have liked it."

Chapter 34
IF YOU GAIN THE WHOLE WORLD

We both went back a hundred and twenty years.
Just two blokes having a pint in the pub, happily, like we were
sitting on the edge of the earth dangling our feet.

When I first went to church with Mark Stokes and his family on the Treasure Coast of Florida a few years ago, it was like everything churned inside of me and a transformation took place. I couldn't stop crying when I heard certain songs. Kind of like the night I was painting Salvador Dali's depiction of Christ on the cross. I told Jane, "Something is inside my heart, my soul, my essence." I didn't know a lot about the Bible, nor how to express my feelings. But I learned that it profits nothing *if you gain the whole world and lose your own soul.*

You may think this matters little in life, but I've found that it is exactly what matters. My question is answered. I am experiencing a new way of life, and I have begun to discover people of faith. Men like Curt Snare, pastor of St. Timothy's in Tarpon Springs, Florida. He sent me this message recently.

> Obviously, God has led Jane to write about you with her descriptive style. I am sure you are humbled by the opportunity. As always, pray, listen, trust the Lord. As best you can, try to discern what the purpose would be and how it might glorify God. People can draw strength and vision from the intimacy of our stories; but in humility remember it is always the Holy Spirit who does the work through our offering. Congratulations! It seems like a wonderful opportunity for you!

"Trust the Lord with all of your heart. Rely not on your own understanding. In all your ways acknowledge God and He will direct your path" (Proverbs 3: 5-6).

In service to Christ,
Curt Snare

John Fleming recently wrote:

Just spent a glorious two days with Greg in Chicago. Me, my Dad, my brother Gary and a nephew all flew to Chicago Tuesday morning and we surprised him outside his college class 2 pm—He turned 21 so we had a blast with dinner and a blues club, not to mention a foot of snow! I got your message as well. Not sure you know, but I am the praise drummer for a local church band—First United Methodist Church—it's the one on Kanner with the pretty tall stained glass steeple. Been there 2 years. Allen & Judy Scott (and her parents) are also members, so it's great to see Allen there every now and then. Paul, you have no idea how happy I am that you are walking your journey with Jesus Christ. I vividly remember almost six years ago to the day when my Dad and brother Wayne flew down to Palm City and the three of us went to see Passion of the Christ one night, and then the very next afternoon the three of us were having lunch in Ruby Tuesday and you walked in having also seen Passion by yourself. Stay in touch and God Bless you brother!

John

John Fleming is from New York. I met him in Palm City, where he and his wife, Anna Susanna, welcomed me with open arms. I stayed at their house during the hurricanes, a good time to get together and really get to know these wonderful people. They have three great kids. I called the two girls, Cheryl and Christine, the Flembots. And then there is their son, Greg. The mischievous one. But wait, Christine was mischievous as well! That leaves Cheryl, the angel.

The storms came, and we watched the wildlife settle under the trees, the bobcat snooping around, doves taking shelter under the bushes, each creature responding to the urgency of preparing for the worst. Amazing and exciting. Listening to the radio, as there was no TV for a few days, we could tell when we were in the eye of the storm. When it came, we took the dogs for a walk in the peacefulness before heading back to watch the other half of the storm from a safer place.

John helped me with Treasure Coast United, did a great job with our books. He also played drums and guitar (not at the same time!) and Greg played guitar. They made some great rock music for us.

John and I went to England for a week. We saw the last game of the season for The Albion as they played Nottingham Forest. Albion had got back to the premiership, and we were thrilled to be there in our executive box. Of course, my kids were there, and we all had a blast.

I took John to the Black Country Museum in Dudley so I could boast of my heritage which, as already mentioned is, so far, traced back to the 1600s, and there is more research to come thanks to Tom Gibbons. Like me, he is a true Black Country lad, who may have direct lineage to the Vikings. The museum is a step back in time in open air with buildings restored and rebuilt suitably on old lime kilns and former coal pits. A real village. It's a page out of history, revealing how Thomas Dudley mastered the art of smelting iron with coal instead of wood charcoal and where iron was first made pure enough for industrial use. The Black Country was not only famous for its iron products, but for the centuries old lead crystal glass industry at a time when the French Huguenot refugees honed their skills in producing crystal glassware. Black Country merchants display artifacts of iron and beautiful lead crystal in the village that sits on the canal basin.

I was once again pleased to return to my roots and the canal-side village where re-enactors clothed in old Black Country attire took us back in time. We went to the little local pub and sat on the wooden benches, listening intently as a garish middle-aged woman dressed for the part told us the story in Black Country dialect.

"The missus looked after the pub whilst the husband werked in the pits. In the evening after a hard day's werk, the blokes came into the pub for a mild or bitter, far better than the wherta at 'um."

We were taking it all in when an ordinary kid of today came into the pub.

"Yo cor be in 'ere. Goo 'um," the woman said.

"Do yo av any crisps?" he asked

"No crisps in 'ere. They ay bin bloody invented yet."

She did a great job.

We sat there listening, munching on a chaise and onion crusty cob, for a lovely hour. We both went back a hundred and twenty years. Just two blokes having a pint in the pub, happy and contented, like we were sitting on the edge of the earth dangling our feet. It was bostin!

As I reminisce further, there was the message from Al Soricelli when I emailed him a version of *Revelation Song* by Philips Craig and Dean that really affected me inside, as if the song came directly from heaven straight into my heart, as if it were a personal message to me.

> Hi Paul,
>
> Great stuff! There is actually an older version of the Revelation Song that I like even better. I blast it on my Bose system and it ministers to me like few other songs can. It is awesome that you have maintained your spiritual walk. When in doubt read Proverbs 3 verses 5 and 6 for a daily reminder of what to do when times get tough. God has given you a gift to translate a beautiful game and deliver it to kids of all levels and abilities. In doing so you are improving lives and opening doors for them that otherwise would not be opened. Imagine if Emily had actually listened to some of her previous coaches who would yell at her and say 'boot it' or 'get rid of it' or 'stop playing with the ball' as she tried to execute Rivelinos, Cruyff's, Matthews and other moves. If you were not there to re-enforce her belief she would not be attending Southeastern University this fall. Look at the impact you made on someone you trained for a few camps and a dozen or so sessions thereafter. Imagine where she would be if she trained with you on a regular basis.
>
> God has given you a gift and soccer is your ministry! Execute it well and lead your charges to Christ via the beautiful game. It doesn't get any better than that!
>
> Al

Tom Wall and I in the Bell Inn in Walsall
Legendary Albion Trip

Chapter 35
HEART STRINGS

*I've learned through the years that home
is not where you hang your hat.
I've had plenty of those non-fulfilling
locations in my adult life.
Home is where you hang your heart.*

Father's Day 2010

I sat in my apartment in Trinity, Florida, where I made my home for eighteen months, opening a lovely gift bag from Nathalie, the card enclosed playing the theme tune from *Match of the Day*, a soccer television programme in England. It was a gentle reminder it's time to go home. Nathalie may not have realized it, but she was successfully pulling on my heart strings. Inside was a daft gift, which we always like. It was a black t-shirt that says *My Dad Rocks* with guitar on the front, too. And if that were not enough to get me emotional, I kept digging until I found three bags of pork scratchings. Before the day was over, I had consumed two of the bags, and they *wor arf bostin!* But there was more. Three Cadbury Star Bars, one of which I walloped down immediately. Nathalie knows her dad is a man of simple pleasures. The littlest things make me the happiest. She said, "Next year, Dad. I want you here next year. I'll run the 5-K for breast cancer again, and you must be here. And for my birthday, Dad—please be here. You've missed so many of them."

I could hear the sigh in her voice when she spoke the words, and I released a few more of those tears that never go away.

I was splitting my time with the Tarpon Springs Soccer Club on the West Coast of Florida with the club on Florida's Treasure Coast. On the way home from the Atlantic Coast one day, I was listening to my favourite radio station, JOY FM. There was a programme on with a lot of talk about family. Father-child relationships. The host was speaking directly to me. About things I needed—wanted—to be doing with my own children, Nathalie, Daniel, and Sean. Things impossible to accomplish with an ocean separating us. They are on my mind every waking moment. Every night Nathalie would send a text message saying, "Goodnight, Dad. I love you. Don't stay away too long."

I have been in The States for over twenty years of my life. And that's how it is for me at the present. The future could hold something entirely different. I have learned not to call the shots on my life. I have *Someone* who leads me from strength to strength, *Someone* who will make those decisions for me now and in the future.

I hear other parents say the kids get married, and off they go with life. That's the way it's supposed to be. And everything changes. But their kids are either next door or not so far away as another country. With me, it's different, I see my kids once every year, twice if I'm blessed to. I've missed a lot of events of importance to them and to me. Those days and special times are gone, and I don't have the luxury of calling them back. I wish I did. As a matter of fact, I am encouraged to press on, to look forward, and that's what I do, with wistful thoughts of those fine moments, days, weeks when I am permitted to spend time with my family.

Daniel said it just right, "Dad, the two weeks you spend with us are the equivalent to a year of love, fun and giggles." I always feel brilliant after just a couple of minutes with Daniel, absolutely brilliant. He is my *Aslan*, just like the Lion in C. S. Lewis' epic *Narnia*, depicted as wise, compassionate with magical authority.

I've learned through the years that home is not where you hang your hat. I've had plenty of those non-fulfilling locations in my adult life. Home is where you hang your heart. Home is where your blood is. It's family. I'll be the first to say I need my kids. Just like I always needed my mom and dad in my life. They died much too soon, before I outgrew a need for their instruction and guidance and love. Quite frankly, I don't know what I would have done without my dad, especially after Mom died. He and Heather were all I had. Of course, Aunt Rene and Uncle Joe and Rob

Marsh and Pat were there for me, they were brilliant. But nothing can take the place of a parent's love and nurturing.

While I cannot live in the past, I have found it cathartic to reminisce, to get pumped for what's coming up in just a short time.

I'm going home to England!

If only for two weeks.

And until then—until I once again lay eyes on my Nathalie, Daniel, and Sean André and all the Gibbons' heirs—to cheer me, I'll keep my laptop handy, where with one click, I can know for sure that my Albion are alive and well, still beating the Wolves two nil!

Boing! Boing!

*Nathalie, Paul, and a "cardboard cut-out" of Daniel
At the Bell Inn in Walsall*

*Daniel, Paul, Sean André
In Palm City Grill, Florida*

My fiftieth in Palm City, 2004.
Nathalie and Daniel popped over to see me.

Chapter 36
MIGUEL LIAM LEMMING

We were all curled up asleep on the bus when the screeching of tires and strange sounds brought us out of our seats in a struggle to get our bearings.

My life has been filled with amazing people. Miguel is one of those who came along and made an impact for the duration. I met him and a couple of other soccer students at Palm Beach Atlantic University. They came and worked in summer camps with me. Migzz, as I have always called him, is a great player, a great coach, a great bloke. His enthusiasm is contagious, just what a summer camp needed to come alive. His *Donkey-Do-Little* story is one that never grows old and is a stock "tale" at my soccer camps, but best told in Miguel's own words.

Donkey-Do-Little

I was born and raised in Zimbabwe by loving parents, Vince and Linda Lemming, who instilled within me a passion for the beautiful game. All my life, family, faith, and friends have been my strong foundation. My brother, Craig Peter Lemming, and friends like Chris Van Atta, Graham Whitehouse, and Ruben Moreno, are just a part of this great support system. And I can never forget Tostao Kwashi, who encouraged me to grow and mature as a player. He and his dad, Steve Kwashi were a major inspiration to me. Steve and my dad grew up together, played together when they were kids. Generational friends are amazing—they remain steadfast and they fill your memory bank to overflowing. And there were others. Blessing Makunike was such an incredible captain and leader who encouraged and inspired players like Benjamin Mwaruwari on to great accomplishments in English Premier League. Blessing died much too young, and a huge hunk of inspiration left a lot of us that day. We mourn, but he would have had us move on and do our best.

We did just that, always remembering the impact Donkey-Do-Little made on us that day.

It was fall of the year 1999, deathly cold out, especially that morning about two o'clock. We were all curled up asleep on the bus when the screeching of tires and strange sounds brought us out of our seats in a struggle to get our bearings. The real wake-up call was a loud CRASH! Followed by the unforgettable sound of crushing metal, a smashed windshield, and the impact of something most of us had never experienced. Gusts of cold air blew through the bus, chilling us to the bone. We scrambled for coats and shoes and then, of all things, the hideous hee-hawing and squealing of a—What on earth? And as quickly as the loud crash and the impact, just so quickly the driver's lap filled up with—a donkey? A donkey—and glass that had shattered and settled all over the front seat, on the driver, and on the floor.

All the players rushed to the front of the bus to remove the poor donkey from the driver's lap. We lifted it up and over the dash, back onto the dark and cold highway. The donkey lay in apparent pain with occasional kicks and starts in an effort to survive. But alas, it finally succumbed and passed away in the cold night.

The comic journey began four hours earlier. Our team, the Zimbabwe U23 National Team, had boarded our eighteen passenger bus in Bulawayo ahead of a crucial 2000 Olympic game qualifier. A must win game. All sixteen players and two coaches boarded Friday night for an overnight road trip to Gaborone ahead of the Sunday fixture. We had no idea what we were in for. No idea we would run over a lost and lonely donkey just three hours away from destination.

We got back on the bus that night, looking back on the dead donkey we had pulled to the side of the highway. We took our seats and covered our faces with track suites and pillowcases to protect us from the strong winds that beat against us for the next three hours to destination. We arrived at our hotel in Gaborone the next morning at six o'clock. The driver turned around to greet us all. We stretched and focused, and he said with all seriousness, "We made it Magents!" His face was covered in dead bugs! They were in his nostrils, the corners of his mouth, squashed and smashed all over his face and spectacles, each one had crashed to its death over the three hour journey from Donkey-Do-Little's final resting place.

Thankfully, we went on to win that game. Benjamin Mwaruwari and Tostao Kwashi capping off a fine game with goals in a 2-1 victory. We lost 4-1 to Nigeria in our final qualifying game that knocked us out, and saw Nigeria go on to beat Brazil in Sydney in the Olympic Game final. Nigeria were deserved winners, with a mesmerizing performance by Jay Jay Okocha and Kanu who had just completed a miraculous comeback from heart surgery.

Donkey-Do-Little played his part in history. The sad part. But my lifetime friend Tostao Kwashi was the goal scorer that day. Blessing and Benjamin were there, encouraging, inspiring, leading. Like Gibbo, whose friends are my friends, we live and love and breathe the beautiful game. I'm glad to be a part of the life and journey of Gibbo. World class!

Miguel Liam Lemming

Chapter 37
SLIDING DOWN THE GLOBE

What we do with what we're allotted is the important part.
How we treat our responsibilities.
My mind loped in a thousand directions . . .

Alex and Nic, the two French lads, came to the Gulf Coast of Florida from Strasburg, France for their annual soccer camps with my teams. Alex arrived first as planned. Nic was delayed by a day. He actually missed his train, let's put it that way. I went to fetch Alex on Saturday and told him I had been invited to go to Botswana but as soon as I picked him up from Tampa airport, it was time for me to zoom off from the same airport the very next day. Sensational the way it fell into place. The trip wasn't actually finalised until the Wednesday before the Sunday I was due to fly. That Sunday was the Fourth of July, Independence Day in America. So significant. I had four days to prepare, four days to try and finish what I had started in Tarpon; I knew my time was up at the soccer club if I left Tarpon that day. Looking back it was up anyway. People in positions of power again. So I followed what Providence had planned for me. I am not going to argue with Him, and besides with him on my side how could I fail. I dare not question, for it was the opportunity of a lifetime. I knew the French lads would understand. Besides, they would be staying in my apartment, using my car, and working with my soccer teams for two weeks.

Sunday came; I was off to the Tampa Airport myself. Alex took my car and helped with my luggage. I would be gone a month with a side trip to England to see my kids. Two weeks in Africa, two weeks in England with my family, how spiffing. The stuff of which dreams are made.

Heaven sent and guided again, this is how it happened, elaborated upon from my diary.

In June, I began email and telephone communication with Lesley Boggs, Director of C4C (Coaching for Conservation), an exhibition and a soccer camp being hosted by the Botswana Predator Conservation Trust (BPCT) aided by Tusk Trust (UK), to be held in Maun, Botswana, an initiative generously sponsored by Investec Asset Management.

His Royal Highness Prince William of Wales, former South African Football Captain and English FA Ambassador, Lucas Radebe, and recording artist Joe Jonas, were scheduled to participate in a day-long exhibition of the work of BPCT, lending support to the innovative sport and social development programme C4C on June 16, *The Day of the African Child*. David Beckham had agreed to come but the World Cup was actually being played in South Africa and things worked out that Lucas Radebe was there in his stead.

The mission of C4C is to conserve natural resources by using sport to engender self respect, teach lessons about wildlife, and inspire a generation of kids who care. Lesley was certain having Prince William, who is also the President of England's Football Association, and Lucas Radebe on the field, would be a great inspiration for the children.

Following Prince William's visit would be a three-day training camp in the bush at the research camp which was situated in the Okavango Delta within the vast confines of the Moremi game reserve and after that, a week-long educational programme at the Maun Sports Stadium with around seven hundred age nine to eleven-year-olds expected to attend. Cleverly, Lesley asked for a fifty-fifty split of boys and girls.

My role in all of this was to head up a team of local coaches who came mostly from the nearby town of Shorobe and then to teach soccer skills and games which integrated self respect, respect for others, Botswana wild animals, and conservation to the young kids from about twelve local schools in and around Maun, Botswana.

C4C was looking for high value, high energy, professional expertise and I was to make it happen on the ground. I had just a few days to achieve all this. I love challenges and this was one of the best. Theirs was to focus on the endangered species. Mine was to do what I do best, coach soccer while teaching life skills.

The day arrived with extraordinary speed, and I was off—Tampa to Atlanta. Sitting 35,000 feet over the Florida Peninsula, I reflected with mixed emotions not only on the past few days and everything going on in my life, but I thought ahead to what surely would be moments to remember. I needed a travel partner to share my adventure. Sometimes it's not brilliant traveling alone. I'll settle for my diary. Kristin Anthony was later to become that perfect partner on our second trip to India.

Climbing the clouds en route to Atlanta on the first leg of the journey, I was off to yet another foreign country. The fluffy whites split, and below us houses, railroad tracks, and coursing rivers appeared then vanished like so many pipe dreams. I was getting the birds-eye view, wondering if this is how God sees us in our humanity. Trifling, small, insignificant. No, not if *He loves us with an everlasting love.* What we do with what we're allotted is the important part. How we treat our responsibilities. My mind loped in a thousand directions as I thought about the sign on the marquee somewhere in Stuart, Florida, "Do what you can, with what you've got, where you are."

Atlanta Airport had not changed one iota from the last time I passed this way—from the many times I had passed this way. All roads lead not to Rome. They lead to Hartsfield Airport, Atlanta, Georgia. In the USA! In Foxworthy country!

At the Baggage Claim I retrieved my luggage and headed for Concourse E14, tired already. Legs not as strong as they once were, but just being in Atlanta Airport makes one tired. I knew I would do much better once I'd talked to Sean in London. With a hefty layover, we could have lunch at Heathrow with plenty of time for catching up. My arrival time was ten o'clock a.m. and I was not scheduled to leave for Johannesburg until seven o'clock p.m.

I called London. No answer. Where might my son be?

That many hours in Heathrow was going to be a long wait with no toiletry. No toothbrush, no deodorant, no Sean. Might be a bit yucky. Perhaps they'll give me a bag on British Airways, I hoped.

Again, my thoughts crowded up the spaces in my mind I had desired to keep blank. Am I really moving from the Gulf Coast back to the Treasure Coast when I return? Knowing the answer to that question was almost one hundred percent *yes*, I quickly turned my ruminations toward England. To Team Gibbons and the heirs. There would be time to think about Treasure Coast when I returned.

I nervously contemplated arrival in Botswana. I had thought about it, but in the rush of leaving with a load of last-minute preparation, I hadn't taken the time to sit and concentrate on the sheer joy of an English-American soccer coach privileged to visit Johannesburg, South Africa during World Cup 2010. Well, when I say visit, I really meant about an hour and a half layover in the airport, okay? I had greater things to do!

I had jotted down an important line in my diary in the Atlanta Airport. I read it again and highlighted it: *I have faith!* That line covered not only my hectic agenda for the next two weeks but for the immediate future. I needed *faith*. I leaned back in my seat, closed my eyes and found some sleep, thankful for lessons hard learned. I didn't want to repeat the India jetlag experience. Those Tylenol PM worked.

When I stepped off the plane into Heathrow Airport, I knew I was at home in my country, though I was still wondering where Sean was and why he didn't answer. I needed a nice cup of tea and a full English breakfast. Gordon Ramsey obliged, and in no time I was sitting down to a proper teacup, proper toast with a toast holder, a rack so familiar to me. It reminded me of a little bed and breakfast where Dad, younger sister Heather and I stayed in Ventnor on the Isle of Wight. I well remember Heather spitting out a mouthful of tea in one of our fits of giggling. I love my Zez. Oh, the toast holder, one that held those little toast points, being triangular in shape, of course. A side of chunky thick mushrooms; two eggs; proper, and I do mean proper, meaty bacon; big fat sausage; and a half-cut thick tomato. Bostin! Again, I was in heaven. My accent returned with full passion, along with my appetite. I certainly hoped I was not an elitist, though I was feeling quite posh.

I indulged heartily and celebrated the event by reading *The Guardian* with proper English comments. Why had everything suddenly become *proper*? I really did read it, though I could have pretended. It was all good until I looked at my bill. £19, something like $27.00. You could get a good steak and ale for that price in Florida. What value for money the good old USA!

I now had seven hours to kill in Heathrow. There were a lot of Africans on the flight Atlanta to Nigeria via Heathrow. They were returning home, I suppose. Nothing personal, but I pledged to make it a priority to ask that some Sure Deodorant be dropped at the next UN food drop. Mind you, I bet I didn't smell much better myself. The air was thick with odours of which I was not familiar. I caught myself sounding in my head like Anthony Bourdain again. Possibly his visit to Namibia. The sights and smells. I was a *footy*. Could never be a *foodie*, not in unfamiliar situations.

I kept looking for my Gate number, for I had a ten hour flight to Johannesburg. Guess it had not been posted. I didn't know where to sit.

Just a few small hiccups! Things can't always be smashing, though I was hoping for such. First, I sent Nathalie a text message trying to locate Sean, who resides in London, for he's attending Camberwell Art College. Like father, like son, only surely he will be very successful with it like his brother Daniel who graduated Birmingham College of Art, was awarded British Airways Student of the Year, and currently runs his own interior design business with such clients as some Albion and Villa players!

I'm feeling more contented, finally finding out that the scamp that is called Sean has hopped over to Denmark to a rock concert, or whatever it is they are called these days. As you do, eh? Nothing to how these younger Europeans do things now a-days, my son being no exception. My furthermost exertion was the Bath Pop Festival near Shepton Mallett (where Babycham comes from, of course.)

First hiccup. My reading glasses are falling apart, screw having gone on vacation. They are now delicately balanced on my nose. If I don't move my head too quickly, perhaps they will not pull a *Transformer* and disintegrate before I can purchase new ones in Johannesburg.

Second hiccup. My computer has only forty minutes of battery time left. Sorry, thirty-nine now. Seems like every minute goes down every ten seconds. And, of course, my universal plug is in my luggage in transit.

Third hiccup. My computer is on, I try to link to the famous www.com and success! What? They want me to pay? Join by paying a monthly fee! No way! I'll wait for free Wi-Fi. The French lads pronounce it *Wee-Fee*. Hilarious!

Fourth hiccup. This was chronologically number one. My mobile phone. Yes, I'm old-fashioned. I don't want to call it a cell phone. Cells are for people behind bars, aren't they?

My glasses are holding onto my nose for dear life. Clinging would be the right word here. My phone is running out of battery. So, yes. I pop into Dixon's and pay £21 for a charger. Exorbitant. I scurry down to the lounge. When you think of lounge, you think of comfort, eh? Of relaxing. Not so. It really should have a sign stating, *planks this way*. The seat was so hard I soon had a numb bum. And, of course, the three wall sockets in the whole *plank* area were not working, so I went back to Dixon's and they charged my phone for me. Ain't (that, remember, is the posh version of 'ay') they nice people? Thanks, Dixon's!

Only ninety minutes for them to announce my gate. Exciting stuff, eh? Bet you can't wait for the next riveting installment of GibboGate.

⚽

Finally, I was in the air once again, making my way upward over beautiful London town, seated next to a lady with the lovely name *Honey Gandy*. She had just returned from cruises to the Bahamas, Panama Canal, and Canada, via Bristol, England. She lost her Ralph a couple of years ago and this was her respite. Ralph was a Top Crown Green Bowler. For the record, she missed her Ralph, a native of Johannesburg. Honey lives by the posh shopping area Sandston, but of course, she doesn't shop there. We chatted and shared our love for wine and proper English tea.

Like so many times before, I looked back at Heathrow, a glass-winged city of its own, London's primary airport since the 1940s. My gaze hung on the colourful reflections of tail wing flags from around the globe. I was proud my country boasted the busiest airport in the world for international passenger traffic, Europe's foremost hub airport.

Paul André Gibbons

With a tailwind pushing us southward, we slid down the globe at 37,000 feet, just so quickly over France, still gliding downward toward northern Africa.

When the Sahara Desert was below us, I paused to wonder what goes on under our slip stream. People starving, kids dying, some struggling to live, murder, rape and pillage? Or maybe a pleasantness of life that one could only imagine. When you know nothing but poverty, think how splendid it is to receive the smallest of gifts. It was fitting that I waited my moment to watch East Clintwood's film, *Invictus*, the story of South Africa and Nelson Mandela. (I hoped you spotted the Clint bit, I love that name with a spoonerism.) He came out of twenty-seven years incarceration and forgave all. (Nelson, not Clint) An incredible lesson I learnt. At age ninety-three, they wheeled him out to watch the World Cup Final. The mission was not impossible. I was thankful for the opportunity to go.

Let Thy will be done.

The rifts in the sand below dissected the landscape symbolically depicting apartheid.

The way it used to be.
I thought of confession.
Of repentance.
Of forgiveness.
Of redemption.
The way it must be.

Chapter 38
Botswana

*Little huts—some square, some round,
some with tin roofs, some thatched—dotted the landscape
below, drawn off like pictures from my old geography books,
then disappeared out of sight.*

Johannesburg Airport was saturated with World Cup gear. The dreaded vuvuzela, the monotone Bflat3 noisemaker trumpets that everybody detested during World Cup, that certain football teams sought to ban. Some of them *were* banned in England. Glad to say my beloved Albion was one of them. But the vuvuzela lined the shelves in the airport commissary in bucket loads, along with other World Cup stuff, a footy fan's Mecca.

I sat down for a bit of lunch at Wandies Café in the airport and just had to go and ask a group of ladies on the next table what the World Cup song was called. I couldn't remember it for the life of me. Six of them were South African. They talk a little different. When I asked them if they saw the World Cup, they all answered as one—"Yiss!"—Hiss, but with a "Y." By the way, if you happen to be in this café, don't order the oxtail stew. I was so looking forward to it. I had to change my order, because I couldn't tear the meat from the bone. My expectations were high. I was hoping it would be like my dad's from years gone by. His always just fell off the bone. Pearl barley, leeks and a pig's foot to boot.

I then boarded the prop jet that would take me to Maun, along with sixteen other passengers, a two hour flight over the Kalahari Desert. Gazing down upon the flat, dry arid landscape where trees were few and far between because of an uninterrupted shortage of water, I watched an entirely different world pass beneath me. Little huts—some square, some round, some with tin roofs, some thatched—dotted the landscape below, drawn off like pictures from an old geography book, then disappeared out of sight. Seventy percent of Botswana is covered by the Kalahari Desert. To the south is its border country, South Africa. To the west and north is Namibia, and Zimbabwe is to the northeast. Botswana meets Zambia at a single point.

The country is a success story of its own making. Small and landlocked, Botswana was one of the poorest countries in Africa until it found diamonds. They received independence from Britain in 1966. In the decades that followed, Botswana transformed itself and is one of the fastest growing economies in the world. With good government and economic growth, the living standard has improved, though many of its people have been left behind, still in poverty, and sadly, HIV/AIDS is pervasive there, the second highest in the world. Education and health are below par considering countries in the same income group. But Botswana is the least corrupt country in Africa.

⚽

I trekked across the tarmac to the terminal, wondering what to expect. No jetlag. Just wonder. An English-American favoured, whilst not with wealth and fame, certainly with comfort o' plenty. I was happy. What about these people? I was not oblivious. I had read *National Geographic* for years. I had been to foreign countries. I had seen poverty. I had watched documentaries about African nations and people. But this was the real scene.

The airport was small, but brilliant. The baggage claim was a hole in the wall, but sufficed.

This was a strange situation. I had talked to these people over the last few days but had never seen them in person. Still we had a striking common bond—football. How would they know me? Of course my big black Adidas bag. A dead give-away for a coach.

Keith and Jen, two Americans, met me at the airport, loaded my bags onto the back of the Land Rover and off we went to the offices, just around the bend, about half a mile from the airport. It was happening so fast. At this rate, I would be back on the plane headed for England in no time. I must slow this reel down if at all possible. To take it all in. To jot it all down. I must soak this all up like a sponge.

The streets were dust, but for a better word, clean dust. No litter, no garbage like some of the other countries I had visited. Inside the Conservation office, I got a great big welcome from Lesley and her husband, Tico. A brilliant Canadian couple.

I noticed right off that everyone was speaking English. They're taught it in the schools. Botswana was once, of course, a colony of the UK; they all speak English; and they are Christians. How pleasant! They will never forget their own culture and language though, quite right too. The people are very polite, respectful, not the least bit intrusive, happy, and always smiling. I was impressed.

I met the coaches I would be training and learned that they play for a local football team sponsored by the BPCT. Their team is "Wild Dogs of Shorobe." An enthusiastic group, they immediately showed a wonderful willingness to learn. An hour later we began packing up the Land Rovers and Toyotas with gear, food, and water.

Soon we were off, riding the dusty roads to camp in the Game Reserve. Lesley and I chatted all the way. We passed through the buffalo fence that keeps the predators in, and interestingly, the first wild animal we saw on the dusty road was . . . Holy Cow! All dressed up in her colour coordinated sporty gear . . . a female jogger. Lesley and I looked at each other and thought the same thing. What would one be doing jogging at six in the evening (dinner time for wild animals) and out here with the predators? Two minutes later, I noticed some sort of cat. We slowed down and turned around. Indeed, a leopard was watching over her cub. Later a big herd of elephants stopped us as they nervously crossed the dirt road just a few small yards in front of the grille of the truck, making sure their little ones got safely to the other side. The young ones scampered across with their tails in the air and their ears out, showing us they were frightened.

I was in awe, though it was business as usual on this road to the camp. We moved on, braking as hundreds of impala pounded across in front of us and zebras gracefully pranced about. A family of giraffes peered down upon us inquisitively. They all looked like females to me with thick, long eyelashes. As we neared the camp a couple of hyenas prowled around, such was their habit of an evening. This was not Busch Gardens. It was reality. These animals lived here, were born here, and raised themselves here. It was their habitat, and we were subject to their rules and whims.

The dry wind blew about like a million hot blow dryers, though the nights were chilly enough for a sweater. It was their winter season, and sometimes the night temperatures drop to freezing this time of year. A camper's dream; at night, that is. We ate our meals under an open canopy. They were beautifully prepared by the cooks, from scratch, all homemade, no electric devices used. No microwaves.

Later we sat by the fire in the open place, jungle drama unfolding mysteriously as some ill-fated impala or buck drew its terminal breath. The shrill barks of the hyenas, wild dogs, a jackal or two were muffled only as they devoured their evening meal, the growls and sighs a background musical score in celebration of the survival of the fittest. My first night and just a few yards away was a *kill*.

A million diamonds sparkling in their courses lit the night sky, flickering radiance exaggerated by the absence of manmade power supplies. Without the stars, our campfires and torches, the nights would have been black as pitch. A group of traditional dancers and singers—and later in the week spirit coaches for the schools and teachers of the songs—dressed in their native attire and performed native music in ancient style. The watering hole below the deck where we sat together and took our delicious meals was backdrop for the delightful attraction. It was all so splendid!

Our tents were firmly attached on wooden platforms with open mesh for windows. For two nights in a row as I lay snug in my real bed about to drop off to sleep, some hungry elephants came and stood outside my tent and proceeded to munch and crunch on the acacia trees. That night I became educated to their eating and digestive habits, though not voluntarily. They were about six inches from the door of my tent. As if they were wired and mic'd for sound, they breathed and regurgitated their food. I could hear with no problem. They were close. I later learned that the elephant's favorite meal is the nut from the acacia tree. The following morning, proof they were there and it was not a dream were the large brown mounds they left as a present outside my door. I learned to be more discriminating about where I stepped after that first morning.

Like the close call with the big cat in a forest in France when I was a kid, the story of my life, I must tell this as one of those frightful animal encounters that, shall I say, keep me on my toes. I should have known better, that is if common sense had kicked in. One late afternoon, I walked with

Sarah, an Oxford University student. We were chatting away. I asked if she had experienced any close encounters of the predator kind. I wanted the information to reassure myself it was okay to be out and about the camp in the late afternoon. In perfect answer to my question, the deep-throated bellow of a growl, a breathy sigh, not a roar, gave us indication of how close the lions were. Too close for comfort, hidden from sight in the four foot high beige savannah grasses. To be sure, we were scared out of our wits. We stopped dead in our tracks, though not a good choice of words at that point.

We were a hundred yards from the main camp and about twenty yards from a couple of the tents, mine included. We couldn't see the lions, but we could hear them, almost feel their hot breath. The soft-low growl was a warning for us to stay away, not to come any closer to the resting pride.

Happy to oblige them, Sarah and I looked at each other, gulped to keep from making a gasping noise, our hearts racing, eyebrows raised, jaws dropped low. Instinctively our bottoms told us to turn and run. But just like a cat playing with a mouse, they would have loved that. Sarah, who had been there a few weeks longer and who knew what to do, said in a low voice, "Stand still and start to slowly walk backwards." We did. And then after a few carefully planned and sensible steps my brain joined my bottom and said, "Run, you fool!" What a situation! But we walked back as slowly and confidently as we could until we saw the main camp. We looked at each other and this time we accommodated our natural instinct.

"Let's get out of here!"

We ran like the blazes.

Foolishly, I had been walking at night to and from my tent armed with only a torch. Roz, a fellow Midlander (East not West) from Derby (pronounced Darby) told me that not even the resident researchers walk anywhere at night. Now they tell me!

I wondered how many times I unknowingly might have been the special on some lion's evening menu and how the gulps and sighs might have sounded with a munch-down on a nice ripe, plump Gibbo for dinner! What a rush, just the thought of the experience was exhilarating, something I could never have contemplated.

During the first week I had seen every bush animal in the Botswana preserve, including Cape buffalo and a family of mongoose. Should that be mongeese? No, sounds too French.

In Florida and other parts of the USA, when you walk in the wild, you're always told, "Don't worry. The animals are more afraid of you. If you ignore them, they'll scurry away." Not so in Africa. That rule does not apply. I confirmed my fears when I was on the plane back to Johannesburg. I sat next to an Australian called Brad Horn from Epic Private Journey. He told me that elephants and lions can and will walk right through your camp whenever they want.

Even considering the lion scare, it was splendid to be away from civilization, from mobile phones, email, and the internet. Just like it used to be. Remember going "on yer hols" for two weeks when nobody had computer or mobile phone? When returning home did not include a fear of coming back to hundreds of emails waiting? Yes, it was a real break in those halcyon days.

Chapter 39
THIS TIME FOR AFRICA

... the delightful kids made Fagin's Band of Scallywags look like catwalk models for Versace or Prada.

I must admit I filled up a couple of times when the kids arrived, some in buses, some in flatbed trucks, some on lorries, most of them dressed in hand-me-downs, not from their older brothers or sisters, but true hand-me-downs from other brothers and sisters around the globe. Clothes that didn't really fit, like those we threw out twenty years ago. Some of them tattered, torn. Boys were wearing girls' sandals. It didn't matter to them. They were shoes. A couple of the girls wore fur-lined boots once owned by some spoilt New England girl. Some wore tights, in eighty degree weather, mind you, though it was their winter, hot and arid, sun so brilliant it was blinding.

With shoes and clothes torn and tattered, dirty at best, smelly at worst, the delightful kids made Fagin's Band of Scallywags look like catwalk models for Versace or Prada. But they were happy and they didn't care. Especially when they were safely inside the artificially lush Astroturf stadium. It was a welcomed respite from their home in the dust and poverty, like a trip to Disney. No dust, no school, lots of water, small gifts, snacks and food.

The kids entered the stadium as the name of their school was announced, each group displaying the banner for their chosen animal. Some of the classes didn't get picked up at all, some arrived late, but long time Maun resident, Peter Dow from the U.S., explained that this was normal course for Botswana. They sang their spirit song and waved their banner at the appropriate time. It was joyful to behold them singing their hearts out, a three-kilometre smile unfolding across each face. The wonderful local spirit coaches did a great job with those kids.

The first-rate sports complex boasted of all the modern conveniences—stands, floodlights, Astroturf, running track, changing rooms, even a VIP lounge, a stadium of which England or the U.S. would be proud. It was a green oasis in a dry desert land.

When they were ready, each school paraded down the red running track where they took turn with their personal team cheer under the guidance of "MC Kyle," a nineteen year old mastermind from Canada, of Indian descent, a brilliant boy. Then as a group, they sang the *Respect Song*—not Aretha Franklin's. The song went like this: respect yourself; respect each other; respect the environment.

Then the coup de grâce came with the camp anthem, no small thanks to Shakira and the World Cup that happened to be going on just down the road in South Africa. They called it *The Waka Waka Song*. Everybody sang; everybody danced. Brilliant! Filled me up! Because this time it was for Africa! And I was there, taking part in something so special and so inspiring.

I taught them the Wayne Rooney song, which became the "footy" coaches' anthem. It got a worthy second place to a truly great song.

When I hear the song, *This Time for Africa*, in the future, I will always think of the happy faces of the African children and the spirit coaches. I will think of Emily and especially Sarah and the day the "Giggle Sisters" were born. I see them now with those famous *Shakira* moves to the rhythm of the great footy anthem.

We had a few celebrities on camp. Queen Latifa was there in the guise of spirit coach Lokey. Then there was Stopper, who looked just like Michael Jordan, and another coach called Dimple was the spit of Eddie Murphy. Dickson became the singing ref, and Ben Stiller was actually Keith, who does the best *Coldsteel*. Keith and I were hand in hand with our philosophies and had a great time together.

*Gibbo at C4C
(Coaching for Conservation)
In Botswana, Africa 2010.
This Time for Africa!*

Chapter 40
YOUTH SPORTS

*... when we come to the realization
that life is not all about filling up our own egos
and leaving our young people to wonder
how we came to be so selfish.*

Looking back at the twelve short days in Maun on the Game Reserve, I know that I was *where I was meant to be* though at short notice indeed. It was a good day for me to go in more ways than one. A quick decision—an easy one to make. My three Amigos, God the Father, Son, and Holy Ghost had given seal of approval, and my children were pulling on my heart strings. This trip meant I could see my family for twelve days on my way back to America. Everything fell into place. All signs pointed in that direction, confirmed as the programme opened in Botswana with Lesley and Tico, who so graciously led out in teaching deserving kids to respect themselves, to respect each other, the animals, and their immediate environment. It was brilliant, just what my intellect and heart needed.

We were blessed with seven hundred kids for four days. Not one parent or parent-driven issue, not one board member calling with reasons why they must be heard for how important they are, not one email I didn't want to open. Just seven hundred happy kids and a good group of volunteer coaches, with everyone appreciating every second.

When I consider *youth sports*, especially in the USA, I say with no reservation they are driven not by the youth, as they should be, but by adults with their petty issues, their spite, and their selfish agendas. It sickens me. And it sickens other coaches who desire to run a wholesome principle-centered, youth-driven soccer community free from politics and troublesome disruption, and it is getting worse.

When will it end?

I saw in the two weeks in Africa *how* it can end. When we come to the realization that life is not all about filling up our own egos and leaving our young people to wonder how we came to be so selfish. It was interesting that the African children said good-bye to their parents at the door of a thatch-roofed hut, a mother sweeping out the dirt floor, a father grinning from ear to ear as he left for work making fifty cents a day, thankful his son could hop aboard the flatbed truck and ride to the grand oasis to participate, to laugh, to play, and to thoroughly enjoy a few days in paradise. These parents would never consider interfering with what these free-hearted workers had planned for their children. To them, it was a gift, one which they received with grateful hearts.

A lesson for us all to learn, thanks to the humble folk of Botswana.

Chapter 41
Fish 'n Chips

When anyone asked concerning my food or drink desires,
my answer became quite Anglo-Saxon
in its precise historical definition.

The second week of camp was fast coming to a close with only a few days left. I was staying in the home of Keith Marshall, a friend of Lesley and Tico for the remainder of the time. Keith is an organiser for big game safaris to the Okavango Delta. He's a great bloke. We didn't see much of him, mind.

Our days were long, hot and tiring. We rose early and arrived at the stadium at eight each morning, sometimes finishing at five thirty in the evening.

Back at the house, I challenged Keith to a jump into the icy pool. It was not just cool—it was so cold my voice went up two octaves. But it did the trick. How refreshing! Winter temperatures in Maun are a grand eighty-five degrees. So dry our skin needed hydrating and what better way than in the lovely pool overlooking the river.

⚽

By now my thoughts were turning toward England. Time was getting short. Of course, my vocabulary joined my thinking pattern. My taste buds were not far behind. When anyone asked concerning my food or drink desires, my answer became quite Anglo-Saxon in its precise historical definition. The terms "cuppa tea" and "fish 'n chips" readily swooshed from my lips like the end of a Nike commercial. I was so close to a departure date for England, I could taste those fish 'n chips wrapped with an inner lining of white paper and an outer lining of newspaper. I drooled at the mention of fish 'n chips served with salt and vinegar.

On our last night we sat together, the staff and about twenty-four coaches and spirit coaches, reliving a week of joy, freedom, and memories we had just made that would last a lifetime. Lesley and Tico were graciously hosting this last gathering. We chattered like chipmunks around the long tables eagerly awaiting the arrival of what we knew would be wonderful food. I never expected what was actually in store.

And there it was!

In the middle of Botswana, Africa.

In a village called Maun, a place I will never forget for many reasons.

Huge trays of food began arriving, balanced securely on the shoulders of our servers. This might well be the first time in history when a plate of fish 'n chips had such a moving and emotional effect on one human being. The gesture filled me up, especially when they brought my plate first—my plate of fish 'n chips with a large portion of tartar sauce on the side. Knowing me as you do now, I never get stuck for words, but this time I could find no words to match the surprise. The delight of this Anglo-Saxon delicacy. Such lovely people. They had listened to me drone on and on about fish 'n chips, served up with plenty of salt and vinegar.

I'll never forget the hospitality and genuine acceptance of me by these wonderful people. My heart will forever sing the *Waka Waka Song*, though perhaps I'll not thrill so much at the shrill sound of the vuvuzela!

Next year in Botswana!

Chapter 42
WORLD CLASS PARTNERS

*He may not speak their language
or their dialect, but his eyes and actions of the heart
speak directly to the moment.*

Hello, Readers! Jane here, speaking words that Paul will never speak, but words that should be said. I've watched him with an eagle eye and an inquisitive mind over the past two years while writing his story. He doesn't like it when I call him *a world class soccer coach*. Maybe I don't understand the true meaning of *world class*. So . . . I've employed a few of Gibbo's own Black Country words to define what I know to be true about him.

I'll start with *bostin*. I like that word. I had never heard it before he came into my world. I thought it was something he made up, but I have since found it to be one of the best, most expressive words for *outstanding*. Besides, it has an "English" ring that I like. Then there's the word, *brilliant*. He uses it a lot, but only in the superlative and when he means *outstanding*. His coaching skills and techniques are *brilliant* and the way he reaches to the heart of young people the world over is, indeed, *world class*. He may not speak their language or their dialect, but his eyes and actions of the heart speak directly to the moment. And they love him. They love him because they have an uncanny built-in God-given mechanism that helps them understand that he loves them right back. Children respond to intellect, but so much more to love and regard. That's Gibbo's forte.

Only a *world class* soccer coach could get to Botswana to make a contribution that will likely affect those young people the rest of their lives, I thought, sitting on the opposite side of Planet Earth from Gibbo those three weeks. I tried to visualize how it might have been so I could write it, but never mind, when he returned, he had it down pat and with all the ease in the world, dictated that chapter of his life straight from his journal.

Out of the abundance of new friends and joined by colleagues from other parts of the world, those present at Coaching for Conservation in Botswana, Africa, Gibbo found yet another *world class* partner—Lesley Boggs, Director of Coaching for Conservation. It was through her efforts and due diligence that Gibbo and the other coaches were there.

These are Lesley's words:

> I had never met Paul "Gibbo" Gibbons when I called him from Botswana on Skype, at the recommendation of Nick Gates from Coaches across Continents, to ask if he might be interested in spending three weeks in Botswana helping run our annual Coaching for Conservation program (C4C). I explained that C4C was a conservation program that uses soccer to engage kids, and that I needed someone to lead the soccer component—first teaching coaches and then overseeing the program for seven hundred kids that translates cool animal behaviors into related soccer skills. He would be one of three coaches: a professional soccer coach (him) an animal coach (virtual) and a conservation coach (a professional educator). He laughed, and with a pause of no longer than ten seconds, said "I'm in!"
>
> When Paul arrived, we went straight to our wildlife research field camp for a five-day initiation and training. I attempted to brief him on that two hour drive into camp, and realized early that my Skype introduction had been vague and he actually had no clue what I needed him to do. He had to learn our entire curriculum including animal behaviours, translating them into football skills, training the local coaches to teach the drills.
>
> During the next week, he would be overseeing the football program for seven hundred kids. "Is that all" he muttered. "Guess we better get started!" Like a kid in a candy store, Paul took in all the experiences of the African bush with enthusiasm. It was a thrill for him to get up in the morning and learn that the lions had milled about his tent

the night before. And at first light of a morning to see the giraffe at the waterhole. He said very little, pinched himself now and then, and smiled a lot.

The annual program was a gigantic success. Paul accomplished the task and more. Within five days he learned it himself, gained the respect and confidence of all the local coaches and taught them the drills. He found his way into the hearts of our whole C4C team (more than twenty-five local and international volunteers), and by the end of the following week, flocks of children were following him around the field chanting his name—"Gib-bo, Gib-bo! We love you, Gib-bo!"

Not everyone gets it. But Paul, in a quiet, caring, and gracious way, simply fell into step and put into place the pieces of the puzzle that were missing to make the parts of the whole come together. His eyes give away his warm heart and we are most grateful. We look forward to next July already to hear the chants of "Gib-bo, Gib-bo—"

Lesley Boggs, Director
Coaching for Conservation

Chapter 43
ONE SPECTACULAR DAY

*My roots are planted deep in soccer.
My father watched it on TV as far back as I can remember,
and he raised me to love the beautiful game.*

I had three of my U19 boys with me. We were in tournament in Land of Lakes near Tampa. Jane and I met up at Crispers in Trinity Crossing Shopping Plaza. It was a beautiful Saturday afternoon, and we chose to sit outside under the Key West fans enjoying some mango tea while we edited the manuscript. I was happy to see Jane. It had been several months since I moved to Stuart from the Gulf Coast of Florida, leaving her alone with her computer and to muddle through without me. We had lots of work to do to get this book finished and published, but I wanted her to spend time with one of my players from Martin County. I introduced her to Breno Figueiredo. A player, yes, but more than that, he's a friend. She and Breno talked while Sergio, Chris, and I ate lunch. I've introduced Jane to so many people, it's a wonder she doesn't dump me and fold up her computer. But she assures me it has all been to her gain. With Breno, I can assure you that *is* the truth. Here's what he said to Jane. He spoke her language.

> I was born in Brazil, came to America when I was four years old, and moved to Port St. Lucie when I was twelve. I hold dual citizenship in these two great countries. To speak of my love for Brazil is to declare my love for football, for that is what we do in the country of my birth. It is not just a game. It is a way of life with legends like Ronaldo, youngest ever to win the FIFA Player of the Year at age twenty-one. He

won it three times. And he is a Brazilian, one of my own countrymen.

My roots are planted deep in soccer. My father watched it on TV as far back as I can remember, and he raised me to love the beautiful game. When I have a problem, I go to the soccer field and get lost in my passion for the game. But far beyond the smell of the grass, the breath of the wind on my face, and the feel of the ball at my feet is my love for the One who has made it all possible. My parents taught me at an early age to know and trust the Lord Jesus Christ. I have to thank Him for giving me life everlasting, and while I am here on this earth, the abundant life and that, of course, includes soccer.

What He does works!

I played in a tournament in December where I did not reach the goals and expectations I had set for myself. In fact, it was horrible, and I hit rock bottom. But I have learned that in every life situation, God has the answers. My faith is not based in what man thinks of me or in how I perform. It is based in what Christ did for me when He died on the cross. I have to realize every day that I'm just a sinner saved by the blood of Christ. And when I attempt to conquer something on my own without Him, I am on a path to nowhere. We are all sinners, but when we sin, we don't have to start all over, go to the back of the line. We ask for forgiveness and—as if there were anything better—He forgives us immediately and tells us again how much He loves us.

I met Gibbo through my coach Matt Walby, and in the real world, Matt gave me that push to man up. Gibbo is the same. He dishes out tough love. I joined his team a year ago, and though my dad is my hero, Gibbo is another father figure. A great coach. He loves me and, at the same time, gives me positive criticism.

I have a driving desire to make my parents proud of me, knowing that no matter what I choose to do with my life, they *will* be proud and their investment will have been worth it. I love the thought that Florida Atlantic University (FAU) watched me play today. It was one of the most spectacular days, and as far as I was concerned, I played the game of my life, and I will play again at two o'clock today. They will be there. Watching every move on the pitch. Making their own decisions. I have to keep looking toward the future, knowing that if you don't look ahead, you get left behind. I will do my part.

While soccer is my love, I do have educational goals and an ultimate calling on my life. I will go to college one way or the other, and I will become a mechanical engineer, God willing. That will be my vocation. My calling is to pastor a Portuguese congregation in America, to Portuguese speaking people, for there is the fear that our Portuguese churches will one day become extinct. I must do everything in my power to keep that from happening. I am grounded in my faith in Christ. I speak Portuguese fluently, and I take my Christian faith seriously. I pray in Portuguese, I memorize scripture in Portuguese, and I will preach the gospel in my native language and in English. God has given me talents that I use for Him. Our piano at my church is on the altar. I do not take for granted that my place is on that altar, playing the piano for His honor and glory. And to work in the kid's ministry is a blessing. My dad is the lead saxophone player at the church and this Brazilian ministry is a huge part of our lives.

I was in kindred spirit with Miss Jane. We ordered our lunch and joined Gibbo, Sergio, and Eric outside for some beautiful sunshine and good food. Miss Jane asked me to pray God's blessing in Portuguese. Even Gibbo was "filled up."

Pura não me envergonho do Evangelho de Cristo, pois é o poder de Deus para a salvação a todos os que crê, primeiro para o judeu e também para o grego (Romanos 1: 16). For I am not ashamed . . .

Breno Figueiredo

Chapter 44
To See Her Face Again

*I was so filled up, so anxious
to round the bend, turn the corner,
and get the house on Greenside Road in my sights.*

Sunday, July 18, couldn't arrive fast enough and when my plane landed in London at seven thirty that morning I knew I couldn't have waited another minute to see my kids.

Heathrow, the great see-through city, brilliant in design, still has that one major flaw in the plans. Same as two weeks ago when I was passing through. None of the wall plugs worked, and as is my custom of late, my mobile battery was down again.

I needed to call Daniel. He should be here to pick me up.

I traipsed down to Dixon's to purchase yet another adapter (I have a plethora now) so I could call. Purchase made, I returned to T5 and with no necessity of electronics of any sort, there stood my son. We hugged and set in to catch up without drawing an extra breath, though it was like sliding into each other's heads as if it were yesterday, so natural, with so much love. We paused only to gather my baggage and head for his Citroën, the family van, which is not unlike every other car in England these days with the internal-combustion engine that ignites diesel fuel using compression alone—the smells, the stains notwithstanding, and the only upside being fuel economy. At this writing, petrol in England is now at a hefty eight dollars a gallon as compared to three, and rising, in the States. We stopped along the M40 to fill up, had a panic attack gazing at the bill, and then moved on.

I've always loved the views along this route. I breathed deep, trying to by-pass the fumes of diesel petrol and capture the fragrance of the green of home, the fields held together by bird-filled hedges that lined the motorway, dating back to medieval times. The hedges; not the motorway. Not so green this time due to a lack of rainfall, the long grasses more the colour of the savannahs in South Africa; either way I felt at home. At least it was the calm and placid sheep that lay in the long grasses of the West Midlands, not the lions, the difference being a fluffy white cloud balanced on four stubby legs—not the best camouflage in the world, right? No camouflage needed in these serene pastures, however.

We stopped at *The Services* and had our annual obligatory bacon sammo and a cuppa tea. It's tradition now. When the tray arrived, we agreed they should have billed it on the menu as *A Massive Pile of Meaty Bacon Sammo* with a cuppa strong tea, accompanied by a tube of brown sauce which, I was certain, came straight from the HP bottle (House of Parliament brand, of course).

Still chatting, Daniel broke the news that the three girls all have had chicken pox, poor kids. That didn't worry me. I was just looking forward to seeing those spotty kids.

We continued our journey on the motorway until we reached the built-up outskirts of Birmingham. I was so filled up, so anxious to round the bend, turn the corner, and get the house on Greenside Road in my sights. And there she was in the window, Maddison Poppy—the Poppy Monster (TPM), waiting for her "Bibbo" to arrive. I could see those little eyebrows go up, a big smile form; and she was off and running to answer the door. She jumped into my arms and in her deep dad-like Ducka Ducka Da Da voice, she said, "Hello, Bibbo!"

That little voice I had only heard by phone for so many months. The precious smile that could only be captured with a photograph, the distance hauntingly separating me from my oldest granddaughter—

To see her face again was overwhelming.

For the next two hours Maddy and I were immersed in our own world of dressing up wooden peg dolls, creating a witch, whose name was Winnie, a schoolgirl who donned a lovely Poppy-special tie, Lady GaGa of some sorts, more like a lady with a pointy white hat, a lovely ballerina who looked like Lady Gaga without the pointy white hat, and a couple of witches with purple tissue paper capes.

This day was moving rather swiftly. I knew I would turn around and it would be gone. Story of my life. Once again, I had to slow it down if at all possible.

We played in the garden house with steps that Daniel built. My job was to accommodate the boss and make her giggle. The twins were inside not doing a lot, which they do very well. They are cute, two of them little characters at the early age of one.

Meanwhile, in the garden house, we were interrupted by the warbling calls of a lesser spotted Daddy Gibbons inviting us in for dinner. Daniel does a lot of the cooking, and it is quality. He served up a plate of baked ham, some roasted spuds, cabbage, broccoli, carrots and Bisto gravy. A few of my favourite things, the gravy being the absolute best, and the roast spuds and cabbage a delicacy now, as I don't often get this fayre in Florida.

After lunch, Bossy Boots and I zoomed off on another Alice in Wonderland adventure. TPM donned her pink *chavesque* track suit with matching pink scooter and bag. Off we scooted.

Back at home the twins were still sitting there doing what they do best. They gurgled and giggled, cried and ate, slept and crawled around and did other stuff from the nether regions while TPM and I took a leisurely stroll around the quiet cul de sac. It took us a good hour as we surveyed and studied the trees, houses, magpies, cars. We stopped and drew pictures for a while, making our nest on someone's garden wall. Wasn't long before Daddy Gibbons came out of his castle to make sure we were okay.

"No, Daddy Bibbo doesn't have Alzheimer's yet, Daniel," I said to him. I knew where I was. We were engrossed in taking a scratchy-lined snapshot of our world.

Back inside Daniel's castle, we watched the stunning images of Botswana from my video recorder until the battery went dead. Yes. It happened again. Time to add yet another size adapter to the collection. The shots of lions, elephants, giraffes, and hyenas were all taken at very close range. Kids singing and smiling. Vivid pictures to go with the joyous sounds will never leave the memory card in my brain. For that I will need no adapter.

Chapter 45
THE VILLAGE OF BLOC

*The school, the butcher shops,
fruit and veggie markets and the pub—
all took me back in time fifty years.*

Nathalie and Matt came to pick me up. It was lovely to see my little polar bear and her handsome chap, who looks more like *Hammy* from *Top Gear* every day. Bountiful smiles and hugs followed. The love we share is brilliant. We traveled in yet another diesel-fed car to the Village of Bloc or Bloxwich as it is now known. I must admit the sound of a diesel engine grates on me so much, but Nat's Little Mercedes found its way happily to her street.

Nathalie and Matt's beautifully terraced place reflects the peace and happiness they share. I was very comfortable there. The house itself happens to be a stone's throw from three significant landmarks. My first love, Lesley Chell's home in Bell Lane; my former wife, Lynda's family lived in nearby Church Street; and the church where Lynda and I were married is just over the road from Church Street. Lots of memories for me.

That night Nathalie and Matt took us to their local pub; we had a couple of real ale pints and on the way home we visited the local chip shop. We dined on a pukka pie of the chicken and mushroom variety (the best pie in the world), pickled onions, curry sauce, chips drizzled in salt 'n vinegar—a feast. What a feast! We slept well that night.

Waking up in the morning was the best of times. I scurried downstairs, put the kettle on. It looked silly on me, so I took it off, made us all a cup of tea—weak tea for Nathalie. Don't know how she can be a Gibbons. It's like warm milk. I took our cups to the bedroom and we chatted away. Then we headed out back to the garden to let the rabbits out. Some things never change.

Paul André Gibbons

We took a nice walk into Bloxwich. Watching the local folk was like walking into a living Black Country museum. Truly Anglo-Saxon England. We visited the newsagents and three butchers all in the same block, the butcher shops fascinating me just like they always had, taking me back to my childhood. There were real cuts of meat and best of all homemade pork scratchings. The temperature was a refreshing sixty-five degrees with a little sun but mostly clouds. I walked with more of a spring in my step, so different from walking in the Florida sauna, drained by the humidity. There was no need for constant hydrating the American way—eight pints of water a day.

The morning walk was a grand production, an everyday occurrence—with characters more of the "Ann and Arn" (my former in-laws) contingent—walking together, shopping, enjoying the company of one another after all the years. It's much more communal, and everybody knows everybody.

After lunch was a different story, for the afternoon shoppers in Bloxwich, while a small minority, are of another influence. The scene became a lot more *chavesque* with Burberry caps and a bit denigrated lifestyle. The *chavs* are characters from the famous café scene in *Star Wars* (creatures from another planet) like the people who shop at Wal-Mart in the U.S. But for the most part, the town is made up of hard-working Black Country people with good values, and it hasn't changed a lot since the Bloc family settled there during the Anglo-Saxon period. It remains a bastion of old England—my England, its people salty, earthy—and it is a stronghold of the British National Party.

We walked past the Church of England Infant School built in the 1950s. The brick wall, with wrought iron bars connecting the stone fence, non-threatening, beautiful. We opened the gates, and it took me back fifty years as I watched the kids running around playing on the grounds, mates screaming. So free. Like it used to be.

At night, we went for a quick pint to the pub in Wolverhampton Road, just up the way from *The Spotted Cow* called *The Turf Tavern*. A glance into the window revealed it was open, though it looked as if it were closed. We walked into the place that had not been painted in forty years. It resembled yet another Black Country Museum.

The wood-topped tables were held up by decorated heavy wrought iron legs, warmed by an old fire grate. The bar itself was traditional with the original pulls. Years ago behind the pub there had been a factory that employed thirty people and, from all indications, those thirty hard-working people still frequent that pub. The ceilings and walls were stained yellow from cigarette-smoking days. The people were like those when I grew up in a pub. I imagined I knew them all, from all walks of life, for here it was all over again. Nothing much had changed. In former days, the Blocs would go into that pub because the gaffer kept a good pint. I closed my eyes and heard the local gossip about the Albion and the Wolves. The school, the butcher shops, fruit and veggie markets and the pub—all took me back in time fifty years.

One night Sean and I went into a local pub about a hundred yards up the road from Nathalie's house, again another living Black Country Museum experience. It was called *The Romping Cat*. The main bar consisted of benches, seats halfway around in a crescent. The pub was literally on a corner and in the shape of a crescent. Everybody was served in the main bar, though there were two other rooms that were never used. The patrons stood at the bar having a drink and watching karaoke, the event of the week. It was hilarious to see people in all shapes and sizes like a remake of *The Adams' Family*. Sean and I just had to giggle at the situations.

They set the speakers all in one corner.

I said, "Are they serious?" as one bloke walked in dressed up to the nines and started to do an Elvis Presley song in a Black Country accent. Imagine that. This guy thought he was Elvis. We had to try and hide the tears falling down our faces as we fought to suppress the laughter. Mainly because there were only three people in the place. The singer, the DJ, and another bloke who was sitting in the corner sipping his pint. And was he deaf! Couples started to come in to enjoy the highlight of their week.

One bloke walked in, stood next to Sean and me. Sean, in his best Viking accent, said, "Dow look, Dad. He's got blud in his eyes."

I said, "And look what he's brought in! Go ahead, Sean, have a look at his missus."

Sean was brave enough to turn around and look at the lady sitting at the table with the bloke.

"He has walked in with a hyena," I said. "And she's wearing a red dress and high heels. A six foot hyena!"

Sean was crying with laughter, so hard that he spit his ale all over his scratchings, which were waiting for him on the wooden bar.

Such characters—including my son! I had just come from Botswana. From the bush. Where hyenas were better looking than the bloke's wife.

But the ale was good. We had to walk out with our heads down. We daren't look. This Black Country living museum was just like the *cirque du Blocko*, a real live *panto*, a real live circus. The bearded lady and all.

When we walked out, we let it all out. I was all nice and sun-tanned and Sean, in the look of a model, put on his famous half-soaked Black Country accent—"He's got blud in his eyes, Dad!"

Sean, as usual, had gotten fully engrossed in the moment, becoming one with the character he saw. A couple of years ago, he became Borat. He's been Gollum (*Lord of the Rings*) and an even better Schmiegel from the same film. So convincingly he took on Russell Brand. Just became the character, so it was not difficult to walk straight into this living pantomime. Instead of *widow twanky* we had a bloke with blood in his eyes and with a wife the image of a six foot hyena in a red dress and high heels, who had just had her hair done, as well.

When we got back to Nathalie's, I needed another cup of tea and I couldn't resist the scratchings. They became my breakfast of a morning.

My little bedroom was just across the landing from Nathalie. Every night instead of getting a text from her—"Ni night, Dad"—I could actually hear the words coming from her lips. The most beautiful sound in the world to me. Nathalie doesn't know it, but it filled me up. It was much better than receiving a text.

Nathalie—
Isn't She Lovely?

Chapter 46
PROPER MOUNTAINEERS

With the tent up and in good condition,
we set off to climb Snowden.
We parked our car and took one of the three trails
that overlooked the beautiful lakes.
My boys were always walking just in front of me.

Daniel said to me, "I'll pick you up at seven in the morning from Nathalie's."

We were going camping. It had to happen. And just as it always *had* happened, here's how it went. My leather journal was getting fatter by the minute.

In the first place, Daniel didn't really mean seven o'clock. We knew he would be late. It was more like seven thirty when he picked me up, and we set out to pick Sean up at his mother's house, about five miles from Nathalie's. Daniel was driving Marvin's BMW. (Marvin is his new brother-in-law.) It's a four-seater and yes, diesel. Sean came out looking like a Bedouin with sheets everywhere, parts of a tent and poles sticking out all over the place, pots and pans clinking and clanking, and his pride and joy, a Bart Simpson sleeping bag. He was dressed in American style Tartan shorts of a light colour, which extended to his scrawny knees. He had on grey school socks, black school shoes; he looked about eight, just off to school. With this get-up, you wouldn't be thinking of a camping trip, but more of an art show at a museum. On the other hand, his brother Daniel had the proper hiking boots, some jeans, and wrapped around his neck a grey and white Arabesque scarf quite similar to ones the models wear. With all the proper gear, he looked like David Beckham prepared to hike up a mountain.

Off we jolly well went. I was the navigator, so we needed a GPS! Daniel was driving—sort of. Sean the Sherpa was snuggled in the back. We started this trip off laughing so hard we missed the turn-off on the A5, nearly ending up in Wrexham. We found our way back to the A5 via a long and winding road, all hills and turns, surrounded by narrow roads of all gradients and bends laced on either side with beautiful hedges with the worst camouflaged animals—you guessed it—sheep. I was doing a *mocumentary* with my video camera as we travelled, interviewing the intrepid adventurers. Watch out Mr. Attenborough!

Now for the funny part. I started to get motion sickness. Of course, as soon as Daniel realized this, his driving became hazardous, making bad matters worse. He was smiling. Sean in the back, all of a sudden joined in, not with nausea, but this poor boy was in need of a rest facility and quick. Sean started Daniel off. He now needed to relieve himself. I joined in with that, too. Of course when you need a lay-by, there isn't one. We eventually found a farmer's gate and a field. There was a line of cars behind us, but at this point, we didn't care. Daniel stopped the car. We jumped the fence. A bull looked at us a little bit curious. We did what we needed to do before the bull could get to us, and it was back into the car. We were hurting with laughter. The farmer's field recorded 3.5 on the Richter scale and the tremours were heard as far away as Rochdale.

We were looking for Capel Curig. The last time I visited Garth Farm was when I was about fourteen, and I had to take the boys to see where I used to camp. We eventually found Garth Farm. The place had not changed in forty-odd years. Even the sheep looked familiar. We were true *muckus* for we were all mucked in together.

The cost was just three quid per person per night. We thought of trying to unravel the cloth and sticks of Sean's tent, which was not Sean's to begin with, and it didn't look that promising for shelter or any other reason. In fact, it would take a NASA scientist to figure out the sticks and bits. Luckily, before we got to the site, we stopped in Betwys-Coed and went into a camping place, walked out with a brand new tent for seventeen quid, and that at half-price. So we used that instead of Seany's piece of flannel and random sticks.

There were no showers, just a toilet block. The only new addition to the place since I was there last was a stainless steel kitchen sink top that had been wedged against the old stone walls. Cold water only, of course. It was bloody hilarious!

For all the lack of amenities, there was, indeed, a beautiful lake and a wonderful stream that flowed into it. I remember when I was growing up, we used to bathe in that stream and wash the plates and pans there. One of us would wash the plate and float it downstream to be rinsed and laid on the towel to dry.

The valleys were made by glaciers that scraped away at the landscape leaving silt, terminal moraine, and eventually Garth Farm.

With the tent up and in good condition, we set off to conquer Snowden. We parked our car and took one of the three trails that overlooked the beautiful lakes. My boys were always walking just in front of me.

The last time Daniel and Sean were there, it snowed four feet. And they walked to the top, real mountaineers, wearing pumps (sneakers) crazy boys. I was in The States, of course, and they called me from the top of Snowden, "Dad, guess where we are."

Some parts of the climb are very scenic. Some parts steep. I had trouble keeping my balance, and my legs started to ache. The higher I climbed, the more I considered that I had been much younger when I climbed it last. In fact it had been forty-something years. There I was in my favourite white Adidas sambas, white ankle socks, a pair of cargo shorts, and some sort of fleece top and my famous tatty pink Adidas cap. I should have been doing much better than this. And eighty percent of the journey all I saw of my boys was their back sides. As we got to the top I had to rest more. My legs, you know. Up in the clouds it started to get a little damp and even congested, if you can believe that. One French family with a dog stopped for a picnic. My boys encouraged me to keep going. We had to make it to the top. When we finally got there, we had something to eat in the café train station.

Jane just said to me, "Did you say train station? I hope you took the train back down."

I said, "Yes, I did."

Steam off the engine fogged into the car, pumping moisture into me, warming me, which was all I needed, so I nodded off, slept, and forty-five minutes later the train was at the bottom of the mountain. And the boys—well, they ran back down four miles. They got the car and picked me up from the train station. Now, that was more like it. My kind of camping.

On the way back to the tent, we stopped in the pub where Sir Edmond Hillary enjoyed refreshments. He and his crew practiced on Snowden before they conquered Everest. It was a beautiful place. We sat on benches in front of a fireplace sipping the locals' ale. An hour I'll never forget. A brilliant moment. Behind us were pictures of Sir Hillary and one of the Sherpas who looked like Sean. Climbing boots hung from the ceiling and more pictures of the native guides of the Himalayan range lined the walls.

We drove toward our tent, stopping along the way to eat. We were supposed to be cooking our own food, but Sean was the cook, so we skipped on that idea, partaking of a beautiful steak 'n chips instead.

I got inside the tent while the boys sat on a couple of stones talking. I could hear them whispering, chatting about the day. I lay down in the Bart Simpson folding Daniel's coat under my head for a pillow, and fell asleep to the muted sounds of my boys. I was safe under the canvass, sleeping well, camping in Wales with no bears, wolves, snakes. Only sheep. I woke to realize we were all in the tent, legs, arms everywhere. Daniel's feet were in my face. Sean's feet were in Daniel's face. We all slept. Me and my lads. I wanted it to last another two weeks.

Next morning, we got up, packed our tent, and off we went. We stopped at a lay-by café on the A5 and had bacon sammos with brown sauce, of course, and a cuppa tea. Surprising enough, the next few days my legs didn't hurt. I thought I'd be stiff. But no, and my knees—they never did hurt. I didn't ache at all.

Chapter 47
For Old Times' Sake

*On the hill we viewed the silence of the valley
Called to witness cycles only of the past*
Jon Anderson with *Yes*—

A Little Diary Talk
Café Ambience

Tucked away on Florida's Treasure Coast is a small town called Stuart, a place I call home for the second time since coming to America. It's the only incorporated city in Martin County. Stuart weathered nineteen hurricanes between 1871 and 2005, not that many all tales being told. I've endured a couple of those Treasure Coast hurricanes myself, thinking that *enjoyed* is a better word *only* during the eye of the storm when all around me becomes quiet and serene. Then the stormy blast resumes. Not so enjoyable. But I've found that one of life's essentials is a proper mixture of storms and tranquility. They give us perspective.

Treasure Coast takes its name from history, a great name for a place that is treasured in many ways, not the least of which is for its natural beauty. In the eighteenth century, Spanish galleons shipwrecked off the coast of what is now Martin County, most likely resulting from some of those earlier hurricanes. They had loads of gold and silver on board. Some of the treasure was lost; some has since been recovered.

I now live on the very south of Hutchinson Island, a barrier island bounded on the east by the Atlantic Ocean, on the south by St. Lucie Inlet, on the west by the Indian River, and on the north by the Ft. Pierce Inlet. The view outside my windows and from my balcony is breathtaking. Sometimes I visualize myself back in the British Isles with plenty of water, if not-so-much ancient history, the exchange being Florida's sunny weather.

To top it off, I've found a little haven over here on the Treasure Coast which has become a pleasant part of my life and times. It's called the Osceola Street Café. Just the next best place to Panera Bread in Trinity, Florida. Except—Jane's not here, and it's not so easy trying to finish off this book via telephone, email, and Facebook. But I've found a generous measure of comfort, great food, and new friends at Osceola Street Café. All things considered, the days are extraordinarily sufficient what with my soccer club, my friends, my place with a beautiful view, and a fantastic church, especially at this time in my life when I long for simpler, kinder moments without all the tension of trying to read minds, make everybody happy, that sort of thing.

A Starting Place. A Finishing Place.

With my white thick china bowl of a coffee cup, which they routinely give me now, warm in my hand, I can relax and observe the different characters a place like this attracts. Downtown Stuart has a magnetic charge and pulse. Boaters, fishermen, golfers, snowbirds, which are migratory folk who live in their second home in Florida from Thanksgiving which is around November 26, a great American family tradition, which is bigger for them than Christmas, Christmas being Christmas Day dinner, then the next day back to work—whoosh—to about Easter time, then it's back up north. For businessmen and women, various groups, and locals—of whom there aren't that many true Floridians about, I mean people who were actually born and bred here—Osceola Café is the place to be. It is not a nationwide Wi-Fi café that has sprung up. Wi-Fi is available, but not advertised except on a small card in the front window.

So inspiring, people actually drop in here for the best coffee. And that comes from an avid hot black tea drinker too, with half a sugar and not too much milk. Strong. The way it should be, fighting to get out of the cup, unlike Natty Barry's!

This café personifies Stuart, the walls decorated with art of the locals, some of it very good. It reminds me of a Bar-Tabac in a small village of rural western France, St. Julien de Landes, the smell of *Cognac* and *Gauloise* or *Disque Bleu* replaced by the aroma of hot coffee and the sound of soft music such as Dave Matthews, one of my favourite bands. Try listening to *Crash* on headphones lying down by the pool in Orange County as the sun warms your soul, as I did at my mate, Tom Wall's place once, and it just hits you. Add to that the warmth of the staff at the Osceola—Marty, Beth, Debbie, Kim—and it *makes lemonade taste like a summer's day*. Cheers, Dave!

Outside of *Café Ambiance*, as I now call it, I'm careful to close the glass doors behind me so as not to let any warmth or character escape, and I continue my day.

This is the starting place to finish the book, my insides are telling me. Starting place to finish? A strange phrase I must admit. It gives me a quiet calming inspiration. It sets me free to work on some inspired action; it helps me balance the thoughts that release themselves within me. It gives me a platform to liberate some energy that will now hopefully be relayed to the universe. Besides that, it delights Jane that we are nearing the end.

That Footy Feeling

Speaking of atmosphere and a good feeling on any level—before, during and after any practice or game, I get my young soccer players to visualize their play and feel it. They have to have a good feeling inside them in order to play their best. I need them to release their individuality and express their unique personality, no matter how important the game. Some coaches take this game far too seriously.

Girls have to feel good to play well, boys have to play well to feel good, however there is a starting point for all this, and that tone is set by the teacher-coach. I get my players upbeat and happy in their approach. That makes the first step into the game so much easier.

A phrase I borrowed from English footballer, Brian Clough, one of the greatest managers of the English game is: "Your mental approach determines your physical attitude."

I ask my players: "What makes you kick a ball? What makes you make a tackle?" The answer, of course, is your brain. If they can get that right, they are halfway there.

I was up in Norcross, Georgia not so long ago with my U18 boys, who in 2009 were number one in Florida and number three in the nation. Not bragging, but *Custard, The Joker, Sponge Bob* and the rest of *the motley crew* deserve a mention. We were by the pitch waiting to play, and we were all having the banter, smiling and laughing, looking forward to the game. I let my captains, Custard and Sponge Bob, organise the warm up, and the three of us chatted about the team selection and formation. We played the game with great style and after the game, a couple of college coaches who were watching us from start to finish, came up to me after the game and said, "We will take any one of your players, as we loved the respect you all have for each other, loved the way you have taught your players, not just skillful footwork in tight situations, but good life skills. Your players love the game and they love you, too!"

That was not the first time coaches had said that to me through the years, but I have never tired of hearing unsolicited observations. They are a true measure of success, a way of knowing I have done my job, thanks to Coerver and the way we deliver. Mind you, one thing that does beat that is one girl on the U10 team up in Port St. Lucie just named her Teddy Bear *Gibbo*. Now, who can beat that accolade?

On Hutchinson Island

So here I am, back in green Martin County. I had eighteen months in Trinity, a place I wasn't meant to be. Having said that I would never have met Lady Jane and you wouldn't be reading this now. I will re-phrase that last statement. "I *was* meant to be there." But I have friends on the East Coast of Florida, some in particular who wanted me back coaching their kids and their community. I am humbled at the thought of such a compliment.

Thomas and Gail Rongen are among those very good friends. I've known them since they moved down. Thomas is Dutch, played for Ajax Amsterdam, and knew Wiel Coerver. He and I are from the same pod. Gail once told me when she and my mate, Thomas, visited FSU in Tampa—we went to the Sponge Docks in Tarpon for lunch, a lovely Mediterranean type atmosphere, with cafés and lots of Greek folk and their descendents loitering with their coffee and beads—that Thomas had really missed his buddy, Gibbo. This touched me. From a human standpoint, I am happy to be back amongst such good friends.

The sun welcomes me outside again, follows me down the street through the music and chime-filled stream that filters from surfer shops and arty establishments, past the myriad restaurants, jewelers, ice cream parlours, then slides unseen beneath the shadows of a boulevard of trees to a favourite restaurant for dinner, *The Riverside Café*. I love the place with its bare bricked walls, white paper covered tables, the last resting place for many delicacies—a bucket of forty mussels done in white wine and garlic, warm French bread upon which is smashed lumps of fresh garlic with butter. And the crème brûlée—*to die for y'all,* as we say in the Southeast USA.

All day long, the river lazily snoozes on its own giant li-lo, making its way to the open arms of the sea, resting, gliding under the rays, the eastern breeze naturally cooling every creature in its path. A boat sails by in the distance, the white foam obediently trailing behind.

It has long been a desire of mine to one day live by *la plage*, and after weeks of promises and let downs I finally stumbled across the perfect place. I loved this peaceful spot the first time I laid eyes on it, and when I visited on my own for the first time, I spent time surveying, relaxing and looking around, not wanting to leave. I walked out onto the third-floor balcony, eye level with the tops of the royal cabbage palm trees, on the top floor, up with the slightly stronger breeze and the birds I love. From the vantage point of the high castle turret, I could see the entire countryside. Below, the ibis were poking around and the sandhill cranes were majestically strutting their long legged feathery stuff amongst the sand dunes and the golf bunkers. To my surprise, in the water below, a couple of otters were showing off their swimming and diving prowess with a great deal of quality.

It's mine now, and from the balcony overlooking a small lake and a driveway over the bridge, the golf course hugs the larger lakes keeping them in check, and in the distance behind a hammock of palm trees and some other newly built condos, I hear the pound of the Atlantic waves as I drift off to sleep each night. La plage is only a walk away; the soothing tropical breeze is good for me, and the turtle doves that are building their own condo in the nearby palm tree, coo their approval.

Nature pampers this castle and moat, amazingly surrounding it and magnifying its beauty. I look forward to the sunrise that greets me of a morning and the wake-up call of the busy white ibis that help the Guatemalans prune and manicure the greens for the golfers. Hundreds of varied birds congregate on this green oasis, chat all day long until the day is done, while chipping and munching and cleaning away at their choice of the luscious landscape.

I recently watched in awe as a group of about fifty or so frigate birds swooped onto the lake gently touching the surface. At first it looked like they were diving for fish, but no, they were taking water to drink and also to bathe. As they rose, they showered themselves and shuffled their feathers whilst in the air. They were bathing themselves on the wing—amazing sight. I'm told if they get into the water, they can't get back up again if they try, as they have such batman-like wingspans and long tails.

On Monday nights we practice at Leighton Park, a beautiful piece of land donated by the Leighton family. It caresses the south fork of the St Lucie River, where some days dolphins give us their rendition of *Cirque du Soleil* and with no exaggeration. I saw a school of them dancing on the water, standing upright out of the brackish, twisting and cavorting as if in a liquid ballet, an incredible sight.

And the giant harvest moon that comes to visit us at certain times of the year—you could touch as it rises up just behind the river. It gives an extra orange floodlighting of the cosmic sort. Matt Walby, my most loyal friend and coach who is a Liverpool fan (my second team behind the Baggies) could reach up and pull it even closer from the black sky to our own green office below.

At the end of a long day, I take my journey to the Marriott, Indian River Plantation, Hutchinson Island and home up there in the cabbage palms, driving past Witham Field the local airport, through Sewall's Point, and over a couple of new bridges which span the Indian River Intracoastal Waterway and, of course, St Lucie River which hides behind a barrier reef that is Hutchinson Island. I don't have much money but I have all the simple natural blessings that surround me all the time, for which I'm thankful. The simple things in life are the best for me.

⚽

On the beach at midnight, the regal full moon hovers close, and the gentle breeze bounces off the sea, searching through my hair like a thousand pieces of lace. Across the swell and under the big light of the sky, a cluster of shining diamonds shimmer and bounce on the surface, and those fluffy white clouds now turned to grey, still comfort me like so many fuzzy soft and favorite blankets.

The sounds, the smells, the warmth, the sensations enliven me.

This is my Treasure Coast.

Another lovely night in Martin County.

Paul André Gibbons

15 March
For Old Time's Sake

I found out a few weeks ago that *Yes* were going to be in concert, that they would be playing just fifteen miles north of me at the top of Hutchinson Island at the Sunrise Theatre in Fort Pierce. Normally I would have bought tickets on day one upon hearing, but I rebelled against the fact that Jon Anderson wasn't going to be in the lineup as lead singer . . . *Yes* is not *Yes* without Jon.

I was scheduled to coach Al Soricelli's team on that night. I called, mind, to tell him that I would not make it. He forgave me. I purchased my ticket at the box office and took my seat about eight rows from the front in a theatre that holds about a thousand. It was perfect.

To say it was nostalgic is an understatement. The lads are all getting towards the autumn of their years, but the music was still as sharp as I remember it some forty years ago, and I was still as captivated as ever. The emotional worth of the lyrics blended with symphonic and other classical structures was immense, crowding my cosmic mind with memories of years gone by. My mate, Dave Hurst, first got me into this band and I am so grateful he did. The night Dave, Adrienne and my darling Pauline all went to see them at Stoke City's ground on a rainy evening, I do believe the sensational Alex Harvey Band opened for them—such loving memories.

I ask you, "What makes *Albion* and *Yes* better than a woman?" My answer: "They never leave you! They make you cry and make you happy, but they will never leave you!"

17 March
St Patrick's Day and My Birthday

The day started well with TR (Thomas Rongen) and me doing our aqua rock workout on the beach, battling rocks and waves, so invigorating. I am getting fitter just like I used to be. Well, not really, but it gives me a glimpse back to the past and how fit I was some forty years ago.

I drove to the office at Livings Insurance run by a soft-spoken southern man, who has me in stitches with quips like *as rare as chicken teeth*. He cracks me up, the Southern fried Billy Wobbledagger (work that one out! I will tell you later). Later—William Shakespeare. Okay, correction here. Jane says I got the quip about the chicken teeth wrong. It is supposed to be *as scarce as hens' teeth*. But in the Black Country, I think we would use my version!

On the way, I popped into the local garage which has food, coffee, beachwear, and it hit me that I have been ordering a coffee, a Twix and a packet of crisps just like I did some forty years ago on my way to Art College. Remember? The only thing missing is a fag cadged off my muckas—and my muckas, of course. How I do miss them all.

So then, it is a good day to bring this part of my life story to a close, though I hate to say good-bye. *Cycles of the past*, Jon Anderson had said in the song, speaking of life. Mine has certainly come round full circle and the journey has been phenomenal, memorable, with heartaches unspeakable and joy that transcends even my own enigmatic imagination. Far from *silent still*; closer yet to *the hill* upon which I will view it one day.

EPILOGUE

Cherish the Moments

*I have discovered the urgency
of cherishing every moment,
of loving intensely,
and of making sure my life counts for more than me.*

In Costa Rica, the greeting is *Pura Vida*—and it means *wishing you the pure life*. Becoming righteous, or as the Americans put it—salvation—is a one-time experience, a free gift of God. Becoming pure takes a lifetime of hard work. I'm reminded of that daily as I attempt to keep everything in perspective. And if I have to work at becoming pure in life, surely I must work at keeping soccer a pure game.

I hail from a very liberal environment, and I was born and raised in the middle of the Counter Culture. Long ago, England dropped her standards, and as *The Lion's Whelp*, America followed close behind. Our young people in both countries are at great odds today because of it. We live in a generation where a less-than-pure life and misbehavior get ignored or even rewarded. We can all speak from experience. I know I can. To that, add the fact that our last freedoms are either being attacked, challenged, or removed. President Reagan said, "You and I have a rendezvous with destiny. We will preserve for our children this, the last best hope of man on earth, or we will sentence them to take the first step into a thousand years of darkness. If we fail, at least our children and our children's children can say of us we justified our brief moment here. We did all that could be done."

The last great world power, before America, to lay hand over heart was Rome—and look what happened to her. The cry was "give us circus and give us food." In essence, entertain us and feed us while you're doing it! Is that not where we are today? There's a breakdown of the moral fibre in both America and England. I have experienced a lot of it, perhaps disqualifying myself to speak. But surely experience counts for something.

While we were talking about this chapter, Jane asked me a question. She has asked me a thousand questions! She may well know me better than anyone on the face of the earth by now. She asked, "If you had your life to live over, what would you change?"

I told her, two things. One I would never have left my children in England. And two, *somehow* I would have made my marriage work. When I walk through the woods and meadows, I see the turtledoves and recall that they mate for life. God gave us the senses—sight, smell, touch, taste, hearing, intuition, pain, temperature and equilibrium. All the basics needed to find and keep the right mate. I know it is supposed to be one man for one woman for one lifetime, like the little turtledoves, and I blew it. If I had it to do over, I would not allow it to happen.

My vantage point is on the far side of all things important, and those things cannot be changed. We press onward.

Dad said to me once in his broad Black Country accent: "Kid, if yow knew y'ode unny got twenty-four hours t' live, 'ow wud yow live it?—yow myte not werk up in the mornin' kid'!"

I've never forgotten what he said. In fact, lately it has haunted me. It aligns with that song that says *I don't want to gain the whole world and lose my soul.*

I pine for the days of Maggie Thatcher, and the Americans speak of Ronald Reagan with the same wistful remembrance. And of women like Jean d' Arc, *The Maid of Orleans*. I visited Rouen, France, where she was burned at the stake and I wonder since men have failed in the job of leadership if the world would not have been a greater place with more of the feminine touch. William Ross Wallace talked about that touch in his beautiful poem when he said, "The hand that rocks the cradle is the hand that rules the world."

Mom

I sometimes imagine how it would have been had Mom lived. And I've probed the past for the least remembrances of her, pushing myself across a threshold of pain to stir memories which before were stuffed away into the far reaches of my mind. In so doing, I have truly *touched* life in a way

I never dreamed possible. Oh, I still cry when I think of her. That will never change, but to bring those memories to the forefront has helped me understand a lot of things about myself, for I am seeing that so much of Mom is inside me.

I have discovered the urgency of cherishing every moment, of loving intensely, and of making sure my life counts for more than me.

Just a few weeks before I met Jane, I sent away for my mom's death certificate. I have no idea why I did so at that time in my life. I had never really known how she died. I only knew she was ill. I had blocked that part from my memory, finding it too painful to even mention.

I met Jane, shall we say by coincidence? In a place called *Trinity*. No, not by coincidence, for it was far too powerful for that. I sat across the room from her just waiting for someone to leave the seat beside her so I could find out what she was doing with the reams of paper. I was compelled, constrained to know. I would never have been satisfied to leave Panera Bread that day without knowing this lady. An hour and a half later, following my passion of emotions, tears, and laughter, she agreed to consider writing my story. The second time we met, which was the day we started writing the manuscript, I brought the death certificate which I received from England the day before. Jane read it then introduced me to her friend, the gentleman sitting at a nearby table.

"This is Dr. Ben, Paul."

"Pleased to meet you, mate."

"Likewise," said the doctor.

Then Jane said to him, "Ben would you please read this death certificate and translate the medical meaning of why Paul's mother died?"

"Sure," he said, and quickly wrote down these words. *Mesenteric thrombosis, mitral valvular disease, rheumatic fever*, then said, "Looks like it was blood clots to her heart, which was obviously not working right, likely from the rheumatic fever."

I explained to the doctor that my mother had lived her entire life in the West Midlands of England, which was the heart of iron and coal country for centuries. He told me that was very likely the cause of the rheumatic fever early in her life.

From that moment, I began to feel a measure of comfort, and with the hard and poignant questions answered and behind me, I knew I would be able to tell my story. In just a few short minutes, I was, for the first time since I was ten years old, facing the fact of my mother's death and the medical reason she died so young. I never really knew, because I had never asked. All I understood was that she died from internal bleeding, that she had a weak heart, was trying to have kids for a few years, and decided to seek a specialist's advice. She was told that if she had children with her weak heart it could kill her, and she went ahead, knowing that fact. What true love she had for my Dad, unparalleled love. Unparalleled, unequalled.

It was not as painful as I thought it would be. In fact, it was liberating and healing. I took a deep breath and gave a sigh of relief. I knew in that moment I was going to dedicate this story to her memory and that I would have an opportunity after all these years to thank her, though posthumously, for what she poured into me the first ten years of my life. I could apologise for repressing the remembrances for so long, afraid of the pain of allowing them to surface.

Thanks, Mom, for these memories, though faded and old. They are what I have of you, the fabric of who I am, and they will suffice for as long as I live. And the memories will live on through the tears and laughter of my own children and grandchildren for years to come.

If I Had It To Do Over—

But I don't have that privilege, so I go on from here, hoping to do the greater good in the time I have left. Will I continue to live *close to the edge*? Probably, but with higher calling, purer motives, and deeper insight.

It's never too late to do the right things. It was not too late for me the day I walked into that church in Jensen Beach. It's never too late to be exposed to righteous living, to be forgiven. The pure life depends on that exercise.

I like this walk. It gives me peace. Allows me to sleep at night. To peace I have added strength. I take life a day at a time, for that is my instruction and my promise. To peace and strength, I have added *power, love and a sound mind.*

I can't change everything; I can in no way understand everything; but I have learned from so many who have crossed my path—the Costa Ricans, the people of India, the Christians in America, the children in Botswana, the AIDS victims in South Africa—that the better life is the pure life. I have not arrived. I'm on a journey like a lot of other people. The night I painted the crucifixion of Christ, the night I came out of that theatre alone after watching *The Passion of the Christ,* I was drained, literally bent over, sobbing with a sea of people reacting the same way. But somehow I knew then there must be purpose to my journey.

I know I don't have the strength of character to perform them, but I like these biblical words—*Greater love has no man than this, that he lay down his life for his friends* . . . In metaphorical essence, my beautiful mother did just that for Heather and me. She risked her life and later died because she wanted to have my sister and me. She loved my dad that much. What love!

And based on what life has given me, I must, from my responsibility with the kids, give in return whether it be in the USA or in England, or in France, Costa Rica, India, Botswana. These kids have nothing but dreams, and perhaps that's all they need. For all that I am not . . . I *have been* a part of that dream, a channel effecting change in those corners of the world that I've been privileged to touch.

Pura Vida

I love you, Mom.

Ma Tante et moi at Pat and Keith's House
West Bromwich, 2010

Printed in Great Britain
by Amazon.co.uk, Ltd.,
Marston Gate.